THE SOVIET WORKER

THE SOVIET WORKER

Illusions and Realities

Edited by
Leonard Schapiro and Joseph Godson

St. Martin's Press   New York

ISBN 0–312–74923–6

Library of Congress Cataloging in Publication Data

Main entry under title:

The Soviet worker.

   Includes index.
   1. Labor and laboring classes—Russia—Addresses,
essays, lectures.   I. Schapiro, Leonard Bertram, 1908–
II. Godson, Joseph.
HD8526.5.S65   1981   331′.0947   80–21546
ISBN 0–312–74923–6

The editors dedicate this book to
Andrei Sakharov and Vladimir Klebanov
fighters for freedom and free institutions

Contents

Acknowledgement

The editors gratefully acknowledge the assistance provided by the Labour and Trades Union Press Service in London and the Advanced International Studies Institute in Washington, DC, which made the research for this volume possible.

Notes on the Contributors

DAVID A. DYKER was born in Aberdeen, Scotland, in 1944. He graduated in economics and modern history from the University of Glasgow in 1965, and pursued graduate studies at the Institute of Soviet and East European Studies, University of Glasgow, and the Institute of National Economy, Tashkent, USSR. In 1968 he was appointed to the faculty of the University of Sussex, where he is now Lecturer in Economics in the School of European Studies. From 1976 to 1978 he was on secondment to the Economic Commission for Europe, Geneva. He is the author of *The Soviet Economy* (1976) and a contributor to A. Brown and J. Gray (eds), *Political Culture and Political Change in Communist States* (2nd ed., 1979).

JOSEPH GODSON was for 21 years a senior Foreign Service Officer with the US State Department, specialising in labour and political affairs. Since his retirement in 1971 he has been living in London, where he is European Coordinator of the Center for Strategic and International Studies, Georgetown University; European Consultant of the Board for International Broadcasting; and Joint Editor of the Labour and Trades Union Press Service.

ALASTAIR McAULEY was educated at the London School of Economics and at Glasgow University; he also spent a year at Moscow State University. He taught at Manchester and Princeton Universities and for the past 13 years has been a member of the Economics Department at the University of Essex. He has written extensively on the Soviet economy; among his most recent publications are *Economic Welfare in the Soviet Union* (1979) and *Women's Work and Wages in the Soviet Union* (1981).

MAX RALIS, a sociologist, is director of Soviet Area Audience and Opinion Research at Radio Liberty. He joined RFE/RL Inc. more than 20 years ago. Earlier he was public opinion consultant to the United States Government in Germany, he pioneered a survey of miners conducted underground in the natural setting of the work place, and he directed cross-cultural research in Indian and Thai villages for Cornell University.

LEONARD SCHAPIRO is Emeritus Professor of Political Science, with Special Reference to Russian Studies, London School of Economics and Political Science, University of London; and a Fellow of the British Academy. He is author of, among other books, *The Origin of the Communist Autocracy* (1955), *The Communist Party of the Soviet Union* (2nd ed., 1970), *The Government and Politics of Soviet Russia*, (6th ed., 1979), *Totalitarianism* (1972) and *Turgenev: his Life and Times* (1979).

MURRAY SEEGER was Moscow Bureau Chief for the *Los Angeles Times* from January 1972 until August 1974 and reported from Eastern Europe from 1975 to 1978 as Bonn Bureau Chief. He graduated from the University of Iowa and was a Nieman Fellow at Harvard University, where he specialised in Soviet affairs. He is now stationed in Brussels as the European Economic Correspondent for his paper.

FYODOR TUROVSKY is a Russian jurist, a former legal consultant to *Literaturnaya Gazeta* and former chairman of the legal committee of the Moscow Construction Workers' Union, who now lectures in Montreal, Canada, where he resides. He emigrated from the Soviet Union in 1976.

PETER WILES has been Professor of Russian Social and Economic Studies, University of London, since 1965; he was Professor, Brandeis University, USA, 1960–3; Visiting Professor, Columbia University, USA, 1958 and City College of New York, 1964 and 1967. His publications are *The Political Economy of Communism* (1962), *Price, Cost and Output* (2nd ed., 1962), *Communist International Economics* (1968), *The Prediction of Communist Economic Performance*, editor (1971) and *Economic Institutions Compared* (1977).

MURRAY YANOWITCH is Professor of Economics at Hofstra University, Hempstead, NY. He is author of *Social and Economic Inequality in the Soviet Union* (1977) and editor with Wesley A. Fisher of *Social Stratification and Mobility in the USSR* (1973); his articles on Soviet economy and society have appeared in *Soviet Studies* and *Slavic Review*.

1 The End of an Illusion

Leonard Schapiro

This volume attempts to discover, by looking at many varieties of evidence, to what extent the working class of the USSR has been the beneficiary of a revolution which was ostensibly carried out on its behalf, and of over sixty years of rule in its name by a communist party. The motive force behind Marx's analysis of society – probably the most potent intellectual influence of the last two centuries – was the desire to put right the injustice presented by the exploitation of the majority in industrial countries, the proletariat, by the minority, the bourgeoisie. Russian social democracy, of course, derived from Marx.

The improvement of the lot of the working class was a fundamental tenet of all Russian socialists. The social democrats, indeed, were only indirectly concerned about the peasants, who formed the majority of the population of Russia before 1917 – they would, it was believed, somehow benefit in the end from the arrival of socialism, provided they abandoned their bourgeois property instincts and accepted the workers' lead. But even the peasant party, the socialist revolutionaries, included a substantial claim for workers' rights in their programme, and championed them no less vigorously than they did the rights of the peasants.

Marx did not live to see the development of social democracy in Russia. It was, in effect, born in the year of his death, 1883, when the League for the Liberation of Labour was founded by Plekhanov and others – and, incidentally, greeted by Marx with great scorn. But by 1895, when Engels died, social democracy had become something of a force in Russia. In that year, Engels recorded that socialism in Germany had passed the point where it could be shot out of existence, as it had been in France in 1871. 'The irony of world history turns everything upside down. We, the "revolutionists", the "overthrowers" – we are thriving far better on legal methods than on illegal methods and overthrow'. But such was not the position in Russia. Plekhanov thundered against conspiratorial plots by a minority, but believed in a

1

revolution which would be accomplished by a whole class – whatever that may mean in practical terms. The more realistic Lenin perceived that the revolution, in which both he and Plekhanov believed, could only be accomplished by the insurrection of an élite which would seize power in the name of the proletariat, and then govern in its name. He laughed to scorn his critics' prognosis that rule by an élite could only lead to tyranny.

Lenin's main opponents – the socialist revolutionaries and the Menshevik, or social-democratic, wing of the Russian party from which the Bolsheviks had split off on the issue of tactics in 1903 – were also to maintain, until they were silenced by force, that Lenin's Communist Party rule was a betrayal of the workers. For the first few years after the Bolshevik seizure of power in 1917, while expression of protest was still possible, there was ample evidence of the fact that the workers in the cities, from whom the Bolsheviks had drawn their main support, were turning against the ruling party. The heady months when Lenin was pitted against the Provisional Government had seen the establishment, with Bolshevik support, of the highly popular 'workers' control' in the factories which proved an excellent way of disrupting the economy and bringing about the general disintegration which helped the Bolsheviks to seize power. After power had been seized, however, a very different pattern prevailed. In the case of the railways, to take only one example of many, the institution of workers' control led to complete chaos, and strict centralized management had to be introduced on 26 March 1918. There was ominous praise for the Taylor system of industrial discipline from Lenin. This unwelcome discipline could, of course, be justified by the Bolsheviks by the argument that since the state was their own, the control exercised by that state over the workers could never be regarded as oppressive – but the workers did not see the matter in this light. Some of them even took up arms against the communist régime – on 8 August 1918 the workers of Izhevsk on the Volga overthrew its communist government and, together with neighbouring Votkinsk, rallied a worker and peasant army of 30,000, which is said to have grown to 50,000 by the following month, and to control a territory with population of over 700,000. This army continued to fight against the communists until 1922.

There is no doubt of the decline in the popularity of the communist government during the years of the civil war – of course, any government would probably have lost support in the face of the appalling hardships which the population had to suffer. The workers endured rather more than the peasants: peasants had to put up with the forcible requisitioning of food, while the workers mainly suffered from the suppression of the trading between town and village on which the townsmen relied to supplement as best they could their often non-existent rations. The effects of starvation told on industrial production, which fell drastically, and the drain of factory workers to the villages in search of food had halved the proletariat by 1920. Over seven million people are estimated to have died of epidemics and malnutrition between 1918 and 1920.

However, that worker dissatisfaction with their communist leaders was not solely the result of such hardships is proved by the steady recovery of their influence by the Mensheviks from 1918 or 1919 until their final suppression by the security force, the *Vecheka*, in the spring of 1921. The six million or more members of the trade unions represented by 1920 the great majority of industrial workers. By that date there was little love left for the Communist Party in the largely non-communist rank and file trade union membership. The Mensheviks, who demanded freedom of the trade unions from communist control, but at the same time advocated radical socialist measures, gained at the expense of the communists. While one cannot estimate exactly the strength of Menshevism in the unions, it can be stated with certainty that Mensheviks, pro-Mensheviks and other anti-communists far outnumbered the communists and their sympathizers. Zinoviev, who was prone to exaggerate and to panic, estimated in 1920 the total anti-communist following among industrial workers variously at 90 or 99 per cent, but other leaders, including Trotsky and Lenin, admitted that the communists had lost the support of the workers. It is usual for this loss of support to be explained solely by the hardships of the civil war, but the growth in influence of the Mensheviks, whose programme of 1919 stood for free and secret participation of all workers in all elections, freedom of speech and press for all workers' parties and abolition of terror, proves that the workers' dissatisfaction was not limited to their material conditions.

The Mensheviks had to fight desperately against arbitrary action by the *Vecheka* designed to silence them. One after another during 1921, congresses of trade unions upon which Mensheviks and their supporters had won majorities were forcibly closed down, the union committees disbanded and then replaced by others on which communists predominated. Repressions against union organizations were followed during 1921 by mass arrests of the workers, who protested in strikes and demonstrations against the administrative acts of terror perpetrated upon their elected committees.

What must have been particularly alarming to the communists was the fact that in a number of instances in 1920 and 1921, communists joined the Mensheviks in the demand for freedom in trade union or Soviet elections and in protests against arbitrary repressive measures. No doubt it was this that prompted Lenin in his notes for a speech prepared for delivery in 1921 to include the phrase: 'Mensheviks and Socialist Revolutionaries:– to be shot if they show their noses.' The final assault on the Mensheviks began during February 1921. In the course of the first three months of the year some 2000, including the entire Central Committee, were arrested and, for the most part, not released but sent into exile. Some ten leaders were permitted to leave the country as an alternative to exile. By the middle of the year the Menshevik organization had ceased to exist. One of the reasons for the elimination of the Mensheviks was, beyond doubt, the fact that for some time before 1921 the Mensheviks had been advocating the New Economic Policy which Lenin put through at the Tenth Communist Party Congress in March 1921. Another was the Kronstadt revolt which coincided with the Congress.

In June 1920 a delegation of the British Labour Party visited Russia. Its members had a full opportunity of meeting opposition socialists. They were also able to witness an example of communist methods of suppressing democracy in the unions. At that date, there still survived in Moscow a separate Menshevik organization of the Printers' Union, with its own central committee – in defiance of the official all-communist central committee set up at a Congress in 1919 which represented fewer than half of the union members. The almost all-Menshevik Moscow Central Committee organized for the benefit of the British visitors a mass meeting of workers which, it was claimed, was the last free meeting of its kind to be held in Russia. This last surviving free trade union paid the penalty while the Labour Party delegates were still in Moscow: its leaders were arrested and the Committee dissolved. The Labour delegation published full details of this incident, but failed to point out that repressive measures of this kind were applied to *all* socialists in the trade unions (and outside them, for that matter). The main purpose of the delegation's report was to urge the end of Allied intervention in Russia, and it confined its comments to pointing out that personal freedom and freedom of speech were 'severely repressed in the case of all those whose activities are supposed to threaten the Soviet régime' – without explaining that this applied to all socialists in the trade unions (and outside) who were critical of the communist dictatorship. In particular, so far as the Mensheviks were concerned, their opposition was strictly constitutional. They did not engage in violent struggle, and individuals who did were immediately expelled from the party. One Labour delegate at any rate, Shaw, remained under no illusions. Speaking at Geneva a few months later, he stated that 'the proletariat has no rights in Russia, and enjoys neither freedom of association nor of press. It has no right to choose its own representatives'. Among the many documents brought back by the delegation was an illegally-printed appeal to socialists everywhere asking for support for nearly 200 socialists and anarchists, imprisoned in Moscow. This document, with hundreds of others, remained buried in the library in which they were deposited by the delegation on its return. The whole exercise was a cruel betrayal by the British Labour Party of their fellow-socialists in Russia in the interests of what they saw as political expediency.

Communist domination of the trade unions therefore anticipated by many years the subjugation of the unions which is usually associated with Stalin. In the course of 1920, some of the communist trade unionists (who were quite content with the domination which the régime encouraged them to exercise over the non-communist majority of union members) rebelled against the central party leadership. The spokesmen for the communist rebels acquired the nickname 'Workers' Opposition' and were led by a former metal-worker, A. Shlyapnikov. There were three subjects on which the communist trade unionists criticized the party leadership. One was the practice, much encouraged by Lenin after the collapse of Workers' Control, of employing non-communist experts and specialists. This enraged radical worker communists who regarded it as evidence of lack of faith in the working class. The second grievance was the growing habit of the central party organs of substituting nomination for the methods of election prescribed in the Rules – though, from the point of view of the centre, it is difficult to see how else they could have maintained a highly unpopular minority in power. The third disagreement went to the core of Leninism. According to Lenin, the voice of organized labour was sufficiently represented by the participation of trade union leaders in the councils of the central party and government organs. The opposition trade unionists demanded that control over industry should be exercised by a central organ elected by the 'unions' – by which they meant elected by those who alone by 1920 enjoyed any voice inside the unions – the communists on the trade union committees. They relied on a passage in the Party Programme, adopted in 1919, to the effect that the trade unions 'must achieve the actual concentration in their hands of all management of the entire national economy'. The 'Workers' Opposition' was somewhat enlivened by the adherence to it later of Alexandra Kollontay, a colourful figure who added a clarion call for greater freedom of discussion within the Communist Party and for a larger proletarian component in a party which she alleged was becoming bourgeois in outlook.

The emergence on the scene of this opposition group with some apparent coherence was brought about by a Central Committee decision to inaugurate an all-party discussion on trade unions, and which called on representatives of different views in the party to submit their 'platforms' for the consideration of the Tenth Party Congress due to meet in March 1921. This unusual decision, supported by a very reluctant Lenin, had been brought about by Trotsky's dictatorial methods as Chairman of the Central Transport Committee (*Tsektran*) in attempting to put the disorganized transport system into order. His efforts had caused uproar among trade unionists. *Tsektran*'s policy had virtually split the Central Committee on the issue of less or more party dictatorship (strong personal conflicts behind the scenes were an additional important factor). No one in the top leadership supported the Workers' Opposition which, after all, directly challenged that leadership. In addition to the 'platform' of the Workers' Opposition, the Congress was presented by a number of other programmes on the trade union issue, including one by Trotsky which bluntly advocated the fusion of trade union organs with the state machinery, and military discipline and compulsion as the normal methods of maintaining industrial efficiency.

Lenin's Theses, which became known as the Platform of the Ten, were a masterpiece of understatement, and held out the hope, at least to the more credulous, that greater freedom would be tolerated: the state functions of the unions 'will gradually increase', but the tempo of fusion must not be speeded up; the principal method for ensuring discipline in industry is persuasion, though 'proletarian compulsion' is 'in no way' excluded; all trade union organs should be elected – but 'of course' under the 'overall control of the party'.

The Tenth Party Congress met under the shadow of a big wave of workers' strikes and demonstrations which took place at the end of February 1921 in Petrograd; and which sparked off the rebellion of the naval and city garrison of Kronstadt, a naval base some seventeen miles west of Petrograd. The insurgents, who (contrary to communist and pro-communist mythology) included workers as well as peasants in their number, demanded, among other things, free and secret elections to the soviets, the basic civil freedoms for all workers' and peasants' parties, liberation of all political prisoners and abolition of all special privileges for communists. The danger of the general situation was aggravated by a peasant guerrilla war, involving tens of thousands, which was then in progress.

The panic-stricken Congress was united to a man on the policy of forcible suppression of the Kronstadt revolt, an operation which claimed many hundreds of victims. The slaughter, directed by Trotsky, was enthusiastically supported by the Workers' Opposition. The fear of the Congress for the survival of communist rule made the acceptance of a number of resolutions, not always consistent, a foregone conclusion. The Platform of the Ten was adopted by an overwhelming majority, as was also a resolution condemning the 'anarcho-syndicalist' deviation of the Workers' Opposition. So was a resolution on inner-party democracy, followed some days later by another one, which severely limited free debate inside the party. Within a few weeks of the Party Congress it became clear that Lenin's apparent moderation was little more than a tactical move to gain time. The hated *Tsektran* (which had been suspended) was restored immediately after the Congress – though it was precisely on this issue that the Central Committee had split, with Lenin ostensibly ranged against *Tsektran*. As regards the Platform of the Ten, which deprecated 'reconstruction of the trade union organizations from the top', events soon showed what this was worth. A conflict arose shortly after the congress between the Central Committee and the communists in the Metal Workers' Union – incidentally, the oldest pro-Bolshevik union. In May 1921, the communist 'fraction' of this union rejected the Central Committee's list of candidates for its controlling committee by 120 votes to 40, whereupon the Central Committee ignored the vote and appointed a trade union committee consisting of its own nominees. It was an ominous precedent for the future. The Workers' Opposition kept up for some time a desultory and uneven struggle against persecution by the police and security forces, and was finally liquidated in 1923.

It is therefore clear beyond dispute that stringent party control over the trade unions and suppression of any critical trade union activity in the interest of the workers where this conflicted with the party's policy had been firmly established by the time the New Economic Policy (NEP) came into existence. The NEP period certainly witnessed a relaxation of the stringency of control in all spheres of life. It was widely supported in intellectual circles and was warmly welcomed by the peasants. The workers, in the main, viewed it with mixed feelings. On the one hand, they approved of the rising standard of living – it has been calculated that real wages in 1927–8 were 111.1 per cent in terms of purchasing power of the 1913 level, and the working day fell from $8\frac{1}{2}$ hours in 1921 to $7\frac{3}{4}$ hours in 1927–8. By the same date (1927–8), ravaged industrial production had reached the level of 1913, which was incidentally not inconsiderable: on the eve of the First World War, Russia was established as one of the five or six leading industrial powers. On the other hand, the workers strongly resented the growing prosperity of the peasants under NEP, persisting in the ingrained hostility towards the villages that Lenin at the end of his life had deplored. There was also strong opposition to the employment of 'bourgeois' specialists in the factory – a relic of the traditional anti-intellectualism of the Russian working class (to which Peter Wiles refers in Chapter 2). So far as Communist Party members in the working class were concerned, there is no doubt that NEP was seen by many of them as a betrayal of the brave, defiant traditions of Bolshevism and as a capitulation to more sordid, bourgeois leanings. Trotsky's criticism of Stalin on these lines during the years that Stalin was supporting NEP (1921–9) would have been more effective among the workers if it had not been for the memory of his advocacy of ruthless dictatorship over them. But with Trotsky out of the way, Stalin could rely on a good deal of support within the Communist Party for his reversal of NEP in 1929.

The saturation of the trade unions by the Communist Party took place during the NEP period. By 1 January 1927, the number of party members enrolled in the unions was 1,190,200 out of a total party membership of 1,212,505 – in other words, virtually all party members were enrolled as trade unionists at a time when, at the very outside, half of all communists were engaged in manual work. Total union membership, which included managerial, white-collar and technical staff, was ten million in 1927. The percentage of communists was very much higher in the trade union organs than their proportionate strength in the unions as a whole. For example, the All-Union Central Council of Trade Unions was 100 per cent communist in 1924, 99.6 per cent communist in 1926; the members of the All-Union Trade Union Congresses were 98.9 per cent communists in 1924 and 87.1 per cent communists in 1926.

Highly centralized party control over the unions was perfected during the NEP period. The trade union communist organization was fully integrated with the ordinary party network, and made subject to the same rules and discipline, as trade union leaders repeatedly emphasized. Trade union organs were forbidden to by-pass the party organs: directions from higher to lower trade union organizations had to go through the party channel, whether the Central Committee or the provincial party committee. The Central Committee, or rather its secretariat (which Stalin controlled after 1922), asserted the right to control both the election of trade union organs and of the key officials, and to effect the transfer of officials from one union to another, or from a union to a party organization. Party control when perfected in this manner gave the Secretariat of the party a powerful instrument for governing the industrial workers. Thus, the party could decide on the expulsion of workers from the unions – a serious sanction towards the end of the 1920s when unemployment was growing, since an expelled trade unionist would almost certainly lose his employment. Recorded cases of expulsion show that this measure was resorted to not only for such offences as drunkenness or unpunctuality, but 'criticism of the work of the union organ', or religious observance as well.

The rôle of the trade unions under NEP was dealt with at the Eleventh Party Congress in 1922 – the last Congress attended by Lenin, who drafted the resolution which was adopted. This resolution recognized the rôle of the unions in defending the class interests of the proletariat against capitalism, in view of the fact that a limited revival of private capitalism had been permitted under NEP. In the case of nationally-owned undertakings, the duty of the unions was to 'defend the interests of the workers, to promote as far as possible the increase of their material welfare' and to correct the errors which flow from the 'bureaucratic deformity of the state apparatus'. Strikes would have to survive for these purposes. But since the object of strikes was no longer the overthrow of class domination but the strengthening of the proletarian state, trade unions must do everything in their power to bring about a peaceful solution of disputes 'with the maximum advantage' to the workers; and if a strike did occur, to promote a speedy settlement. The resolution laid down further that unions were not to interfere in the running of individual enterprises – their rights were to be strictly limited to promoting candidates for election to state organs; and they must do all in their power to encourage harmonious relations with bourgeois specialists. They must also win and maintain the confidence of non-party union members: their main method should be persuasion, but they 'could not refuse to use methods of compulsion'. A further resolution enjoined the party organs to undertake a 'renovation' of the leading trade union organs – blandly ignoring the resolution or the absolute inviolability of the electoral principle in composing trade union organs embodied in the Platform of the Ten, adopted by the previous Congress.

The policy laid down by the Eleventh Congress, even if it was intended to be more than window-dressing, did not prove easy to carry out in practice. Trade union communists were not always inclined to obey the part of the resolution which forbade their interference in management. This was not surprising, particularly when it came to dealing with non-party management ('bourgeois' specialists, for example) in view of the encouragement which the party leadership had always given to communists to behave as members of a privileged caste. Criticism by the Central Committee of undue interference by trade union organs in management was made repeatedly during the NEP period. But the most difficult precept to put into practice was the dual responsibility of the unions, both as protectors of the workers' interests and as participants in a government which was building a socialist order. The need to develop industry with the little capital available to do it necessarily acted as a brake on wages and benefits, and stimulated demands for greater production. The union leaders were repeatedly placed in the difficult position of having to side with the management in their capacity as party members, when their duty and often inclinations as trade unionists made them sympathize with the demands of the workers. Although strikes remained legal under NEP, it became impossible for a communist, on pain of expulsion from the party, to support them, though there is evidence that many trade unionists sympathized with the strikers and secretly or even openly tried to side with unofficial strikers. In October 1925, a stern warning that their action would be followed by disciplinary measures, including expulsion from the party, was sounded by the Secretary of the Moscow party organization.

The trade unionists never succeeded, as enjoined by the Eleventh Congress, in winning the confidence of the mass of non-party workers. For the rank and file worker, as repeated official statements acknowledged, the union, like the party and the management, remained 'the bosses' – an attitude, incidentally, shared by many rank and file trade union communists. Indeed, the trade union leaders, and in particular Tomsky, who remained Secretary of the All-Union Central Council of Trade Unions during the NEP period, did not conceal the fact that support by the union of the interests of the management and of production, where this was dictated by party policy, had to take precedence over the interests of the workers. Yet many trade union leaders, and especially Tomsky, had the interests of the industrial workers at heart. That they were able to give loyal service to the party in the way in which they did was due both to their faith that they were thereby helping to build the full socialism of the future and to the fact that wages and work conditions were, under NEP, slowly improving.

The improvement was not, due however, in any way to the efforts of the unions, but to the slow recovery of industry in the more relaxed conditions of NEP. If during NEP the unions had in effect become instruments to enable the party to exercise control over labour, this function of the unions became even more essential to Stalin in 1929, when he embarked on his sudden reversal of NEP, enforced collectivization of the peasants and industrialization at break-neck speed. The suffering which this 'Third Revolution' imposed on the industrial proletariat (which, however great, was much less than what the peasants had to endure) called for the kind of iron stranglehold over workers that even Tomsky, who had loyally put party first as duty decreed, could not be expected to support. Characteristically, Tomsky was by implication attacked by Stalin for his undemocratic methods in December 1928 and removed six months later. Stalin always liked to disguise his tyranny as defence of 'democracy'.

Since then Soviet trade unions have remained faithful instruments of the party, who play little, or even no, part in advancing the prosperity and welfare of the industrial workers. They act as agents of the party in carrying out party policy which always sacrifices present benefits to measures which are supposed to ensure a golden future with the advent of communism. Whether, after the trauma of the 'Third Revolution' and the mass terror which followed it, one can still credit present-day trade unionists with the idealism that inspired men like Tomsky to believe that the sacrifice of the present to the future was justified, is a matter for guesswork. For collectivization and terror have left a permanent mark on society and engendered the cynicism, careerism, opportunism and servile conformity which some internal critics of the Soviet régime see as its main characteristics. Be that as it may, one must not forget the recent courageous effort, described in Chapter 5 by Joseph Godson, by a small group of Soviet trade unionists to set up a free, genuine trade union. It was immediately and brutally suppressed by the Soviet authorities, and did not receive the kind of international support from the free trade unions of the West which it expected. But the fact that this attempt could happen at all, after sixty years of ruthless party dictatorship over the unions, is proof that the notion of what a genuine trade union movement should stand for is not yet wholly dead among Soviet workers.

Certainly the present which the Soviet worker is expected to be content with after sixty-three and a half years of communist rule is meagre enough. The chapters which follow attempt to assess various aspects of the workers' lot in the USSR, including welfare and education, as it is at present. If David Dyker is right, it is difficult to be optimistic about the future – especially so if the level of state expenditure on military requirements remains as high as it is. Certain other features also seem destined to survive, at least until the advent of that utopian and barely credible age of plenty called 'communism' which the Programme in 1961 boldly predicted as scheduled to begin to appear in 1980, and to be mainly completed in the decade. Such features as extreme inequality of earnings, welfare provisions which are designed to encourage effort at work rather than to cushion the weak, or an educational policy which mainly favours the children of the white-collar employees and the intelligentsia (see Chapters 2, 8 and 6 respectively) are not likely to disappear in the foreseeable future. For a quick assessment of the position of the Soviet worker in relation to his counterpart in several of the major Western industrial countries the reader is recommended to turn to the Supplement, especially pages 276–85. Here he will find an analysis, based on meticulous research into all available evidence on wages and prices, between the number of minutes or hours which a Soviet worker is required to work in order to be able to purchase various commodities or services in Moscow, as compared with his counterpart in London or Washington (and some other capitals). This graphic method of assessing standards of living tells one much more than figures of earnings, which have to be transposed into different currencies with the aid of a largely meaningless rate of exchange for the ruble.

The question has to be asked, why does the Soviet worker put up with such a low standard of living? There is no one answer to this question. For one thing, it is not true that he always puts up with hardships without protest. There was enough protest during the first few years of the Soviet régime, before the party dictatorship was fully consolidated. But ever since then, there have been outbursts of protest. Fyodor Turovsky refers to several, major and minor, actions of resistance in Chapter 7, and David Dyker accepts the view that strikes and other pressure by workers may influence government economic policy (Chapter 3). A graphic illustration of this trend has been the decision in past years to buy grain abroad, which has to be paid for in hard currency or gold, rather than let the population go short. It is unlikely that this policy is based on considerations of compassion.

Another factor is the vital importance of privilege, in a system in which the government controls the distribution of all scarce commodities and services, and uses them as incentives to desirable behaviour. Privileges, like foreign travel or a holiday on the Black Sea, have to be earned by good behaviour and conformity. Few are ready to risk the loss of them for the sake of a protest which is unlikely to achieve its object. Again, it is the case that there has been slow but marked improvement over the years: there is therefore always the hope that, given patience, further improvement will take place. One should also not ignore the fact that the Soviet citizen may sometimes admire austerity of living and, bolstered by national pride and patriotism, can see compensations in his own life as compared with the 'decadent' materialism of the West – though it seems very probable from all recent accounts that Soviet society is fast becoming every bit as materialistic as any Western society.

There are several other factors to be considered. As Fyoder Turovsky, Max Ralis and Murray Seeger all show in their chapters, an important part of Soviet life is knowing how to 'work the system'. Many have learned this art and, for them, life in Soviet conditions is far from bad – if risky. All recent evidence points to the fact that this prevalence of 'fiddle' is on the increase. The main factor for the passivity of the Soviet worker, as several of Max Ralis's informants pointed out, is probably the sense of security which he has. He may not earn much, but he has the confidence that a job will always be available, with a pension at the end of it, however small. Besides, however much the Soviet régime may have exacted sacrifice from the workers, they still remain in many ways the most privileged class. The peasants have been repeatedly exploited beyond endurance. The intellectuals, of course, earn much more than workers, and their privileged position is to a certain extent, by way of educational opportunities, inherited by their children. But when trouble starts the intellectuals become the first victims of the purges and the witchhunts; the workers, at any rate, are relatively immune.

Indeed, it is ironical, as Engels observed in 1895, to note how much more the workers of the Western industrial powers have gained through free trade unions, industrial struggle and the ballot box than the Russians who, led by Lenin, were induced to believe that nothing but extreme revolution led by the communists would ever change their conditions. It is true that much poverty remains in some sections of some Western industrial societies, including our own. But it is doubtful if even life on welfare subsistence in our societies is of as low a standard as that endured by many Soviet workers in employment and not classified as poor. Besides, in view of the improvements that have taken place in the condition of the poor in our societies over the past two or three generations, there is reason for confident hope that their conditions will continue to improve and that the inequalities which still survive will ultimately be eliminated.

The material in the chapters which follow is of two kinds. In some chapters, academic experts on Soviet society assess the standards of the

Soviet worker on the basis of carefully checked and sifted evidence. In other chapters, a journalist or former (or actual) residents in the Soviet Union give their impressions of those standards from their observation or experience. These impressions necessarily suffer from the absence of reliable factual material. For example, such matters as food prices are classified as secret information by the Soviet authorities, and the foreign journalist in the Soviet Union has no access to the kind of facts that he can readily obtain in any Western capital. The general secretiveness of all Soviet authorities and the absence of a free press means that Soviet citizens in their own country have to rely on gossip, rumour or conjecture in order to build up a picture of the reality which surrounds them. The facts described and the conclusions reached in the two different kinds of chapters sometimes coincide, and sometimes do not. No attempt has been made by the editors to harmonize the two forms of exposition. It is hoped that the reader will be the better enabled to form his own judgment by looking at the different kinds of material which we have assembled side by side.

NOTE

For the sources of the facts asserted about the early years of the Soviet régime in this chapter, the reader may refer to my *The Origin of the Communist Autocracy* (London, 1955) and *The Communist Party of the Soviet Union*, 2nd ed., (London, 1970).

2 Wage and Income Policies[1]

Peter Wiles

THE MARXIST TRADITION

Income distribution is one of those rare fields in which Marxism is all in all, Russian tradition nothing. With what preconceived Marxist ideas did the Bolsheviks take power in this field? They were primitive Marxists who adhered to Marx' original views as published, not what we gather from his posthumous writings and correspondence. Owing to the concentration of capital, society is supposed to be becoming more and more dichotomous. Further, in the oppressed part, the independent craftsmen, whose wages are differentiated, are yielding to a simple undifferentiated mass of machine-minding proletarians. Thus, already under capitalism, technical progress has produced a good deal of equality among the future victorious class. It is the business of the revolution to confiscate the profits on capital and put them at the disposition, not of individual workers, but of the workers' state. From 'surplus value' it becomes 'surplus product'. Management, again, is not a great skill and need not be paid much or cosseted. On the contrary, capitalist development has simplified it, and socialist democracy requires that such jobs be rotated; indeed, all jobs should be rotated in the name of abolishing the division of labour, which is one of the ill-effects of the market. Since machinery has simplified all tasks, not merely management, the frequent interchange of all jobs would abolish alienation and be quite practicable.

Towards the end of his life Marx, and still more Engels after Marx died, admitted that industrial capitalism was, on the contrary, producing an aristocracy of specialized labour, and even that management is an independent factor of production, quite distinct from capital. But these arguments did not make much impression on Lenin's mind, and it was the earlier complex of doctrines that carried over into Russia.

In particular, one very celebrated late work by Marx, his 'Critique of the Gotha Programme' (1875), seems to have made very little impression until Stalin came to power. This is the only Marxian text to deal with the period between revolution and full communism. Under full communism, it should be explained, self-interest no longer moves the new man, and he works for altruism or pleasure, not direct economic reward. Consumers are so reasonable and workers so productive that there are no shops and no money. We help ourselves to our agreed needs from warehouses, even without rationing. This was Marx' vision and it remains Brezhnev's. The rapidity of our approach to it is a major permanent internal issue of Soviet politics. Now Marx thinks of this approach as a short period called the Dictatorship of the Proletariat (Stalin thought of it as a long one called socialism). His main concern in this document is with labour. Everything is to be nationalized at the moment of revolution, but men's minds have not yet been reformed, so they continue to be paid directly in accordance with their work. But since their productivity is unequal, their pay is unequal. Simply, there is no unearned income from capital and so only one class.

Marx is very brief. Notably he does not make it clear whether there is to be a true labour market, with pay inequalities being used also to entice labour to appropriate jobs and places; or merely a labour incentive system to entice workers to put forth effort once in jobs to which they have been administratively assigned. My feeling is rather the latter, and certainly the talk among Soviet labour economists is mainly about this problem, not about job choice – notice the curious term *ustroistvo* (placement) in David A. Dyker's chapter in this volume (Chapter 3). *Ustroistvo* is a weasel word signifying that one is neither enticed nor directed – both meaningful terms – but 'placed', whatever that means.

In contrast to Marx's foresight and moderation, the Bolsheviks tried at first to leap straight into full communism, with an equal national dividend (we must not say wage, because a wage is a payment conditional on work performed) for all. In the then unregenerate state of the people, this meant that appeals to altruism had to be supplemented by force – a very characteristic combination when appeals to self-interest are disallowed. There was first and foremost administrative direction of the unwilling and unprepared labour force, which in a mild form is an obvious consequence of even successful full communism. But force was also used: the 'militarization' of labour. This whole vast socio-economic experiment failed completely, and was later renamed war communism – a name not used at the time – in order to establish the false pretence that the Bolsheviks had done all this out of the necessities of the civil war. It is indeed true that the dates of 'War Communism' (summer 1918–spring 1921) and the civil war coincide; but that is due to the historical accident that the Kronstadt revolt (by which the rebellious proletariat convinced Lenin to abandon the system) occurred immediately at the end of the civil war. There is nothing in the Bolshevik literature of the period to suggest that they were not trying to establish their final, peacetime version of society on the spot. A more thorough reading of Marx would have saved a terrible disaster.

In an essentially non-historical chapter, we must pass over the New Economic Policy (NEP) period. As an avowed step backwards into 'state capitalism', it has little resonance today. We pass directly to Stalin's 'socialism', of detailed command from the centre, constantly bumping up against true markets for consumer goods and – what is essential for our purposes – labour, at the periphery.

The USSR is still in the period of 'socialism'; indeed, Brezhnev's new constitution of 1977 even emphasizes how long it will still last. That is, the goal of full communism has retreated since Khrushchev fell (1964). Nevertheless, full communism casts its shadow before it. Things that contradict it are regrettable if necessary concessions to expediency. Thus Soviet incomes and labour policy is distinguished from capitalist policies by:

   (i) unwillingness to come to terms with supply and demand, indeed, to admit that a labour market exists at all;

  (ii) egalitarianism in wages and salaries (or at the least such extreme hypocrisy and sensitivity about inequality that egalitarianism is clearly the felt principle);

 (iii) a consequent tendency to direct or nearly direct people *to* a job, and to neglect this aspect of pay differentiation (at least in theory: this is *ustroistvo* as in Dyker's chapter);

 (iv) hostility to labour turnover, as damaging to the *ustroistvo* principle and simultaneously, of course, costly to employers;

  (v) an almost absolute failure to provide for unemployment, on the false ground that it does not exist (it does exist, in very moderate amounts, but mainly as a result of labour turnover);

 (vi) sheer direction of labour to jobs, notably of young graduands;

 (vii) appeals to sheer altruism, in the occasional form of unpaid overtime, and the regular forms of a nationwide unpaid Saturday's work (*subbotnik*), student help with the harvest, *Komsomol* campaigns to 'go East, young man' – especially directed at soldiers at the moment of demobilization;

(viii) an unusually heavy emphasis on incentives to effort once *in* a job:

bonuses, piece-work, promotion scales;
- (ix) a larger weight of social services in total incomes;
- (x) a sharply progressive income tax on private income only (which is seldom paid, since most private incomes are 'black').

Note that points (ii)–(vii) all arise out of point (i). Note also how essentially Marxist all these points are. The remainder of this chapter illustrates them seriatim.

OTHER RUSSIAN LEFT-WING TRADITIONS

But before we leave intellectual traditions for practice we should look at the main other left-wing Russian[2] traditions in general.

- (a) Anarchism. A Russian is fundamentally an anarchist who does not trust himself, so takes refuge in authoritarianism. This underlying anarchism is plainly evident in the tax evasion, plan violation and drunkenness of nomadic Siberian building workers, and in the occasional spontaneous eruptions of popular fury against the government – it would be a misnomer to call them strikes. The Bolsheviks suppressed overt anarchism with an iron hand in 1921 (Footman, 1959).
- (b) Anti-intellectualism, perhaps more pronounced in the Russian left-wing tradition than in other European ones. With them alone, it acquired a name: Machayevism.[3] People with spectacles, people with briefcases, people above all with technical degrees, were highly suspect to Machayev and those of his tendency. The Bolsheviks, he said, were just such technocrats: they wanted to expropriate the capitalists who owned physical goods in order to substitute exploitation by the owners of intellectual capital, themselves. Machayev supported the workers by hand, not brain. He was wrong about the Bolsheviks, who shared and share his suspicion of the technocracy. What they favoured was not the simple proletariat but a third force, the party. So, in practice, the Machayevist element in Soviet communism has been reduced to a few rhetorical flourishes. After all, it originated as an attack on Marxism, and is wholly incompatible with it.
- (c) Taylorism, or the treatment of men as machines. F. W. Taylor[4] was an American management expert who, working unabashedly for capitalists, showed how to break down an unskilled or semi-skilled

worker's movements when, say, hammering into small sequences. The best choice from the variety of these sequences could then be strung together by the 'scientific manager' by 'time and motion' study into a movement sequence compulsory for all hammerers. Subsequent research by ergonomists and labour relations experts has tended to refute everything he claimed, even in relation to short-run efficiency; while in terms of the alienation and dehumanization of the worker, Taylor stood at the exact opposite pole to Marx. It is thus with astonishment that we see the Bolsheviks taken in by Taylor. The engineer-cum-literateur Alexei Gastev[5] wrote 'The Poetry of the Worker's Stroke' (*Poezia rabochego udara*, published in 1918) before the revolution and, after it, while still not a party member, turned to the advocacy of extreme Taylorism in practice. He was given an institute, funds and publicity by Lenin himself! Truly the movements of the human mind are very complicated. Probably what we have to deal with here is Russian self-contempt, hinted at in (a). We are woolly, indisciplined, self-indulgent people, thought many Bolsheviks. What we need is discipline, good time-keeping. And so Taylor and Gastev became powers in the land, and revolutionary enthusiasm yielded to the metronome, nay actually embraced it, in a fit of ergonomic Puritanism. Russian Taylorism, with its emphasis on skill and incentive, tended rather towards inequality.

(d) Was there any tradition of workers' self-management? Yes, but only for craftsmen, that is, for semi-peasants with nothing of the proletarian life-style. These were habitually organized in *artels*: effective producers' co-operatives, protected by law and custom, with a primitive technology and a democratic management. The strictly agricultural population had its traditional village community (*obshchina*), a far more individualistic set-up than the *artel*, by no means the socialist model that romantics held it to be. While the Bolsheviks totally rejected the *obshchina*, they tried to incorporate the *artels* as a transitional form, even in light industry. But they employed only 1–2 million people and very little distinguished an *artel* from a state factory in Soviet practice, and they were all nationalized in 1960. Other communist countries have taken this form more seriously, and even in the USSR it is now making a comeback. Again it cannot be said that the Bolsheviks encouraged experiments with self-management among the established proletariat. What English-speakers mistranslate as 'workers' control' (*rabochi kontrol'*) was workers' audit: Lenin asked the victorious proletariat, during the first six months of Soviet power when little was nationalized, to make sure that the capitalists were not misusing their profits, concealing their outputs etc. Yugoslav ideologists, who claim that this is a Leninist precedent for Titoist self-management, are in grievous error. There was thus very little tradition of this sort to counter Bolshevik centralism – *and this fact has in the long run worked for equality*. For decentralization necessarily creates little groups with favourable and unfavourable positions in the market, which are thus able and unable to improve those positions by investment; the result *must* be inequality. But centralization works, as we shall see, the way the boss happens to want it to work.

The most remarkable fact about these other traditions is that they have contributed so little to Soviet practice. Only Taylorism/Gastevism has had influence. We are left with the strong conclusion that *Russians are good Marxists*. It is, of course, a highly pragmatic Marxism, but then what serious practical government can adhere exactly to an *a priori* doctrine? Rather can they say, with Cole Porter: 'I've always been true to you, darling, in my fashion'; as opposed to, say, Tito or Mao Tse-tung or Deng Hsiao-ping, who have gone whoring after strange gods and have but the slenderest claims to be Marxists. It comes as no surprise, then, to see the USSR turning back to equality after Stalin's death, simply on these grounds.

THE LABOUR MARKET AND THE INEQUALITY OF EARNERS

To proceed now with our numbered points. First, the refusal to use the phrase 'labour market' is in itself wholly ideological. On a market, Marx says, a man sells his 'labour power', that is his whole working day, and gets back only his subsistence, which it needs but a fraction of a working day to produce. The rest of his product, the surplus value, is also the capitalist's property and so the worker is exploited. This lore is so fundamental to the religion that no shadow of it may appear under socialism, even though all the surplus value or product is the property of the proletarian state. But language has long-run consequences, notably in the very practical points (iii), (iv), (v) and (vi) above. That is, it prevents the government from looking straight and clear at its problems.

Soviet ideology is at its worst here: labour moves around on a non-market, where it is also non-directed!

The truth is that there is a (very imperfect) labour market, over which planners have little control, as Dyker shows in Chapter 3. We may add that Siberia is always emptying, with however much effort and propaganda it is filled up; that the agricultural surplus drained away to the towns far more quickly than the five-year plans laid down; that building labour is a law unto itself, and evades both taxes and wage-limits; that turnover is much the same as under capitalism; that despite careful planning of the annual output of technical education, much of the expense is wasted since people take quite unrelated jobs etc. etc.

Second, inequality is the natural product of a market, but no one can deduce the degree of inequality appropriate to a particular country's labour market. There are many reasons for this disconnection.

(a) Skills can be arranged in different packages; thus there is so much effective demand, public or private, for medical attention in a given country, but Russians will satisfy that demand in part with *feldshers*, the semi-skilled doctors that capitalist doctors' trade unions have driven out. Surely in this case the Russians are quite right, but the point here is that where *feldshers* exist the distribution of income will be different; since a whole big new group exists whose pay is between doctors' and nurses'.

(b) The supply of skills depends on public decisions as to how people shall be educated. These decisions make this one (say secretarial skill in the USSR) relatively scarce and that one (say engineers' training in the USSR) relatively plentiful. For if you want any education at all you must adapt yourself, in all countries, to a menu of courses subject to public decision.

(c) There are wide bands of tolerance within which we prefer a given career and, above all, stick to it once we have chosen it.

(d) The productivity of very senior men is unknowable – indeed, with one decision they might lose, and with another gain, a million rubles. So their worth to the enterprise is unknowable and their salary arbitrary.

Perhaps the greatest reason why the inequality of earnings is so loosely related to the job structure is the so-called backward-sloping supply curve of labour. This doctrine states that *homo economicus* gets accustomed to a certain income, and treats leisure as a luxury, not a necessity: so if you pay him less per hour he works more hours, and if more, less. Both economic history and careful statistical study confirm pure reason. At least there is a very slight backward slope, provided that people are given time enough to settle down at their new wage rate, cannot substitute other employment (including housework and do-it-yourself) and cannot emigrate. The Soviet state, whether it is aware of the backward slope or not, certainly controls all substitute employment and prevents emigration. Therefore, if it raises or lowers the wage rates of a group and its competitors, it gets but little less or more work from them. Therefore, relative hourly wage rates may be set with other goals in mind.[6] But the piece-rate case is more complicated.

So what has the party had in mind? First, as we saw, a period (1918–21) not only of almost perfect equality of pay rates, but also of achieved income: in other words, no reward for performance, even at equal hourly or piece-rates. This extravagance produced the catastrophe we have seen.

There followed the NEP, towards the end of which inequality among workers and employees exceeded the level of the UK in 1966. And here we choose as our measure of inequality the number of times that the income of the ninetieth man in a random sample of 100 exceeds the income of the tenth man, if all 100 are arranged in ascending order. This number is called the *decile ratio*, and the ratio in the USSR in 1928 was 3.8 (Table 2.1) and that in the UK about 2.7,[7] both after tax.

This was substantial inequality by any standards. In the absence of internationally comparable statistics, the authorities may or may not have felt this. Certainly during the first five-year plan they did nothing to change the situation. But at the end of that period, Stalin felt compelled to introduce yet more inequality, and probably landed his country in the position of the least equal in the world.

It is not easy to establish his reasons for doing so from his own words.[8] Tradition assigns his turning point to his speech of 23 June 1931. But here he based wage differentiation exclusively on the need to reduce the then very high labour turnover – or at least that is what he said (Stalin, pp. 362–3). His only actual argument was that:

> The consequence of wage equalization is that the unskilled worker lacks the incentive to become a skilled worker and is thus deprived of the prospect of advancement; as a result he feels himself a 'sojourner' in the factory, working only temporarily so as to earn a little and then go off to 'seek his fortune' elsewhere. The consequence of wage equalization is that the skilled worker is obliged to wander from

factory to factory until he finds one where his skill is properly appreciated.

This is not wrong, but there are other weapons against high labour turnover, and he mentioned some of them. It is inconceivable he should have thrown over so central a part of the party's and Lenin's tradition just to have one more weapon against labour turnover.

In fact, until 1934 nothing much changed, as Table 2.1 shows. Inequality may even have fallen. What there seems to have been is substantial differentiation within each grade, including the possibility of earning less than the previous minimum. This was as an incentive to produce more there and then, at that job, rather than to work for promotion, let alone transfer (Schwarz, 1953, pp. 145–52). Much in this spirit, in January 1934, Stalin addressed the Seventeenth Congress and said, in a very long passage on industry, only this: 'No, it has also its defects. . . . The fact that bad organization of work and wages, lack of personal responsibility in work, and wage equalization have not yet been eliminated . . .' (Stalin, pp. 475–6). He also condemned rural communes for their unpractical degree of egalitarianism and defended their conversion into producers' co-operatives (pp. 500–4).

In August 1935, Stalin invented the Stakhanovite movement. The objects of this were: to raise to exemplary heights the productivity of particular people within their present occupations; to break the remaining traditions of trade union restrictionism; and to swell the numbers of people with a social if not a political stake in Stalin's continued leadership. Fantastic wages were paid, and fantastic costs in disruption of the work process incurred, for these aims. Most of Stakhanovism was bogus, in that Stakhanovites were given artificially easy conditions by management to secure their improbable results. The movement spread wider and wider until 1952, when whole factories were Stakhanovite and 'everyone had a medal', albeit on complicated piece-rates that made even Stakhanovites very unequal to each other. The movement's main legacy was surely no increase of productivity but the extraordinary peak of inequality after the late 1930s. On the whole, managerial, bureaucratic and academic salaries kept ahead of Stakhanovite wages, thus adding to the inequality and giving Stalin another layer of social support.

The date of this peak is not known, since from 1934 to 1956 no distribution surveys were made. Rabkina and Rimashevskaya (1966) put it in or just after the Second World War. They did not mention Stakhanovism, which in 1966 had only been dead a decade and may still have been a sensitive subject. They ascribed the peak to incentive payments in munitions factories at a period of very low real incomes. This would be in stark contrast to British wartime developments, but we must remember that in the USSR ration cards were more important than money until September 1946, so that monetary inequality had little meaning.

Was Stalin's behaviour rational? There is no reason whatever to think so, and those today who, from whatever intellectual position, defend him are guilty of sloppy reasoning, since:

(i) he started from considerable inequality;
(ii) he made no changes during the first five-year plan, and not many until the end of the second (Table 2.1);
(iii) he had labour turnover mainly in mind;
(iv) he barely raised the rate of industrial growth over 1927–9 (Table 2.1) though, of course, so composite a variable has many causes. Indeed, inequality was still higher in 1950 than in 1934, yet the growth rate had fallen.

Stalin set the demands for this and that labour skill, but hardly their supplies. Was he perhaps reacting rationally to changes in supply? The decile ratio of earnings in the state sector has moved as shown in Table 2.1, which includes an appropriate index of performance and series indicating the main influences from the supply side.

The period of high Stalinism was 1931–54 approximately. The main influx of peasants, which might rationally have raised the decile ratio, began in the eighteenth century and lasted until about 1956. It was particularly great in the 1930s, and these movements are indicated in the fourth column. The main influx of graduates took place during 1928–36 and should have depressed the decile ratio, but did not do so. Thereafter, the Great Purge struck very hard at the number of experienced graduates properly employed, since it sent them to cut firewood, and the Second World War diminished the production of new graduates. So some part of the 1946 (we should probably say the 1938–54) peak has a rational explanation. But some again does not for there was, according to all evidence, no equalization until 1956 (Stalin died in 1953). Furthermore, industrial growth pursued its usual S-curve, apparently irrespective of all movements of inequality. Or at least the other influences were much more important.

There are larger points too against Stalin's policy. First, a correct set of incentives, operating on each worker and employee at the micro-level,

TABLE 2.1 *Soviet decile ratios of earnings in the state sector, industrial performance and supply of engineers, 1928–70*

	Decile ratio of earnings		Rate of growth (% p.a.)		Engineers, etc. in industry, as a percentage of production workers	
	Industrial workers	All workers and employees	Industrial output	Industrial labour force[d]	Engineers, technicians and managers	Graduate engineers
1928	3.23[f]/3.7[e]	3.8[e]	12[j]	8.3[k]	3.6[l]	0.5[l]
1932	–	–	–	–	5.5[l]	0.8[l]
1934	3.17[f]/4.1[e]	4.2[e]	18.1[m]	8.7[m]	7.5[l]	1.7[l]
1936	–	–	12.0[n]	4.0[n]	8.3[l]	1.5[l]
1946	–	6.0[c]	–	–	–	–
1950	–	–	8.9[o]	4.0[o]	10.6[g]	1.9[h]/2.2[g]
1956	3.38[b]	4.4[a]	10[h]	4.0[h]	10.8[g]	1.5[h]/2.1[g]
1961	2.75[b]	–	7.5[h]	4.5[h]	–	2.2[h]
1964	–	3.7[a]	7.0[h]	4.0[h]	–	2.3[h]
1966	–	3.2[a]	7.0[h]	3.5[h]	–	n.a.
1968	–	2.7[a]	7.0[h]	3.0[h]	–	n.a.
1970	–	3.2[a]	7.0[h]	3.0[h]	–	3.2[h]

a. Wiles (1974) lecture IV, table 4.
b. Kirsch (1972) pp. 181–2.
c. Reduced arbitrarily from the original 7.24 (Loznevaya, 1968) to allow bread rationing, that is, for the far greater purchasing power of the poor man's ruble. Cf. Wiles (1974) Introduction.
d. Three-year average about the given year, unless otherwise stated.
e. Bergson (1944) pp. 227–8.
f. M. Mozhina (1961).
g. Dewitt (1961) pp. 496–7, 500–1. In contrast to source [h], the last column includes managers.
h. Joint Economic Committee (1973) pp. 280, 508 and 568; includes construction.
j. Wiles (1966).
k. Schwarz (1953) pp. 31–2
l. 'Large-scale' industry only; source as in [g].
m. Rate for 1934 on 1933 only. 1933 on 1932 is vitiated by the fall in the industrial labour force (by 7.6 per cent) due to the famine: production also fell, by 3.6 per cent. 1935 on 1934 is incredibly high: output rose by 39.9 per cent and the labour force by 10.0 per cent.
n. 1935–7 only; see footnote [m]. That is, when Stakhanovism became widespread, in 1936, output growth fell.
o. Source for footnotes [m, n, o]: Powell (1963) pp. 187–8. I have averaged the 1928 and the 1937 weights.

need not render them very unequal overall. For it gets the best out of each on the basis of his (equal) starting rates, so each earns more.

Then there is the fact, referred to above, that the more we are paid per hour, the fewer hours we devote to work of all sorts in the long run. This paradoxical truth was not accepted by Stalin and is not by his successors. But it exercises its influence at all times: so that inequality is not anywhere, and was not under Stalin, closely related to incentives and productivity. If he made the poor work longer, he let the high-paid relax, just as greater equality would have done the opposite. It was not the fanning out of hourly pay or monthly salaries, it was the introduction of piece-rates and various penalties, that enhanced effort overall; and these latter, as we have seen, had no very obvious connection with the fanning out.

Consider in particular the raising of the promotion steps, which was necessarily a part of the fanning out of salaries. Suppose this was superimposed on a constant supply of suitable labour and that the actual number of high-salary jobs was also constant. Then a larger number of candidates for promotion, not all of them quite suitable, would be all that could be observed – and indeed it was observed. There is obvious waste here, in the sense of overpayment. But it would be difficult for an administrator to deduce that all top salaries might well be lower: for had any particular post been offered at a lower salary, fewer candidates would have appeared.

When Khrushchev came in he founded the State Committee on Wages in 1955 and actually lowered some top salaries (Loznevaya, 1968; Kirsch, 1972, p. 184). He also abolished the 'progressive' piece rate, which increased with output (Kirsch, 1972, p. 32). As this happened everywhere, his appointments committees had no particular difficulty, since applicants had nowhere better to go. As to the labour supply of the successful candidate, he was caught as usual by the indivisibility of the labour contract, but must have been more tempted to moonlight; that is, the charms of leisure had diminished, but otherwise the supply of labour was probably unaffected.

So there would appear to be little reason to consider distribution as a variable affecting Soviet economic performance. It varies greatly, but at the behest of ideology and politics. Nothing suggests that Stalin was right, in terms of growth, to reverse the trend to equality, or that Khrushchev was right to start it up again. They expressed thereby their own personalities and perhaps yielded also to some vague social pressure.

Only the really extreme 'War' communist step of cutting all links between pay and productivity had a noticeable effect – predictably a negative one.

LABOUR DIRECTION

Under War Communism, as we saw in the absence of differential incentives, Trotsky directed labour. It is fortunate for the Soviet citizen that so many unpleasant possibilities of communism are labelled

Trotskyite! Direction vanished with the NEP and did not return with Stalin's system. But he did introduce, or retain, certain exceptions. We might wish to say that here, too, full communism (a form of Trotskyism!) casts its shadow before it. But that is hardly so, except for cases (f) and (g) below. Full communism will certainly not use the market, but neither will it use the police, since the state will have withered away. Instead of orders, the planners (who are no part of the Marxist concept of the state) will persuade people, nay merely inform them. Even such an institution as (c) will cease to exist, since young doctors will *want* to go to Norilsk (where anyway we shall have changed the climate – for climate control is part of full communism).

Be that as it may, Stalin's exceptions were (and Brezhnev's are):

(a) Corrective labour (*ispravitel'ni trud*) in a camp or colony. This, based on Marxism, is the ordinary penal sentence (a very few top political prisoners go to isolators, where little work is done). The numbers are quite unknown today, but certainly much smaller than under Stalin, when they reached about 6 mn. in 1939, which implies 10 per cent of the adult male population.[9] But there is very little reason to suppose that even Stalin went to the expense of arresting and sentencing people for 'cheap' labour: it was and is not cheap, since cold climates disable and guards must be well paid. Corrective labour is a crucial penal device with, today, small economic consequences.

(b) Deportation to a place (*ssyl'ka*). This is the fate of legally innocent people judged by the KGB to be security risks, or even merely by the comrades' courts to be ne'er do wells. The sentenced are nominally permitted to choose any job on arrival, but are often 'found' work by the militia. They are at all times exceedingly numerous, perhaps more so than (a). Indeed, released prisoners ordinarily go into *ssyl'ka*, and whole nations like the Crimean Tartars did the same. This institution too is mainly legal, though perhaps the cloven hoof of economic motivation is more evident: *ssyl'ka* does populate Siberia to a minor extent, but it does not spare the state the necessity of removal costs, and the considerable regional wage differential is paid also to the deportee – though usually in a much worse job than before.

(c) The one real serious case of economic direction is the leavers of technical schools and universities. These are sent by the ministry in charge of their professional function (for example, the Ministry of Health for young doctors) to an assigned post for the first three years. Much excitement, and much corruption, attend this moment. Plum assignments, say to Moscow or Leningrad, go to the children of the most influential parents. The rest suffer, but as a solution to the problem of, say, rural doctors, it is certainly more efficient than the free market. No society pays rural doctors a big enough differential to keep them: the Soviet distinction is merely that it does not try. The system is of Tsarist origin and clearly does influence income distribution.

(d) There is also a minor penalty called forced work (*prinuzhdennaya rabota*).[10] This is a short sentence to work at one's normal place of employment at reduced wage, in order to cover some fine, say for absenteeism or the destruction of working material. It is also a court sentence, and so again hardly concerns us except to show the Draconian character of Soviet law.

(e) Party officials can be directed to specific jobs by the party, for political rather than economic reasons. This affects the distribution of people to jobs, but does not alter the number of jobs on offer or their pay differentials.

(f) Then there are the many mobilization campaigns, for the Virgin Lands, the Great Building Sites, and what not. These collect, in a fairly voluntary way, Komsomol members entering the labour market and soldiers being demobilized. They are conducted by *Orgnabor*. Since people thus mobilized cannot be prevented from leaving again, they are a very weak substitute for pay differentials.

(g) Lastly, the enthusiasm of students and Komsomol members (the latter include nearly all the former) is often mobilized for a *subbotnik*: an unpaid Saturday's work cleaning something or harvesting some minor crop.

Different from any of these, and outside our subject, is the prohibition on the *kolkhoznik* to leave his *kolkhoz*. Never well enforced, this has been lifted region by region since 1 January 1975. It was the greatest of all forms of Soviet directed labour, and most severely depressed *kolkhozniks'* incomes.

Note that in every one of these cases the state is ordering or persuading the individual to *go* to a particular place, or to *adopt* a particular occupation. It is not commanding his degree of effort within that job. This applies even in corrective labour camps, where bonuses and other incentives reign supreme, with particular inhumanity. Everybody must be rewarded for effort within his job, and this necessity is more imperious than that to reward movements between jobs. But, of course, it too will disappear under full communism!

TURNOVER AND UNEMPLOYMENT

The state's hostility to labour turnover follows directly from this: people should be influenced by bonus systems to put forth effort, but they should not wander around in the job market, not even if the state's own pay differentials tempt them. But, further, no worker is of much use for the first few days: indeed, he takes up the time of others who must teach him. So there are excellent economic reasons for reducing turnover. Stalin took many measures short of labour direction towards this end (Schwarz, 1953, Ch. 3): loss of entitlement to social services, instant eviction from the employer's housing etc. He had a partial success, and the harshest of these measures have been repealed; but turnover remains, at around 20 per cent p.a. of leavers for all causes, about the same as in the UK or USA.[11]

Among Stalin's measures for reducing turnover was greater inequality of pay, as we saw above. The author has never followed the logic of this, unless Stalin meant seniority pay. But logic or no logic, we have no reason to doubt his word that this was one of his motives.

The interval between a man leaving one job and taking the next one is the commonest sort of unemployment. But the formal definition of that phenomenon is to be 'genuinely seeking work'. This is so highly subjective that the volume of unemployment is about the most arbitrary magnitude in capitalist economies. The USSR officially abolished unemployment in 1930, except for underemployment on collective farms. The boast is not wholly true, since turnover persists at a high rate and there is a longish interval between jobs.[12] However, much of this is, as elsewhere, voluntary.

As Dyker shows, unemployment is low and an essentially local problem, fought by local investment in areas where it threatens; also by sheer orders to enterprises to employ more people in return for a state subsidy. There is, of course, no macro-economic policy of a Keynesian kind, since investment and employment are according to detailed orders, not general monetary incentives. But what is the effect on the distribution of income and the functioning of the labour market of Soviet unemployment?

On the one hand, the amount is small but, on the other, there is no dole, so distributively these effects cancel out. The dole was abolished by

Stalin in October 1930, officially because he had abolished unemployment, in reality to reduce labour turnover. Without a dole or genuine trade unions, the government can run the economy at very full employment without cost inflation. But the subsidized, unwanted labour is a nuisance to the enterprises ordered to hire it and engenders many managerial protests. When, however, we look at the fate of the unemployed under capitalism, we may ask ourselves if the micro-inefficient system is not more macro-efficient, or at least more humane.

The USSR is an extremely large country, with great differences of climate and with ethnic minorities that, having occupied a particular territory for centuries, have had an economic history that favoured or disfavoured them. It is much to the credit of the system that there are no substantial earnings-per-worker differences at all, except in the co-operative sector. Here, productivity still reflects inherited differences of education, fixed capital and, of course, climate-cum-land fertility. But in state farms and outside agriculture there is substantial uniformity of real pay.

The cost of living differs across regions: partly because *kolkhoz* market prices are lower in good climates, partly because the housing shortage varies a great deal. But care is taken to differentiate wages accordingly. Nay more, needs (in food, clothing and housing) rise as the climate gets colder so that, on top of a price compensation, a need compensation is also paid (in fact they are lumped together). In the study of these matters the USSR seems to lead the world.[13] But it would be foolish to ascribe any of this to ideology. The very real regional differences that exist are almost wholly due to variations in the size of the family: Protestants – or people in that tradition – have far fewer children than Moslems, and the family allowances are far too small to level up the difference.

INEQUALITY OF FAMILY INCOME PER HEAD

Accordingly, we turn to the second great question: how has income per member of family, or family income *per capita*, been distributed? In a modern welfare state of whatever political complexion, the distribution of earnings per earner is only very loosely connected to that of family income per head. Law and custom intervene with enormous effect. Take two societies with the same inequality of earnings per earner; but in the first, let rich men habitually marry poor women, and everyone marry someone and have two children. All this spells equality by contrast with the second society, in which the rich marry each other, but not everyone marries at all, and the poor have more children than the rich. Differences in state pensions, children's allowances and income taxation further complicate the picture, even before we get to that last great 'complication': is the society capitalist or communist? Have the rich, in addition to their larger salaries, substantial unearned incomes from the private ownership of the means of production?

Not even the later, almost revisionist, Marx and Engels lived to see the capitalist welfare state and redistributive taxation. So Marxists have felt bound to deny their importance altogether. This had two practical results for the USSR. The first is surely beneficent: there is scarcely any redistributive taxation, on the grounds that the state already distributes income justly, and will move towards full communism by further equalizing gross wages, by means of central directives. The second is what we observe in McAuley's chapter (Chapter 8): the Soviet social services are less egalitarian in intention or effect than the British, since they are essentially the fringe benefits of the proletariat, that they enjoy because of their membership as workers of this or that grade in the single enterprise constituted by the victorious proletarian state. The distribution of these services is nevertheless, of course, more egalitarian than that of wages themselves. This is practically a matter of definition: you have to be poor at present to qualify (but the higher your wages were, the more you get now).

The prime contrast between capitalism and socialism is the private versus the public ownership of the means of production. However simple and old-fashioned this point is, however boring the stale Marxist iteration of it, it takes pride of place in ideology, ethics and law. So must it too in the study of income distribution.

It is true that Marxists grotesquely exaggerate the importance of capitalism in this field. We have not the relevant figures for the USSR, but Table 2.2 shows how wages, incomes from capital and social services are distributed in the Polish socialist sector and in Britain as a whole. In all known respects the Soviet and Polish socialist sectors are much alike, so we can say that both these societies have a very 'British' distribution of family income right up to the top 5 per cent. The social services, scattered capitalist incomes among poorer people (particularly pensioners) and wages themselves make the bottom 95 per cent very similar. But then inherited wealth takes its toll, and produces at the very top of British society, fantastic extremes of wealth. Unfortunately for all sound reasoning, this is just the point at which the extremely high and little-known special fringe benefits of the Soviet élite begin! It seems that these

TABLE 2.2   The composition of household income by source – all UK, £ per week, 1967 (in order of household incomes)

	Range of income (£)												All households	60 + as % of total
	0–6	6–8	8–10	10–15	15–20	20–25	25–30	30–35	35–40	40–50	50–60	60 +		
No. of households	246	328	311	710	893	1149	1004	818	574	699	319	335	7386	4.5
Average income per household	5.17	6.85	8.95	12.54	17.64	22.51	27.48	32.35	37.50	44.37	54.45	83.31	28.25	13.4
No. of persons	258	391	535	1555	2473	3725	3406	2723	1927	2605	1234	1303	22135	5.9
Composition of income (%)														
Wages and salaries	1.9	5.1	10.1	39.2	72.7	81.2	82.4	84.0	86.2	84.5	81.2	64.6	75.8	11.4
Self-employment	0.4	0.97	2.2	4.3	4.9	3.8	4.8	4.9	3.8	4.9	5.6	15.3	6.0	34.4
State retirement, old age and widows' pensions	68.1	56.0	49.7	24.9	6.9	3.5	2.8	2.0	1.5	1.5	1.3	0.97	4.9	2.6
Other state benefits	20.3	22.9	18.8	11.9	4.3	3.5	2.4	1.4	1.1	1.2	1.3	0.59	2.9	2.8
Investments	2.7	4.1	4.4	4.3	3.0	1.8	1.5	2.0	1.9	2.2	5.3	11.9	3.7	42.5
Non-state pensions and annuities	1.7	3.3	7.4	7.6	3.4	1.5	1.5	1.2	1.3	1.7	1.2	1.7	2.0	10.5
Sub-letting and/or owner occupation	3.3	4.8	3.8	3.2	2.1	2.1	2.3	2.3	2.2	2.2	2.0	2.1	2.3	12.3
Other sources	1.9	2.9	3.7	4.6	2.7	2.6	2.5	2.2	1.9	1.8	2.1	3.0	2.4	16.1
	100	100	100	100	100	100	100	100	100	100	100	100	100	13.4

approximate median by no. of people

Urban, socialized, non-pensioner, Poland, thousand zlotys p.a., 1967 (in order of household incomes per person)

	Range of income per person (thousand zlotys p.a.)							Polish total	UK total	UK £60+
	0–7.2	7.2–9.6	9.6–12.0	12–15	15–18	18–24	24+			
No. of households	152	474	606	745	562	591	326	3 456		
Average income per person (zl.)	6 978	9 359	11 880	14 424	17 662	21 548	30 922	14 508		
No. of persons	765	2 057	2 297	2 563	1 585	1 347	538	11 180		
Composition of income—(%)										
From work or employment	77.9	80.6	84.5	86.5	89.6	90.1	90.5	87.1	81.8	79.8
Social benefits	15.2	13.0	9.8	8.9	7.3	5.6	3.8	8.4	9.8[a]	33[a]
Other income	6.8	6.3	5.7	4.7	3.1	4.4	5.7	4.5	8.4	17.0

approximate median by no. of people

a Treating private pensions as if they were state pensions.

SOURCE Wiles and Markowski (1971) table 24.

benefits have as great a weight as inherited capital–so long as a man is in office! On retirement or dismissal, they cease very abruptly, so that their social, as opposed to their statistical, effect is very different indeed.[14]

We had no data until very recently for the distribution of family income. We give it, therefore, at a point of time in Table 2.3, with an international comparison. Before the 1970s, we must suppost that the equality–inequality pendulum swung as follows:

(i)   At the moment of revolution it was violently equalized, as the property of capitalists and aristocrats, even in the means of consumption, was confiscated. Then for about seven months there was a sort of stable chaos in which social policy was quite moderate.

(ii) Then followed the near total equality of 'War' communism, described above (June 1918–March 1921).

(iii) The NEP brought this inequality back to what it had been in (i).

(iv) The differentiation of earnings per earner under Stalin's new system did not set in with the system (early 1929), but in about 1935, as described. But in 1929–34, social services worsened (suppression of the dole), so family incomes must have become more unequal. Then came the differentiation of earnings. Its impact on family income was somewhat mitigated by the continued expansion of the new social services until the war.

(v)   In the war (1941–5), earnings were further differentiated and social services stagnated. But there was very little to buy with the inflated money and, while bread and a few other basic articles were still sold at frozen prices, the real inequality was the rather considerable one of rations and administrative privileges. The USSR concluded the war a very unequal society.

(vi) Earnings were apparently equalized when bread rationing was abolished in 1947, but simultaneously bread prices rose, to take away the poor's gain from the extra money. In 1948–54, civilian production increased enormously, but the increase was divided equally among all groups by lowering retail prices instead of raising the lowest incomes. Nothing really changed until Khruschev (1954–64), who

(vii) Froze retail prices, and raised minimum wages and social services

(viii) Finally, Brezhnev, with his predilection for a long period of 'developed socialism' before full communism comes, took a very short step backwards towards unequal earnings and relatively smaller social services.

TABLE 2.3a Per capita income

	USSR[b]		UK		Italy	Hungary		Poland	Czecho-slovakia	Bul-garia	Sweden		Canada	USA		FRG	Aust-ralia[c]
	1958	1967	1953–4	1969	1969	1967	1972	1971	1965	1965	1967	1971	1971	1950	1974	1969	1966–8
$P_{95}/P_{50}\%$	n.a.	n.a.	251.1	251.4	331	?201	?206.5	n.a.	190	174.5	231.1	226.0	300.0	315.6	289.8	266	273.1
$P_{90}/P_{50}\%$	190.6	179.4	194.5	204.4	234	171.5	173.3	167	167	152.2	197.0	182.5	226.7	200.0	229.4	209	226.3
$P_{75}/P_{50}\%$	137.5	128.3	143.2	149.2	154.7	134.2	140.8	130	133	127.1	148.4	138.1	153.7	160.0	153.0	146	165.8
$P_{25}/P_{50}\%$	68.1	76.6	73.3	71.2	61.5	75.3	76.7	74	72	77.6	71.7	74.5	64.8	58.0	63.5	71.2	71.3
$P_{10}/P_{50}\%$	46.7	57.7	52.9	52.0	39.9	57.3	57.0	58	53	58.0	53.7	51.0	38.4	28.1	36.7	54.5	52.5
$P_5/P_{50}\%$	n.a.	n.a.	43.5	42.5	29.5	?50	?48.4	51	42	47.8	35.8	25.3	?25.0	?15.7	?23.9	47.0	39.2
P_{50} in local money	39.2	56.35	3.29	9.05	394 000	1 080	1 403	18 700	8 400	624	7 140	10 131	2 002	826	3 311	5 464.60	979
(period)	(month)	(month)	(week)	(week)	(year)	(month)	(month)	(year)	(year)	(year)	(year)	(year)	(year)	(year)	(year)	(year)	(year)

a. All sources except the UK omit imputed owner-occupiers' rents. All figures are net of income tax and national insurance unless otherwise stated.
b. McAuley (1977), excludes households headed by pensioners and students, and state and collective farmers. Deducting 5 per cent arbitrarily to allow for the income tax on P_{95} and P_{90}; 2 per cent on P_{75}. For the probable actual impact of *Polish* income tax, cf. Wiles and Markowski (1971) pp. 361, 364. Communist figures always treat the income tax as an expenditure out of income.
c. From Podder (1972) p. 191. All other columns from Wiles (1978) table 7.17.

We see that not only Marxism governs the Soviet régime in these matters; but very much depends on the given Marxist in charge. It is in all seriousness difficult to explain the whole story except in terms of personal decisions.

NOTES

1. This chapter is confined to the socialist sector and excludes the incomes of collective farmers. It deals not only with the inequality of wages per earner, but also with that of income from all sources per household. 'All sources' includes legal private enterprise, illegal private enterprise, social services, deposit bank interest and do-it-yourself.
2. 'Russian' is of course a word describing a particular Soviet nationality. The minorities have other traditions, but these have not left their imprint on policy or legislation.
3. J. W. Machayev (1867–1926) (alias Machajski, for he was a Russified Pole) preached these doctrines in 1898–1900, see Utechin, 1958.
4. 1856–1915, see Bibliography.
5. Skillen, 1980; Bailes, 1977.
6. One qualification to this surprising but well attested doctrine is that the better we are paid, the better the quality, not quantity, of our work. The qualification is big, but not overwhelming.
7. Wiles and Markowski, 1971, p. 506. I have set the average rate of income tax in UK at 5 per cent on the tenth, 30 per cent on the ninetieth, centile. This reduces 3.4 gross to 2.7 net. The Soviet income tax is very low, and hits also low-paid workers, so it needs no allowance.
8. From here on I reproduce, with permission, pp. 55–6 of my *Stalin and British Top Salaries* with a very few corrections.
9. Preliminary results of my own workings.
10. In all European languages there is a 'work' word (*œuvre, Werk, trud, opera, opus, ergon*) and a 'labour' word (*labeur, Arbeit, rabota, lavoro, labor, ponos*). The latter is less honourable and creative, and it is used in the contexts of alienation and childbirth. In modern usage, the distinction is very blurred, but in different ways: thus worker, *ouvrier, Arbeiter, rabochi, operaio.* 'Labourer', a depreciatory word, has no equivalent except, incompletely, *laboureur.* But in 'Labour Movement', labour is a good word, as in German and Russian – but French and Italian use *ouvrier* and *operaio. Trudyashchiesya,* a word of praise meaning workers plus peasants, that is, non-idlers or non-bourgeois (literally 'toilers'), has no equivalent either. This is the sense of *trud* in *ispravitel'ni trud,* above.
11. But paternalistic Japan and self-managed Yugoslavia have much lower rates, about 5 per cent per annum. Rates also vary very much by occupation, with building far in the lead in all countries. This is natural since a building enterprise is only a nucleus of administrators and skilled craftsmen, while other workers are hired according to the job in hand and to the place where it is.

12. Also new entrants take time to find their first jobs, and old people leave before retirement.
13. Cf. Wiles, 1980, appendix D.
14. Numbers are anonymous: they only tell us that each year there are so many people who earn more than so many rubles or pounds. They do not say if these are the same people as last year, or whether they owe their good fortune to political power, inheritance or any other thing such as theft, thrift or sheer ability.

BIBLIOGRAPHY

Kendall E. Bailes, *Soviet Studies* (July 1977).

Abram Bergson, *The Structure of Soviet Wages* (Harvard, 1944).

Janet Chapman, *Wage Variation in Soviet Industry* (Santa Monica, 1970).

Nicholas Dewitt, *Education and Professional Employment in USSR* (Washington, 1961).

David Footman, *St Antony's Papers* (Oxford, 1959) No. 6.

Joint Economic Committee of Congress, *Soviet Economic Prospects* (Washington, 1973).

J. Leonard Kirsch, *Soviet Wages* (New York, 1972).

M. Loznevaya, *Sotsialisticheski trud* (October 1968).

Alastair McAuley, *Soviet Studies* (April 1977).

Karl Marx, *The Critique of the Gotha Programme*, Letter to Bracke (5 May 1875).

M. Mozhina, *Byulleten Nauchnoi Informatsii: Trud: Zarabotnaya Plata* (October 1961).

N. F. Podder, *Economic Record* (June 1972) p. 191.

Raymond P. Powell, in Abram Bergson and Simon Kuznets (ed.), *Economic Trends in the Soviet Union* (Harvard 1963).

N. Rabkina and N. M. Rimashevskaya, *Voprosy ekonomiki* (December 1966).

Solomon Schwarz, *Labour in the Soviet Union* (London, 1953).

Daphne Skillen, 'Patterns of Urban – Rural Opposition in Russian Literature in the Early Twenties', Ph. D. thesis, London University, 1980.

Joseph V. Stalin, *Problems of Leninism* (Moscow, 1953).

Frederick W. Taylor, *The Principles of Scientific Management* (New York, 1911).

Sergei V. Utechin, *Soviet Studies* (October 1958).

Peter J. D. Wiles, 'Statistiques sur l'économie Sovietique', in *Analyse et Prévision* (1966).

Peter J. D. Wiles, 'Stalin and British Top Salaries' in A. B. Atkinson, *The Personal Distribution of Incomes* (London, 1976).

———*The Distribution of Income East and West* (Amsterdam, 1974).

———'Our Shaky Data Base', in Wilhelm Krelle and Antony Shorrocks, *Personal Income Distribution* (Amsterdam, 1978).

———*Anti-Systemares Verhalten in der Sowjetwirtschaft*, Bundesinstitut für Ostwissenschaftliche und Internationale Studien (Bonn, 1980).

Peter J. D. Wiles and Stefan M. Markowski, *Soviet Studies* (January and April 1971).

3 Planning and the Worker

David A. Dyker

INTRODUCTION

The Soviet system of economic planning is based on the principle of command. Developed during a period when, to quote Oscar Lange's memorable phrase, the Soviet economy was '*sui generis* a war economy',[1] the system operates through the dimensions of hierarchy, subordination and obedience/disobedience, through vertical rather than horizontal links. It is also, of course, a highly centralised system, and matters peripheral by any normal standards may come within the purview and competence of the authorities in Moscow. There is, then, in general terms, a complete contrast between such a system and systems characteristic of Western societies, where vertical and horizontal links mingle to form a picture of bewildering complexity, where the market remains the ultimate nexus of economic activity, even for state-owned enterprises, and where government concerns itself with operational details only in circumstances of emergency (for example, a real war or ecological disaster). In the field of labour, the contrast is not quite so complete in terms of the operational elements of the planning system. Despite the prevalence of the command principle, for example, there is little direction of labour as such in the Soviet Union today. But other contrasts, related to the long-term strategy of planning, make their appearance. We start by detailing the key characteristics of labour-force planning in both its operational and strategic contexts.

In the Stalin period there were, notoriously, many elements of coercion of the workforce. Labour camps apart, legislation was introduced in the late 1930s and early 1940s which made provision for the direction of 'free' labour, especially of apprentice labour, and placed serious obstacles in the way of any worker wishing to change his job. Peasants on collective farms were subjected to 'organised recruitment' (*Orgnabor*) for industrial work – not in practice terribly coercive – and passport restrictions which meant that no peasant could leave his farm without permission from the political authorities. Even under 'high Stalinism', however, the bulk of the working population were constrained by essentially negative controls, rather than active direction as such. Since the death of Stalin, the situation has become simpler and we can say that, in general terms, only members of the Communist Party and new graduates, for the first three years after graduation, are subject to active direction. Constraints on free movement no longer affect urban workers to any significant extent, and collective farm peasants are, in principle, now entitled to an internal passport (permitting free movement within the Soviet Union) on the same automatic basis as urban dwellers. The police *propiska* (registration) regulations may still make it very difficult for an individual to settle in the town of his choice (especially if it happens to be Moscow[2]), but this acts as a constraint on speculative drifting, rather than on free response to advertised job vacancies.

Of course, the predominance of the command principle in the economic system as a whole can spill over into the labour sphere in ways which the central authorities may, indeed, not approve of. A letter from an irate father published in *Pravda* about twelve years ago (that is, in the period of post-Khrushchev liberalisation) revealed that local political establishments may decide that, for example, all the boys at a particular school are going to be apprenticed as building workers.[3] The particular case was reported with censure, but what is clear is that hierarchies themselves under pressure from superiors to report fulfilment of plan targets may be tempted to try to apply pressure on subordinates on the same basis, legal or not. To counterbalance this, however, it is evident that the provision for direction of graduates often has little real bite. Good graduates and children of influential people may get directed to where they want to go anyway, and many of those directed to less desirable positions, particularly in the less hospitable regions of the USSR, simply do not turn up.[4] In any case, the process of allocation appears to be extremely inefficient, and there are many examples of graduates being directed to enterprises that do not need them.[5] It is not difficult to argue that this inefficiency is wholly explicable in terms of the over-centralisation of the planning system as a whole (see below) and of the peculiar degree of organisational fragmentation of the process itself – a multitude of administrative bodies in addition to the Ministry for Higher Education itself are involved.[6] It has, however, been suggested that a desire to break up potentially dangerous groups of student dissenters and reformists may have contributed to the rather hit-

and-miss 'send everybody somewhere' pattern.[7] Finally, it should be borne in mind that the concept of efficiency is a limited one and that this particular institution of the Soviet system must, like other institutions, be evaluated in terms of the strategic goals of the system – of this more in a moment.

Coercion, then, is not a key element in the process of labour planning in the contemporary Soviet Union. Total control over the educational system, and a much higher degree of preparedness than is common in the West to pressurise school children into following particular specialities does, of course, give the Soviet authorities a powerful means of conditioning the basic composition of the labour force, particularly its more highly-qualified component. But when it comes to the allocation of the given labour force between jobs, between enterprises and between regions, it is hardly surprising that the wage system does, and is meant to, play a fundamental role, as it does in the West.

We can distinguish between three elements in the system of wage planning. The first is the basic structure of wage and salary rates for given jobs, qualified by a system of, in most cases, seven grades (*razryad*) relating to seniority, experience etc. The second is the system of bonuses and incentive payments. The third is the complex of special rates and payments for those working in inhospitable regions. In practice, the distinction between the first and second elements is not always clear-cut, with the increasing incidence of various kinds of payments-by-results schemes. In construction, for instance, the share of basic wage in total wage payments has fallen from 85–90 per cent in 1969 to 55–60 per cent at the present time.[8] Radical changes in differentials between major occupational groups are not very common, but the Soviet authorities have, in particular cases, shown no hesitation in backing up general economic strategy with appropriate wage policies. An example is the 1969 decree significantly improving the relative position of building workers, which formed part of a general drive to improve efficiency in the construction sector. On the other hand, pressure and arm-twisting are bound to play some rôle, if only a supporting one, in connection with any major policy initiative in a Soviet-type politico-economic system.

The effectiveness of regional coefficients and other special payments as levers for solving the crucial, but rather uniquely Soviet, problem of inter-regional labour distribution has been a difficult issue in Soviet economic planning for some years now. It was noted by researchers working in the 1960s that as many people were leaving Siberia and the far north as were arriving, and this prompted investigations which showed that, for example, the cost of living in Eastern Siberia was 20 per cent above that of the Central Moscow region in 1966, while money wages were only 18 per cent higher.[9] Thus the real standard of living in Eastern Siberia was lower, even without taking into account factors like inaccessibility, inhospitable climate etc. A 1967 decree strengthened the regional coefficient element in Siberian and far north pay packets and, in the course of the 1970s, special length-of-service increments have been introduced for outlying regions, while regional pay coefficients have been established for 'semi-inhospitable' areas like the Urals and parts of Kazakhstan.[10] Despite these and other measures, however, Soviet workers continue to display a strong penchant to stay in the big European cities, or to drift down to the climatically more salubrious Caucasus or Central Asian regions.[11] Inadequate incentives apart, it is clear that one of the reasons for the lack of bite in Soviet labour policies for the regions has been the absence, until recently, of any kind of systematic labour placement (*trudoustroistvo*) service.

When unemployment was officially 'abolished' in the USSR, so were labour exchanges. This no doubt reflected a prejudice familiar in the UK – namely that labour exchanges are there to find jobs for the unemployed, rather than to improve the allocation of a scarce resource. In any case, job information has in the past been purveyed largely on the basis of posters and radio and press announcements, usually emanating from enterprises or other grass-roots organisations. Not only has there been no national network of labour exchanges, but there has not even been, as far as we know, any central bank of detailed information on supply and demand for different kinds of labour. *Orgnabor* has changed its character since it specialised in bringing peasants into the growing towns in the 1930s. In the post-war period, it has concentrated on getting people out to Siberia and the far north, and latterly on finding workers for areas of severe labour shortage in the European parts of the USSR.[12] The work of *Orgnabor* has not, however, been of very high quality,[13] and the organisation has been unable to make a permanent impression on the labour shortage in the outlying areas. In the period 1966–70, *Orgnabor* placed just 573,000 workers, as compared to 2,833,400 for 1951–5.[14] Recruitment through the Komsomol operates in a similar way to *Orgnabor*, and accounted for 500,000 placements in 1974–8.[15] There are forty-two officially designated Komsomol 'shock' projects in Siberia and the far east, and 30,000 young people annually are recruited for these projects by the Komsomol.[16] As with *Orgnabor* recruits, however, the pattern with Komsomol 'volunteers' is to go east or north for a couple of years and then drift west or south.

Since 1966 there has been a new development with the establishment of employment offices (*sluzhba truda*) under the aegis of republican committees for labour resource utilisation. By 1970, this service was processing more than a million workers annually in the RSFSR (accounting for about half the population of the USSR) alone.[17] *Sluzhba truda* has shown good results, for example in reducing frictional unemployment, but the fact that it is organised on a republican basis, with no union-wide organisation as such, must weaken it as an instrument of inter-regional allocation of labour. In 1977 the republican committees for labour resource utilisation were subordinated to a reorganised All-Union State Committee for Labour and Social Problems (*Goskomtrud*).[18] Recent planning measures (see discussion of 'mini-reform', below) aim to give republican and local 'labour organs' more teeth. Whether these contrasting developments will lead to a reinvigorated development of *trudoustroistvo* remains to be seen.

Labour supply in the Soviet Union has, then, been to a considerable extent unplanned. To the extent that it has been planned, it has been planned, it seems, rather ineffectually. But this situation must be viewed in the context of the pattern of Soviet economic development over the past 40–50 years. Stalinist industrialisation presents a classic example of 'extensive' development, with high rates of economic development being achieved largely on the basis of pulling into industrial circulation ever larger and larger quantities of the basic factors of production–capital, land, raw materials and labour. Between 1927/8 and 1937, total employment (not including private and collective farm employment) increased from 11 to 27 million.[19] To underline the nature of extensive development, it is perhaps worth quoting the calculations of Abram Bergson, which show that in the period 1928–37, covering the height of the industrialisation drive, labour and total factor productivity at best grew slowly and may even have virtually stagnated (see Table 3.1).

'Labour planning' in the 1930s and 1940s, then, reduced to little more than the aim of maximising the rate of absorption of new workers, with subsidiary targets like maximising the output of graduates etc. In a situation where the strategic emphasis is on resource *mobilisation*, it is hardly surprising if questions of resource *allocation* get pushed into the background, and we shall return to this theme in a moment when we discuss the evolution of the Soviet planning system as a whole. By the 1950s, however, success in terms of quantitative growth was already bringing the Soviet economy up against resource constraints and, in particular, up against an impending labour shortage. In 1976, specialists on Soviet demography could write that 'the labour shortage is serious and will become even more so in the future as the supply drops precipitously . . . .With all other major sources exhausted, the dependence on the able-bodied age group is total.'[20] In other words, with female participation rates as high as they can go and the end of the flow of 'new' labour from the countryside, labour supply can increase only as fast as the population of working age. But a declining birth-rate has meant an ageing population and a lower ratio of able-bodied to total adult population.

TABLE 3.1

	Index numbers of growth of		Labour prod.		Total prod.	
	Net national product, 1937 prices	Net national product composite price base*	1937 prices	comp. p. base	1937 prices	comp. p. base
1928	67.1	38.1	92.6	52.6	96.3	54.7
1937	100.0	100.0	100.0	100.0	100.0	100.0

* With output for each year 1928–37 calculated in the prices of that year.
SOURCE   A. Bergson, *Productivity and the Social System – the USSR and the West* (Cambridge, Mass.: Harvard University Press, 1978) p. 120.

Measures are now being taken to encourage higher birth-rates, and female fertility rates did rise slightly in the early 1970s. But higher birth-rates must, *ceteris paribus*, reduce female participation rates, so that the immediate effects on labour supply of any success in pronatalist policies may be negative. It is, in fact, estimated that the Soviet labour force will increase by just $10\frac{1}{2}$ million in the decade 1980–90, as compared to $20\frac{1}{2}$ million in 1970–80.[21] These figures put into clear perspective the increasing concern on the part of the Soviet planners with the labour supply variable. Recent measures offer considerable incentives to people beyond retirement age to stay in the workforce,[22] but ultimately the problem presented must be one of how to do more with given resources. While in the past an essentially political control over the workforce may have been considered enough, contemporary problems push the system in the direction of planning for optimal allocation. But just as labour is not the only resource that is getting scarcer and scarcer, so it is not the only variable that Soviet planners would like to plan better. In order to understand the kind of world that the Soviet worker lives in and make sense of the way that world is evolving, we must look at the overall framework of Soviet economic administration.

THE GENERAL SYSTEM OF PLANNING AND
MANAGEMENT

The way that the centralised command system takes shape at the level of
enterprise and plant is through an ubiquitous system of targets.
Everyone has some kind of a target – upper management has an output
or sales plan backed up by a formal bonus system that can affect take-
home pay by between 25 and 50 per cent of basic salary.[23] Ordinary
workers or groups of workers, at least those producing easily measured
output, face corresponding targets, often backed up, as we have seen
already, by piece-rate systems. Local political cadres, especially the
professional Communist Party secretaries (the *apparatchiki*), face less
formal, though not thereby less compelling, pressure from their
superiors for 'success' in their 'parish' – and this pressure may ultimately impinge on the workers through political campaigns for higher
performance imposed under the rubrics of 'socialist competition'
and 'counterpart planning' (*vstrechnye plany*). One way or another, the
'success-indicator' is the key way in which the system is concretised, and
up until the start of the planning reform movement in the 1960s the
primary form it took was that of *gross output*.

   Gross output is defined as total production, in physical or value terms,
including the amount or value of brought-in materials. The almost
exclusive emphasis placed on this success-indicator in the 'classical'
period of Soviet planning reflected a studied crudeness in development
strategy which still evokes controversy. It is easy to run off a list of weaknesses of gross output as a planning indicator – the obvious incentive
it introduces for the producer to go for maximum 'grossness', avoiding
anything small and fussy, the insensitivity to costs, quality and new
technology it is bound to induce.[24] Observers trying to establish the
ultimate reasons why Stalinist architecture was so grotesquely 'heavy',
why in the past children's shoes and spare parts of all kinds have been
particularly difficult to obtain, why Soviet beer is frequently ruined
because bottles are not properly sealed, have found little need to go
beyond a discussion of the gross output success-indicator. But other
factors have undoubtedly been present. Pressure from the centre for
maximum growth has filtered down to the shop floor in the form of
targets which may in some cases have been simply unfulfillable except
through systematic neglect of, for example, the quality dimension. The
very high degree of centralised control imposed on the system has meant
that complete consistency between the component parts of the plan
could not possibly be guaranteed. Concern to maintain maximum

'tautness' in the system has meant, however, that planners have often been quite happy to leave 'holes' in the plan, as a way of introducing tension, of 'goading the goaders',[25] thus intensifying the problems of the 'planned' customer. These various characteristics are, indeed, simply aspects of a strategy of economic development based on a preparedness to pay a high price for big short-term output increases, for the kind of total control over strategic variables that a high level of centralisation makes possible, and to take a chance on 'unbalanced' growth. Though we introduce the concept between quotation marks, it is fair to say that the work of a number of post-war economists, particularly Albert Hirschman,[26] has provided evidence and analysis to support the argument that in a developmental context the virtues of imbalance may outweigh those of balance. The evidence and analysis has not, perhaps, been wholly convincing at a general level, but the present context does not demand a clear-cut resolution of the balance/imbalance controversy. Rather, it simply requires that we recognise that when you have potentially abundant resources to mobilise, planners' tensions and bottlenecks may be valuable mobilisatory tactics, just as 'over-centralisation' may be an essential element in mobilisatory strategy. The history of the British war economy 1939–45 presents a strong supporting argument to this effect.[27] Rather than arguing that the Soviet way was the best way or even a good way, we need simply note that, at least in terms of aggregate growth figures, it was a successful way. This success was, however, bought at a definite cost. The crudeness of the gross output success-indicator may not have mattered too much in relation to highly homogeneous producer goods like steel and electricity, but it certainly mattered in relation to consumer goods, where the scope for poor quality and distortion of specification are almost infinite. Equally important, the risks involved in planners' tension could only reasonably be taken as long as there was an ultimate fail-safe that could be brought into operation if imbalance threatened to turn into dislocation. This fail-safe took the form of the famous 'priority principle'.

The operation of the priority principle is based on the clear definition of a number of priority sectors and a number of non-priority sectors in the economy. If a dislocation threatens, resources are simply physically shifted from non-priority to priority sectors. Thus the priority principle is more than just a general strategic orientation. It is, in fact, a vital *functional* characteristic of the Stalinist approach to planning. And, of course, the designated non-priority sectors had to come from the consumer-good side of the economy, because cutting production of goods that come at the 'end of the line', in input – output terms, has no indirect 'linkage' effects on other production sectors – it simply reduces the standard of living.

One rather special but extremely important feature of the traditional Soviet planning system relates to technology. The stress on bulk meant disincentives not only to high quality, but also to innovation. In addition, the shortness of the operational planning period (usually one month), coupled with the pressure to maintain even rates of plan fulfilment so that bonuses could be maximised (see discussion of 'ratchet principle' below, pp. 53–4), meant that any sort of stoppage, for example for retooling, would be frowned upon by management and workers alike. So shop-floor resistance to technical change must be taken to be a systematic element in the 'classical' Stalinist planning system. Of course, in a highly centralised command economy, the authorities are in a much stronger position to impose technical change from above, and you don't have to worry about shop-floor resistance in the case of new plants, where the technology is selected before the shop floor comes into existence. At the strategic level, then, the innovation problem may not have been of crucial importance, at least in the early stages of Soviet development. It may, indeed, have seemed an acceptable price to pay for the '*sui generis* war economy'. But it must have had a serious effect on the kind of small-scale continuous innovation that is so important with respect to consumer goods. Here again, then, we see how the planning system was systematically unsuited to delivering the goods on the consumption side.

What does all this mean in terms of basic macro-economic proportions? Soviet Marxist discussion of these proportions tends to be couched in terms of industrial groups *A* and *B*–the former producing producer goods and the latter consumer goods–and faster growth for group *A* has in the past been posited as some kind of economic law, with appropriate reference to some of Marx's writings. In fact, groups *A* and *B* are not very useful macro-economic concepts. They are limited to industry and involve a lot of double-counting–group *A* includes all intermediate supplies as well as investment goods. Nevertheless, we can be fairly confident in asserting that a movement in favour of group *A* as against group *B* will imply a movement against consumption. Table 3.2 gives a broad picture of the breakdown of Soviet national income recalculated in terms of the conventional Western GNP (Gross National Product) concept. We must be careful not to place too much interpretative reliance on these bald figures–we have already noted the tremendous importance of the quality factor, or perhaps we should say the non-quality factor, in the strategy of Stalinist extensive development, and

TABLE 3.2　*Breakdown of GNP by end use (factor cost), total GNP = 100*

	1950	1955	1960	1965	1970	1974
Consumption	62.4	62.1	61.1	58.2	57.2	56.5
Household consumption	52.1	52.0	51.2	48.8	48.4	48.1
Communal consumption	10.3	10.1	9.9	9.4	8.8	8.4
Fixed investment	14.8	19.4	23.9	26.0	27.0	28.4
New fixed investment	11.9	16.4	20.2	21.7	22.6	23.2
Capital repair	2.9	3.0	3.7	4.3	4.4	5.2
Research and development	1.8	2.0	2.8	3.3	3.5	3.7
Administration and other services	6.2	3.7	2.9	2.6	2.6	2.5
Defence, net exports, changes in inventories and reserves, unidentified outlays and statistical error.	14.8	12.8	9.3	9.9	9.7	8.9

SOURCE　R. V. Greenslade,'The Real National Product of the USSR, 1950–1975', in Joint Economic Committee, US Congress, *Soviet Economy in a New Perspective* (Washington, 1976) p. 277.

NOTE　R and D includes defence R and D, and other items may conceal defence elements. The CIA has estimated total Soviet defence expenditures at 12–13 per cent of GNP in 1970.

this is something the statistics cannot properly reflect. In addition, there are all sorts of problems in the interpretation and recalculation of Soviet raw data–see, for instance, the discussion of the 'defence problem' in the note to Table 3.2. At a very general level, however, the Soviet economy is evidently characterised by relatively high investment ratios and relatively low consumption ratios. For the UK and USA in 1970, by comparison, the fixed investment ratio (the proportion of national income going into new machines etc.) was,respectively, 18.6 and 17.3 per cent. The corresponding household consumption ratios were 61.8 and 63.1 per cent.

We should note that Soviet investment ratios are by no means uniquely high. The fixed investment ratio for West Germany in 1970 was 25.6 per cent, and for Japan it was as high as 35.6 per cent in that year. But the West German and Japanese economies are, of course, characterised by a very low level of defence expenditures and, in fact, the household consumption ratio for these two fast-growing Western economies was, in 1970, respectively 54.2 and 52.5 per cent.[28] It is the combination of a relatively high investment ratio, and a consumption ratio that is low, and which in any case exaggerates the extent of the true 'consumption effort', that sets the Soviet economy apart from other major national economies. It should be clear from the earlier discussion that this picture is to a great extent determined by the nature of the planning system.

Equally striking are the trends in consumption and investment. The period 1950–74 encompasses the movement from a post-war reconstruction phase in which extensive development was still the keynote, through to a mid-1970s period when the theme of public pronouncements and decrees is uniformly technology, quality, 'intensification' etc. Yet the trends in the two major components of national income are continuously upwards for fixed investment and downwards for consumption. What kind of counterpoint between policy and reality is reflected in these trends? To answer that question we must go back and look in detail at the development of the economic reform movement in the USSR.

DEVELOPMENT OF THE GENERAL PLANNING SYSTEM, 1957–65

It was the falling rate of return on investment rather than labour productivity trends as such that initially prompted Khrushchev to institute the first changes in what had become a rather sacrosanct Stalinist planning framework, and Khrushchev's modifications, which largely took the form of reshuffles of the executive planning hierarchy, hardly affected the enterprise, never mind the shop-floor worker. Concern with the increasingly apparent wastefulness of the gross output régime led to the introduction of an explicit cost-reduction success-indicator in 1959, but it quickly became clear that the main effect of this change was to intensify the quality problem, as enterprises discovered an incentive to cut costs by skimping on materials. By the end of the Khrushchev era, trends in capital productivity, labour productivity and growth rates were uniformly downwards (see Table 3.3), and a more radical approach to the problems of the planning system was presaged by the mounting in 1964 of an experimental profit-based system in two famous textile factories, *Bol'shevichka* and *Mayak*. But before these experiments could produce definitive results, Khrushchev fell from power (September 1964), to be replaced by the triumvirate of Brezhnev, Kosygin and Podgornyi.

What ultimate factors lay behind the worsening macro-economic trends of the late 1950s and early 1960s? Khrushchev may have actually made things worse through excessively frequent reorganisation, but

TABLE 3.3	*Average annual percentage rates of growth of GNP, factor inputs and factor productivity, 1971–5*

	1951–5	1956–60	1961–5	1966–70	1971–5
GNP	6.0	5.8	5.0	5.5	3.8
Inputs					
Total	4.5	3.9	4.1	3.9	4.1
Labour (man-hours)	1.9	0.6	1.6	2.0	1.9
Capital	9.0	9.8	8.7	7.5	7.9
Land	4.0	1.3	0.6	−0.3	−0.9
Factor productivity					
Total	1.4	1.8	0.9	1.5	−0.2
Labour (man-hours)	4.6	5.1	3.4	3.4	1.8
Capital	−2.7	−3.6	−3.3	−1.9	−3.8
Land	1.9	4.4	4.4	5.8	2.9

SOURCE	R. V. Greenslade, 'The Real National Product of the USSR, 1950–1975', in Joint Economic Committee, US Congress, *Soviet Economy in a New Perspective* (Washington, 1976) p. 279.

there can be no doubt that fundamental long-term tendencies were at work. The very success of the Soviet planning system in mobilising resources for rapid extensive growth was increasingly *creating* problems, for a number of reasons. Though slightly more people joined the labour force in 1960–5 than had done so in 1955–60, there were already signs of strain in the labour market, particularly in the old-established industrial areas. Khrushchev's Virgin Lands scheme during the 1950s, which brought into cultivation large areas of marginal land in West Siberia and Kazakhstan, represented the last possible extension of the cultivated area of the Soviet Union. Easily accessible raw material and energy supplies which had provided the basis for the industrialisation drive were beginning to run out, and the capital costs of bringing Siberian mineral and hydrocarbon riches on stream threatened to be enormously expensive in capital terms. Nevertheless, the development of West Siberian oil had already started in the early 1960s, and oil was flowing by 1964. On all fronts, then, the Soviet economy was coming up against supply constraints and increasing marginal costs.

In addition, the growing size and technical complexity of the economy was reflected in an increasing sensitivity to the weaknesses of the traditional planning system. As emphasis shifted away from basic intermediate goods to more complex and heterogeneous items, so the scope for distortion of quality and specification, under the gross output success-indicator régime, became broader, and the reality of this problem was reflected in the increasing build-up of stocks of unsaleable goods in the late 1950s and early 1960s. As inter-sectoral relationships became more complex, the dangers of leaving elements of inconsistency in plans became greater. This problem presented itself in a more acute form inasmuch as political developments were tending to weaken the force of the priority principle. Pressure for better living standards, and a recognition of the need to do something decisive about the neglected rural community, meant more emphasis on light industry and agriculture, while emphasis on the latter demanded more investment in agricultural engineering, chemicals etc. Priorities were escalating and there were fewer and fewer 'soft' sectors left that could be permitted to take the strain in times of crisis.

In the investment sphere, the downward trend in the marginal productivity of capital was the steeper inasmuch as purely implementational problems became increasingly evident. In particular, the tendency to *raspylenie* ('spreading') – that is, excessive breadth on the investment front– became even more obtrusive. Intermediate planning bodies struggling to keep investment plans going in the face of supply uncertainty, and unconstrained by any systematic charge on capital, took refuge in a policy which amounted to little more than getting as many projects going as possible, so that you would always have something on hand to complete. Supply uncertainty plus the gross output success-indicator régime meant that projects officially passed as 'completed' might be anything but ready for full-scale production.

A planning system designed to be insensitive to static micro-economic considerations, designed to buy growth at the cost of imbalance and neglect of consumer goods production, was clearly unsuited to grappling with the problems of the day, and it came as no surprise when the new leadership announced a comprehensive planning decree in September 1965.

THE KOSYGIN REFORM

The key elements in the new system were as follows:

(1) Sales to replace gross output as the basic 'direct' planning indicator.
(2) Profit to be introduced as a key 'synthetic' indicator.
(3) A new emphasis on material incentives, with bonus funds to increase all round, for managers and workers alike.

(4) A limited marketisation of the system in relation to some minor sub-sectors of the economy, like subsidiary industrial activity in the countryside, and a certain proportion of industrial investment.
(5) A new emphasis on 'direct links' between enterprises.
(6) The price system to be rationalised with, *inter alia*, the introduction for the first time of a systematic charge on capital.
(7) Special incentives for innovation to be introduced.

There is a rich literature on the subject of the 1965 planning reform,[29] and there is no need for a comprehensive treatment in the present context. The reform clearly aimed to effect a change in economic course, with the sales indicator plus direct links sensitising the output effort to customers' needs, and the profit indicator plus price reform bringing in, not just a new approach to cost-consciousness, but a whole new orientation towards improved resource allocation. Improved bonus arrangements were to ensure that private and public profit coincided, and the limited retreat on the part of the state from certain peripheral but important sectors was calculated to introduce a new and welcome flexibility into the system. In a word, there was to be a switch from extensive to intensive development. But the trends we noted earlier in relation to consumption/investment ratios, which are confirmed by the more sophisticated statistics on factor productivity in Table 3.3, indicate that this has not occurred. We have to be a little careful in interpreting the slow-down in Soviet growth rates. The world energy crisis, and the imperative need to push out towards more and more marginal energy sources in Siberia, have exacted a price which could not but have reduced growth rates and increased overall capital–output ratios. But after a brief improvement in the late 1960s, which may be attributable to certain once-and-for-all effects of the reform decree, it seems that the new planning system has done little to counter 'objective' trends. In relation to labour productivity, we see from Table 3.3 that the secular decline in that variable was only arrested, but not reversed, in the late 1960s, and is now continuing. It is difficult not to agree with the secretariat of the *Economic Commission for Europe* when it states that:

Among the most frequently quoted qualitative factors contributing to an increase of labour productivity are the introduction of new technology, increased use of production capacities, changes in the structure of manpower by skills, decrease in the number of lost working hours and days, reduced unit inputs of energy and raw materials and reduced material costs in general, rationalization in management and allocation of resources, and improvement in the organization of production processes. There are plenty of references in policy statements, plan and plan-fulfilment documents, and in the professional literature . . . to this dimension of labour productivity growth, economic efficiency and the quality of growth, and also to the notable results obtained in this regard in many enterprises or branches. Nevertheless, the contribution of these factors to changes in labour productivity and efficiency in the economy . . . is usually presented in purely qualitative terms. It appears that up to now their contribution has been potential rather than actual.[30]

Why so? It is not, in fact, difficult to pinpoint key weaknesses in the way the planning reform was implemented. Direct links, as it turned out, were not to mean real autonomy in inter-enterprise relationships, and in that context the sales indicator was not much of an improvement on gross output. It was still a 'gross' indicator, and if customer enterprises are tied to a particular supplier and still have their own plans to fulfil, it is unlikely that they will refuse to purchase any but the most abjectly sub-standard deliveries. The price system, despite modifications, remained basically an administrative one, not directly linked to any concept of scarcity price, and there was no question of allowing the market to do the job which the planners themselves could not do. Consequently, the new profit success-indicator was effectively strait-jacketed and neutralised. Because of their reluctance to decentralise the system of plan construction, the planners were unable to eschew reliance on the famous 'ratchet principle'. In a situation where over-centralisation implies a need for an enormous volume of detailed information, while enterprise managers can be trusted only to disclose 'information' likely to produce a plan that can be comfortably fulfilled, planners are forced back on observation of figures on past performance as their main form of 'objective' information, and the process of plan construction often amounts to little more than the mechanical addition of a standard percentage mark-up to the 'achieved level'. With every turn of the ratchet, of course, the output 'floor', below which a given enterprise would not be permitted to drop, is raised irreversibly. It is mainly for this reason that a Soviet manager will always try to go for steady, even levels of fulfilment – the manager who fails to fulfil in period 1, thus losing his basic bonus, may make up a little in period 2 through overfulfilling by a large amount and making extra overfulfilment bonuses. He is, however, likely to find himself in a lot of trouble in period 3, when the planners may have extrapolated from period 2 performance to produce a target that is very demanding indeed. We noted earlier the importance of this kind of reaction to the ratchet situation in inducing resistance to innovation at the enterprise and shop-floor level. Reform measures aimed at creating stronger inducements to innovation came up not only against the problem of defining 'innovation',[31] but more fundamentally against the vigorous survival of the ratchet principle over into the new system.[32] The importance of this survival, however, goes beyond the sphere of technical change. The various marginal elements of genuine 'pluralisation' of the economy were also neutralised by the fact that industrial managers would still feel reluctant to get involved in any kind of 'special order', say for equipment relating to a decentralised investment venture, as long as they were aware that the planners were peering over their shoulders, looking for an excuse to jack up plan targets.[33] Finally, there was virtually no effective change on the troublesome investment planning front.

In one way and another, then, the planned 'change of gear' in the Soviet economic system did not, in fact, take place, and the increased emphasis on material incentives has meant little enough in the absence of a clear orientation as to the direction in which those incentives should be pushing. A forceful illustration of the tenacity of the old planning system is provided by the history of the 1971–5 five-year plan. In the original plan document, the time-honoured primacy of department *A* over department *B* was finally broken, with a higher planned rate of growth for production of consumer goods than for production of producer goods. When overall plan fulfilment ran into trouble around 1974, however, the old priority on producer goods was quickly re-established. This helps to explain why consumption as a proportion of GNP was actually lower in 1974 than it had been in 1970 (see Table 3.2). It also underlines the extent to which the Soviet economy in 1974 was still a command economy, crucially dependent on the priority principle, and the systematic difficulty of orienting such an economy to a consumption revolution.

There is, of course, a political dimension to this story of a planning reform *manqué*. Around 1968, the *apparatchik* group, the professional Communist Party cadres, whose main function has always been oiling the wheels of a creaky economic mechanism, decided that the reform had gone far enough and that their group interests would be threatened by substantial decentralisation or further modification of the command principle. The history of the reform movement in Czechoslovakia indicates that they were correct in so thinking.[34] In any case, we can characterise the post-1968 position as one in which the framework of a rationalised planning system exists, but remains essentially a dead letter, because of the lack of the kind of meaningful economic pluralisation that would have given life and content to that framework.

*   *   *

We have, then, looked at the way labour is planned and the way in which the economy as a whole is planned, noting considerable contrasts in relation to the predominance of the command or market principle and so on. Putting the two together, what is working life in a typical Soviet industrial enterprise like? It is easy to put together a plausible picture of Soviet labour, white- and blue-collar, pushed fairly hard in the desired direction of specialisation as early as school days, constrained in its freedom to move around geographically, bound (once settled in a job) to a strenuous round of plan-target chasing, egged on by the carrot of material incentives and the stick of social and political pressure. There would, indeed, be nothing specifically incorrect in this picture, but in its totality it would be fundamentally misleading. The fact that many Soviet enterprises report annual rates of labour turnover (*tekuchest'*) of between 70 and 90 per cent suggests lots of problems, but it does not suggest serious constraint on labour mobility. Indeed, some of the regulations alluded to earlier, for example the *propiska* regulations, should perhaps to some extent be interpreted as reactions to the nomadic tendencies of many Soviet workers. Nor should the degree of strain and tension in the typical Soviet working day be exaggerated. The following 'photograph' of the working day of a three-man brigade of machine operators at a Perm' factory illustrates the point graphically:

7.45	Start work (only one member of the brigade was there on time).
9.20–9.40	Break for a smoke.
9.40–9.55	Work
9.55–10.20	Break for a smoke.
10.20–11.05	Lunch break.
11.05–11.20	Aimless wandering around the shop.
11.20–11.40	Tuning a press.
11.40–13.00	Work.
13.00–14.00	Smoking and aimless wandering around the shop.
14.00–14.30	Cleaning up.
14.30	Finish work.[35]

This is no doubt a somewhat extreme case– after all, it did get into the papers–but it reflects an important aspect of Soviet industrial reality and must surely bring a smile to the face of any reader who has ever worked in a British factory. The picture of men working very hard for just three to four hours and spending the rest of the working day simply filling in time is, indeed, by no means unknown in American industry.[36] Faced with any kind of payment-by-results system and suspecting, no doubt with some justification, that outstanding performance in the short run may create serious problems in the long run, workers in Western countries typically evolve a 'bogey', or unofficial quota, which is considered to be the safe limit of individual output beyond which the danger of a ratchet-based mark-up in output norms becomes excessive.[37] As we have already noted, the ratchet principle has, for systematic reasons, a universality in the Soviet economy which it does not have in Western economies, so we must not be surprised if we find Soviet managers and workers alike acting in a similar way to Western workers. The Soviet manager fulfils his plan, but endeavours to give the planners no inkling of what he may have in reserve, and the Soviet worker does enough to earn any bonuses that are going and as little beyond this as possible. Even intermediate planning bodies may join in this kind of 'conspiracy'. The following report comes from an in-strument-making enterprise in the Tadzhik republic.

> Many workers simply could not answer the straightforward question, is the factory fulfilling its plan? In fact, the situation is not exactly fantastic as far as the plan is concerned. Last year the enterprise 'fulfilled' its target only because *Soyuzstroiinstrument* [the im-mediately superior planning body–D.A.D.] managed to correct it in time. This year the plan has already been reduced twice. Even this has not been enough, however – they have done even worse than last year.[38]

Of course, the political dimension of socialist competitions and so on present a serious countervailing force to the bogey, but it is not a predominating force.

What, then, of the supposedly growth-maximising characteristics of the Soviet-type economic system? It is, in fact, recognised in the West that, despite the universality of the bogey principle, payment-by-results is still the best way to maximise short-term output performance,[39] and that conclusion assumes a zero level of political pressure. The example from Tadzhikistan, indeed, though illustrative of attitudes, is surely not typical of situations. Many individual Soviet workers, particularly the young and inexperienced, may find eight hours barely enough to make the bogey, and the pressure on particular enterprises or sectors to perform outstandingly can still be very severe. Input–output analysis has proved that Soviet plans may still, even in the 1970s, be 'impossibly' taut.[40] On the other hand, there are enterprises which overfulfil targets by up to 25 per cent,[41] which indicates a degree of slackness in plans so great that even the dreaded ratchet does not have to be feared. It was recently reported in *Pravda* that the norm stated in the 'passport' of a machine is often 200 per cent higher than the norm adopted in the workplace.[42] In situations like these, there is no incompatibility between bogey and high growth rates of output.

It must be remembered in this context that a Soviet director, still basically induced to place priority on the fulfilment of an output-based target, and faced with the combination of short operational plan periods and uncertain supply links with other organisations, can be expected to be loth to part with any resources, however marginal. 'Storming', the mad rush at the end of the plan period to ensure plan fulfilment at any cost, is still a key characteristic of the Soviet economic system,[43] and storming is difficult if you do not have spare workers to throw into the mêlée when the situation becomes desperate. Thus the gap, in terms of productivity and responsibility, between a crack worker and a marginal worker in a Soviet enterprise may be much greater than it would be in a comparable Western enterprise. Exactly the same can be said about the gap between the best and worst plant in a given 'corporation'.

We would not expect a Soviet-type economy to suffer from the kind of unemployment problems that afflict Western market economies–after all, aggregate employment level, price level and so on are all under direct government control, and it is not surprising that in the early 1960s Soviet unemployment on American definitions was no more than 1–2 per cent.[44] Though comparable data for more recent years are not available, the figure can hardly have risen. The preceding discussion fills in the micro-economics of Soviet full employment and indicates that the kind of full employment characteristic in the USSR may be, from the point of view of a government concerned to redirect the economy towards extensive development, extremely disturbing. This is the background to the Shchekino experiment and other experimental systems aimed at raising the efficiency of utilisation of this increasingly scarce resource, labour.

KEY LABOUR PLANNING PILOT SCHEMES, 1965 TO THE PRESENT

The essence of the Shchekino system, first introduced in the Shchekino chemical combine (*Tula oblast'*) in 1967, is very simple. On the basis of a *de facto* integrated wages/bonus fund, management is conceded the right, previously unknown in post-1930 Soviet economic history, to make workers redundant, without necessarily finding them alternative employment, and using the funds thus economised, at least to the extent of 50 per cent, to increase incentive payments to others. In the light of the earlier discussion of the problem of labour shortage and the increasingly crucial significance of the labour productivity variable, the importance of this scheme can hardly be exaggerated.

Since 1967, the scope of the Shchekino system has expanded slowly. In October 1969, the Central Committee of the Communist Party passed a decree recommending the system to all party workers.[45] But in 1971 only 121 enterprises were on the experimental system,[46] and by 1977 the figure had risen to just 1000,[47] though in the chemicals industry itself 70 per cent of total sales in 1975 was accounted for by enterprises on the system.[48] As of 1975, Shchekino-system enterprises employed only 3 per cent of the total labour force.[49] On the other hand, the scheme has been extended outside the industrial sphere, including the state farm sector,[50] this underlining the increasing universality of the labour shortage problem.

How has the Shchekino system worked in practice? The *Bashneftekhimzavody* association reported in 1975 that, after five years of the system, 7000 workers had been made redundant, while labour turnover had been reduced 20 per cent.[51] During 1974, in mineral fertiliser enterprises under the USSR Ministry for the Chemical Industry, 50,000 skilled workers were transferred from established to new production units.[52] In the Shchekino association itself, 1039 men were made redundant and transferred to other departments in the period up to 1970, and labour productivity increased by 2.3 times in 1966–70. In the succeeding five-year period, 1971–5, 475 workers were made redundant, while labour productivity rose by 47 per cent.[53] A 1977 report indicated that labour productivity plans had been overfulfilled by 8.8 per cent in a Shchekino group of forty-six oil and petro-chemical enterprises over a period of three years. Excellent results in terms of reducing labour turnover were also reported.[54]

Among other notable developments in the sphere of labour-force planning are the Zlobin system of brigade *khozraschet* (autonomous accounting) and the Orel system of continuous planning, both applied largely in the sphere of construction. Under the Zlobin system, brigades (of perhaps twenty to thirty men) are given a clearly defined task, the necessary supplies and permitted to get on with it in a fairly independent manner, with material incentives calculated on a brigade basis. The Orel system is essentially a form of applied critical path analysis, providing an operational basis for calculating the best sequence of activities in relation to the defined task. In practice, the Zlobin and Orel systems are often used together. As of 1977, the Zlobin system was being used in 50,000 construction brigades, 26 per cent of the total number, and predominated in the field of residential construction.[55] By 1978, the system covered 33 per cent of construction brigades.[56] Application in the field of industrial construction remains limited, however, and outside construction the system is still very much experimental. Productivity in Zlobin brigades is reported to be around 20 per cent higher than average.[57]

Why has the extension of these apparently admirable schemes been so limited? The question is most easily answered in relation to the Zlobin and Orel systems. Brigade *khozraschet* is all very well, but it remains unclear how even partial autonomy at this grass-roots level can be fitted into a system in which the power of arbitrary disposal is a key operational element. The Soviet press has carried numerous reports on Zlobin brigades whose operations have been wrecked by sudden administrative transfers of groups of workers from one brigade to another.[58] The paradox of trying to combine grass-roots autonomy with the maintenance of a fairly traditional planning system at higher levels is reflected in the fact that only in residential construction where, with modern technology, operations can be very easily broken down into small, self-contained units has the system really taken hold. Perhaps most important of all, the system can only work if supplies are reliable,[59] and the Soviet planning system, as it is, cannot guarantee supply certainty. In practice, then, the successful Zlobin brigades are generally those which have been 'guaranteed', in an essentially political way, the necessary supplies.[60] What this amounts to is simply a modified version of the traditional priority principle. Much the same can be said in relation to the Orel system. Continuous planning can obviously only work in the context of continuous supply and of freedom from the kind of pressures, discussed earlier, that tend to lead to storming.[61]

The importance of the Shchekino experiment is manifestly greater than that of the brigade-level experiments, and success in this case seems to have been virtually unqualified. Why, then, the caution with respect to general application? Bureaucratic conservatism on the part of the industrial ministries is certainly part of the answer, but of greater importance may have been the crudeness of ministerial planning. There have been a number of cases where Shchekino-type experiments have been wrecked because ministries have imposed capital extension plans involving an increase in labour intensity, hence a *ceteris paribus* drop in labour productivity, without making corresponding changes in plans for wage fund and so on.[62] No doubt enterprise managers are wary of anything that may reduce scope for storming in times of crisis. More generally, however, it is difficult to avoid the impression that the key difficulty has been the nature of redundancy. Of all the reports on the Shchekino system that the author has read, only one states explicitly that redundant workers had eventually found jobs *outside* the given enterprise. In the great bulk of cases, it is made quite clear that the spare labour made available has been absorbed within the enterprise or association. Given the strongly regional complexion of the Soviet labour shortage problem,[63] however, purely intra-organisational redistributions of manpower cannot be of much more than marginal importance. There is evidently a political reluctance to go the whole way with Shchekino, and this may be related to a fear that a Western-type unemployment problem might develop.

The idea that large-scale unemployment might result from a measure that simply aims to get higher productivity from a workforce that is already fully employed in terms of the balance of vacancies and job-seekers may seem rather bizarre. But there is, as we have seen, some unemployment in the Soviet Union, though it is clear that it is largely frictional unemployment, that is, temporary unemployment between jobs. Now Shchekino-system enterprises have claimed considerable success in reducing labour turnover and, to this extent, the scheme could be expected to reduce the incidence of frictional unemployment. On the other hand, if outright redundancy were to become a dominant feature, as would follow inevitably with a wide generalisation of the scheme, then men might, even in the context of a general labour shortage, find themselves out of work for more than just a few weeks. On balance, the redundancy effect would surely tend to outweigh the reduced turnover effect, unless a very radical improvement in facilities for the redeployment of labour were forthcoming. This puts into perspective the importance of the development of labour-placement services, as described earlier.

A report from the early 1970s claimed that *sluzhba truda* had generally reduced the average time between jobs to a significant extent,[64] and a

1975 report from the city of Kaluga cited a reduction in the average period of frictional unemployment from twenty-four to fourteen days, through the work of the local bureau.[65] But the organisational weaknesses in the *sluzhba truda* system discussed earlier have reduced its potential, while conservative attitudes have sometimes distorted its purpose. Thus one report from Odessa stated that the local bureau was restricting information to those already out of work, this in order to reduce turnover (*tekuchest'*)![66] Interestingly enough, such an attitude might be appropriate in a depressed market economy where employment agencies had more than enough on their plates trying to find something for the outright unemployed. But in the Soviet context, where the problem is to improve the allocation of a virtually fully-employed labour force, it seems preposterous – and, after all, Shchekino has been reported as reducing labour turnover! Here, in fact, we have an example of old-fashioned attitudes going back to the Stalin days when control was considered more important than planning. In that context, workers who wanted to move around and improve their lot were seen as some kind of threat. But in the present context, and so long as the appropriate arrangements exist, they might rather be seen as potential saviours of the Soviet economy.

As noted earlier, rates of labour turnover have often been excessive in the USSR, and in many cases this has been related to infrastructural problems, particularly housing,[67] and to general feelings of alienation,[68] no doubt in turn related to the generally low level of wages. More specifically, however, drifting has often been, in the absence of adequate job information services, the only way to look for a better deal (so that the policy of our Odessa bureaucrat was probably likely to increase, rather than decrease, the level of *turnover*). A survey based on 1631 questionnaire responses from workers looking for jobs, conducted by the labour-placement bureau in the Belorussian town of Borisov, reported that over 50 per cent of the requests to be relieved of duties in old jobs had originated from dissatisfaction with job or pay.[69]

Better labour placement must surely, *ceteris paribus*, tend to reduce labour turnover, as does well-organised Shchekino. On the other hand, too much Shchekino without enough *trudoustroistvo* (labour placement) would surely lead to an increase, perhaps a considerable increase, in the incidence of frictional unemployment (= turnover times the average period between jobs). In fact, *sluzhba truda* seems to have in practice been somewhat less successful in reducing turnover than it has been in reducing the time between jobs. Figures are few and far between, but the Kaluga bureau succeeded in reducing turnover only from 17.3 to 15 per cent over the period 1970–4.[70] Clearly the time between jobs variable would be the crucial one in the event of generalised Shchekino producing large-scale redundancies, but the apparent failure of the labour-placement bureaux to make a big difference to the turnover figures would suggest a continued information gap, which in the context of a nation-wide redeployment campaign could be disastrous.

Why, it may be asked, should the prospect of an increase in the unemployment rate to, perhaps, 2–3 per cent seem so awful? Western societies are, for better or worse, learning to live with unemployment rates two or three times as high. Political conservatism and a surviving ideological distaste for the whole idea of labour exchanges may explain why the labour-placement backup to the Shchekino system has not really been forthcoming, but does that really matter? It does indeed, but in order to understand why, we must dig deeper into the subjective position of the Soviet worker and also reflect on the difficult question of the sources of legitimacy of the Soviet state.

Soviet workers are, on the whole, poorly paid. They may be subjected to considerable pressure to attain demanding targets, often in the context of unreliable supply and uneven work tempi. Political campaigns relating to socialist competition and so on must often irritate, as well as contribute to the objective problems of the situation. On the other hand, as we have seen, many Soviet workers may, for most of the time at least, have a fairly 'cushy number'. We should certainly not exaggerate the degree of alienation of the Soviet worker. Surveys from the late 1960s and early 1970s suggest that, in general, more than one-third of Soviet workers regarded themselves as participating in socio-political activity.[71] But whether we formulate the search in terms of why is there not a critical degree of alienation or, alternatively, why is prevalent alienation not socially and politically destabilising, we must clearly look for some element in the Soviet worker's situation which is distinct from the dimensions of salary and work conditions. That element is surely job security.

It is estimated that losses in labour productivity resulting from 'infringements of work discipline', turnover and 'bad organisation of the production process' amount to 15–20 per cent.[72] Significantly, it has been calculated that introduction of the Shchekino system in the chemicals industry has permitted an 18 per cent economy in personnel. For all the political muscle of the Communist Party hierarchy, it is quite common for irregular and indisciplined workers to 'get away with murder'.[73] This is partly related to that fact that, pre-Shchekino, and even in the darkest days of Stalinist one-man management, directors had no independent legal power of dismissal over workers. That many directors did, and still do, try to dismiss illegally is surely primarily a reflection of frustration. Equally important has been the simple fact of virtually full employment. The prospect of having to find a new job has not offered any terrors, so that potential turnover has been as important as actual. The kind of systematic uncertainty about job futures which characterises the position of the blue-collar worker in the West and which marks him off from the tenured white-collar worker who may well have inferior remuneration, has clearly not been present in the Soviet Union. Just how intolerable the position of Soviet workers can be in areas where, for local reasons, there is unemployment and a lack of job opportunities has been documented in the Soviet press.[74] But the kind of basic job security normally present represents more than just a compensation for poor pay and conditions. The Soviet state is still very concerned to assert its status as a socialist state, and in West and East alike full employment and job security is generally seen as a necessary condition for any kind of socialism. Unemployment was officially 'abolished' in the Soviet Union around 1932-3, just after the start of the industrialisation drive and just before the proclamation of the first 'socialist' constitution.[75] Any development, however desirable in itself, which introduced even the possibility that the Soviet state would have to admit that there was a significant level of permanent unemployment in the country would once more call into question the somewhat be-leaguered socialist credentials of the Soviet Union. It is hardly surprising that a régime which is still deeply concerned about its own legitimacy has been unwilling to risk the loss of such a major political asset.

THE LABOUR FORCE, THE PLANNING SYSTEM, AND THE SECOND ECONOMY

Up to now we have largely been discussing the mainstream of the Soviet economic system, and most of our empirical material has been drawn from the area of the heavy-industrial core of that system. Even so, reference to problems of supply, quality of inputs and so on has raised the question of how the system is 'made to work', how the wheels are oiled. This takes us deep into the sphere of the second economy, an area which, as is increasingly being argued with respect to Western economies, needs to be viewed dispassionately as an integral and essential part of the economic system.

There are three major elements of the second economy which affect the life of the Soviet worker in essential ways, the first two relating to his life at his place of work, the third to the quality of his leisure time. Perhaps the most important single way in which hard-pressed Soviet managers try to cope with their supply problems is through use of the services of pushers (*tolkachi*). These are men who try to by-pass, or at least speed up, the official supply system and obtain, by semi-legal or even outrightly illegal means, the key supplies needed to ensure plan fulfilment. 'Grey' labour supplies are also often involved, and these may vary from illegal overtime (legal overtime is normally limited to 120 hours a year), especially when a 'storm' is on, to full-scale 'lump' operations, reminiscent of tax-dodging building teams in the West. Illegal overtime is often paid at double, treble or even quadruple time,[76] and *shabashnik* (spiv) operations can attain quite a grand scale, particularly in the countryside. Around 1971, no less than 200 illegal subsidiary enterprises were operating in Odessa *oblast'*.[77] Widespread forms of unlawful act include

> deals between *kolkhozy* and private go-betweens involving the sale of *kolkhoz* production or the acquisition of materials. Violations of the second type are particularly common, which is largely explicable in terms of deficiences in the organisation of material–technical supply to *kolkhozy*. The people who act as commercial go-betweens have, as a rule, no link with the *kolkhoz*, and are usually parasites.[78]

How, it may be asked, in a centrally-planned economy, can organisations get the funds to finance operations of this kind? In fact, the traditional orientation to output rather than costs has meant a degree of preparedness to wink at financial irregularities on the part of successful enterprises. More specifically, however, the wage and bonus funds have often been misused to provide finance for shady deals.[79] One report from the Caucasus, the 'home' of the Soviet second economy, talked of 'dead souls' – fictitious workers on the payroll – and illegal payments to individuals of up to 14,000 rubles.[80] Thus Soviet managers have had a clear incentive to maintain the 'extensive employment' pattern, not just so as to have a reserve in times of need, but also to help to provide the financial leeway needed to oil the wheels.

We have noted that spare labour is a handy thing to have around in cases where storming patterns are characteristic. Directors may, however, prefer a significant degree of overmanning for another, in some ways more fundamental, reason. The main alternative to pushing as a way of solving supply problems is do-it-yourself, and the dwarf-workshop, where humble but essential supplies like nuts and bolts and castings are made, is a widespread phenomenon in the Soviet economy. There is nothing strictly illegal about dwarf-workshops. As long as only enterprise investment funds are involved, the director can set up more or less any production operation he likes, and even where higher approval is required, it is clearly often forthcoming, if only on the basis of who-you-know. 'Just look at what a good guy I am, and how passionately I support the idea of specialisation. But for old times' sake – let me build just a wee castings shop at the factory. . . .'[81] It is, of course, recognised at all levels that the Soviet economy could no more operate without dwarf-workshops than it could without pushers. But there is a price to be paid. The cost of making nuts, bolts and tools in dwarf-workshops is at least two to four times that in specialised factories and, in some cases, the factor involved is nearly 100![82] Here, by the way, is yet another reason why Soviet managers may have reservations about wholehearted implementation of the Shchekino system.

In private life, the second economy may be significant for the Soviet worker in two ways. Firstly, like every other Soviet citizen, he may be able to procure certain goods and services only on the basis of unofficial transactions. Secondly, he may be able to make money on the side by purveying services like painting and decorating or television repair which link up with his day-time job. This is not the place to embark on a detailed discussion of an aspect of Soviet society which merits full-scale study in its own right. Suffice for present purposes to emphasise that although some elements in the post-1965 economic milieu, for example so-called commission trade, do to an extent formalise and legalise hand-to-hand transactions, there is no evidence that the general incidence of strictly illegal deals of this kind is falling.

Soviet workers may be involved directly in any of these specific second-economy activities, but the more general implication of the rôle and importance of the second economy is the reinforcement of the labour-intensive, low-productivity profile of Soviet industry. Notoriously, the most up-to-date plants, with high-technology, highly capital-intensive main production lines, may still be making their own nuts and bolts in poorly equipped side-shows. The second economy helps to keep the marginal Soviet worker in employment but, by the same token, it helps to keep his wages low. The dimension of the second economy does, in fact, help to explain the lack of success of the Soviet policy-makers in relation to labour productivity. Until an economic reform sufficiently radical to obviate supply uncertainty supervenes, Soviet industry cannot afford high productivity.

PLANNING AND INFLATION

It is obvious from the preceding that the whole Soviet economic system
is, in a sense, inherently inflationary. Taut planning, 'holes' in the plan,
the whole apparatus of planners' tension, represents the imposition of a
kind of excess aggregate demand. Pushers' pay-offs, extra money to
workers for illegal overtime and so on mean that excess demand may
filter through to affect specific markets in specific areas. It has in the past
been the conventional wisdom to assume and assert that Soviet-type
economies suffer from a permanent inflationary gap, which is simply
repressed, essentially through administrative control over prices.
Research done by Richard Portes and his colleagues does, however, call
this thesis into question. The most obvious and readily observable
indicators of an inflationary gap (the excess of aggregate demand over
aggregate supply) in a Soviet-type economy are the length of queues and
the difference between state and free market prices, say, for agricultural
products. As pointed out by Portes, the queues would have to be getting
longer and longer, and price gap bigger and bigger, if the existence of a
permanent inflationary gap was to be proved, since build-ups of cash
balances can be carried over from one period to the next.[83] This is
observably not the case for the Soviet Union. Of course, queues and the
free-market price level are not the only variables involved. Savings
deposits in the Soviet Union grew annually by an average of 19.9 per
cent in 1966–70 and 14.3 per cent in 1971–5.[84] Concealed price
increases through the introduction of 'new' models and brands, a
phenomenon not unknown in the West, have certainly meant some
degree of 'concealed open' inflation. It is very difficult to put an overall
figure on this but, in specific cases, its importance is very clear.
Notoriously, the extra money made by building workers during bouts of
storming is often spent largely on vodka.[85] Surely not unrelated is the
fact that in the early 1970s a 'new' and much more expensive brand of
vodka called *Ekstra* (Alec Nove reports that this is said to be an
acronym for 'Ekh kak sud'ba tragichna russkogo alkogolika' – 'Oh how
tragic is the fate of the Russian alcoholic'[86]) was introduced. Now, on
some pioneer building sites in the back of beyond there may be very little
to spend your money on except vodka, so that the price of this
commodity may, for all practical purposes, be the 'price' of consumption as against saving. Whether the Soviet authorities have or have
not been concerned to discourage drinking or encourage savings, the
fact is that they may be able to mop up a great deal of local excess
demand through changing one key price.

Another important variable affecting interpretation of the inflationary gap situation ties in with the preceding discussion of the second economy. There is considerable anecdotal evidence suggesting that the scale and vigour of the activities of pushers and other types of spiv in the Soviet economy has increased since the 1965 planning reform. This may appear paradoxical in the context of a 'marketising' reform, but this paradox can be resolved analytically.[87] In any case, part of the explanation may be that the Soviet authorities have finally accepted that the system cannot work without pushers, so that the profession might as well be 'legalised'.[88] Be that as it may, it is clear that if there is a secular trend for, let us call them 'broking' activities, to become more widespread and more efficient in the Soviet Union, then the existence of a permanent inflationary gap might be consistent with queue/price evidence suggesting the contrary.

The world that the Soviet worker lives in is not, then, a world immune from the phenomenon of cumulative and generalised price increases. Whatever the statistics and econometrics say, anyone who has ever lived in the Soviet Union knows that shortage is an all-pervasive phenomenon and a dominating influence in the life of the Soviet consumer. Whether the worker/consumer contributes in an organised way to cost-inflationary pressures as he does in the West through trade union and political activity is a more controversial point, but Portes argues that, despite the absence of autonomous corporate organisations,

> . . . there *is* pressure from urban workers for wage increases, from consumers for higher living standards, from peasants for industrial consumer goods. There *are* ways in which these pressures may be transmitted, and planning is itself a bargaining process in which they are certainly taken into account. . . . The infrequency of (illegal) strikes is matched by the prevalence of slacking and slowdowns when workers are dissatisfied or simply see no material incentive to work harder.[89]

(This latter phenomenon is, of course, familiar in the West under the name of 'goldbricking'.[90]) It would be an oversimplification, then, to see inflationary pressures in the Soviet Union emanating purely from the strategy of taut planning. By the same token, a movement away from taut planning would not necessarily mean the disappearance of inflationary pressures. On the contrary, a Soviet system which seeks ultimate ideological legitimisation in terms of some future transition from the sphere of necessity (scarcity) to that of freedom (abundance) may have as many problems with increasingly high, and incompatible, aspirations as any other.

THE 1979 PLANNING DECREE AND THE FUTURE

As we noted earlier, the consolidation of Brezhnev's political ascendancy in the late 1960s was closely related to the *apparatchik* group's reaction against any idea of ongoing economic reform, and the rule of the 1970s seems to have been that administrative bodies could mount as many little planning experiments as they liked, so long as they did not expect to be permitted to generalise them.[91] As growth rates continued to fall and the pressure on resource availability to mount, further reform seemed inevitable. But it appeared likely that such a development would have to await the galvanising influence of a change in political leadership, so that it came as a surprise when a comprehensive planning 'mini-reform' was announced in July 1979.[92] In fact, the new planning decree bears all the marks of a compromise between liberalising economists, economists who think that centralised planning can be perfected and *apparatchiki* who simply want to sit tight. But it is full of fascinating, though often contradictory, details, which set in perspective the preoccupations of the Soviet leadership.

Labour policy and planning receives considerable attention in the new decree. The Shchekino system, which as we noted has been essentially marking time in recent years, is again singled out as a priority development, and a new and more radical version of the system, recently reported in the Soviet press,[93] seems destined for generalisation. Under this new variant, wages fund for each sub-division of the enterprise is planned purely on the basis of growth of productivity, historic wage – output ratio and planned level of production. The size of the labour force does not enter into planning at all. These arrangements clearly mean the complete disappearance of even a formal distinction between wage fund proper and bonus fund. The 'wage fund' can now be used, for instance, to pay special bonuses for high-quality work. Total funds made available will presumably vary directly with the level of labour productivity, so that maximum scope will now be available to management to plan in complete freedom for maximum productivity. On the other hand, there is no indication of any basic change in the attitude to redundancy, with Shchekino enterprises still, typically, absorbing all of the labour resources freed themselves. Shchekino still seems, then, to be something special that can be applied in highly dynamic enterprises, rather than something which is going to revolutionise the labour supply/productivity problem in the Soviet economy as a whole. Under the new planning arrangements, republican and local labour placement organisations are to be enjoined and empowered to take on a more active rôle in aiding and monitoring efficient allocation of labour resources, and more comprehensive labour resource balances are to be compiled at republican and *oblast'* level.[94] There is, then, still some impetus on the overall labour placement and planning front which may in the future provide the basis for a further generalisation of the Shchekino system at enterprise level.

The contradictory nature of the 'mini-reform' emerges most clearly if we look at its provisions relating to some of the crucial elements in the general planning system as discussed earlier. There is a definite attempt to get away from the ratchet principle, with 'stable norms' once again a key slogan, as it was in 1965. This time, however, it is to be given more teeth, and coefficients for bonus funds and payments are to be fixed for the whole of the five-year plan, with any unused monies being carried over from year to year. Ministries will now be able to allow enterprises to reduce the level of physical production if this permits greater emphasis on high technology or the production of high-quality goods. Greater freedom is to be left to the working collective to decide exactly how bonuses are to be allocated. On the other hand, socialist competition and counter-plans are given great stress in the decree, and counter-plans, once adopted, will now be counted as being part of the official plan for purposes of assessing plan fulfilment, bonuses due and so on. It is true that in recent years there has been an increasing tendency to try to orientate socialist competition more towards qualitative indicators, and the ZIL system of socialist competition, which is heavily oriented to technical progress, has been officially recommended by the party since 1974.[95] On the other hand, socialist competitions are still often judged on the basis of not even just fulfilment, but indeed degree of overfulfilment of quantitative targets, thus exemplifying the crudest form of growth maximisation strategy.[96]

At the grass-roots level, special bonuses are now to be introduced to encourage workers to 'rate-bust', that is to go all out for maximum short-term output performance, deliberately ignoring any unofficial quotas normally respected on the shop-floor. In the light of the earlier discussion about basic worker attitudes in the Soviet Union, one might be inclined to scepticism as to the possible effect of such a measure. In fact, Soviet material suggests, as does corresponding Western material,[97] that while you will always get some rate-busters, it is

impossible to make everyone a rate-buster.[98] It was recently observed in
Pravda that the acronym NOT – *nauchnaya organizatsiya truda* –
scientific organisation of labour, a form of Taylorist time and motion
study, is frequently ironically rendered as *normal'naya organizatsiya
truda* – 'so-so' organisation of labour.[99] In any case, the very intention
of this part of the decree seems at odds with the anti-ratchet orientation
of its general provisions.

What lies behind these paradoxes? There can be no doubt of the
clarity and firmness of purpose of the Soviet leadership in relation to the
need to raise labour productivity. But in an age of secularly declining
growth rates – not just in the Soviet Union – the leadership seems to
have taken fright at the prospect of having to pay too high a price, in
terms of the continued quantitative growth that is undoubtedly
necessary if the Soviet Union is ever to 'catch up' with the West, for
intensification. Add in a good measure of political conservatism, the
continued prevalence among the cadres of the conviction that people
can be 'chivvied up' to deliver the goods, and interpretation of the
hotchpotch becomes easier. The ratchet has got to go because it
ultimately makes planning more difficult, but the easy way, to the
apparatchik mind, to increase labour productivity is through political
pressure and organised rate-busting. It is surely significant that the latest
major decree relating specifically to labour problems mentions the need
to improve labour placement, but places primary emphasis on the need to
improve labour discipline.[100]

The same kind of contradictions are present in some of the other
general provisions of the new planning decree. Direct links between
client and customer are to be stressed, as is the further development of
'free trade' in industrial goods – all this implying some degree of
decentralisation of the system. At the same time, the number of
commodities centrally planned is to increase, and there is to be a new
emphasis on detailed physical planning indicators for the enterprise.
This latter element ties in partly with the desire to place greater stress on
quality factors, but it is difficult to see how it can do other than increase
the weight of centralisation and command on the producing unit. If
'natural' planning is successfully introduced, it will revolutionise the life
of the Soviet worker and will, indeed, require a complete rethinking of
the whole approach to incentive arrangements. But in practice, given
that planners are still going to have far more to do than they possibly
can, while managers and workers will continue to receive 'messages' in
the form of commands, it is difficult to see how 'natural' planning can
mean anything but a return to the classical *gross* output system, with all

its faults. And how does this tie in with the introduction of normed *net* output as the basic aggregate output indicator? In fact, although normed net output (hereafter NNO) will be the universal basis for calculating labour productivity, it is only for the five-year plans (now being given more teeth) that NNO will be the clear basic output indicator. For annual and quarterly plans the precise status of NNO is not fully defined, but it is explicitly stated that gross output in physical terms will still be used operationally in some cases. To make the whole situation even more complex, *realizatsiya* (that is, gross value of sales) will still be used to assess fulfilment of contracts.

One last special area to which the decree devotes particular attention is that of capital investment. As we noted earlier, there is plenty of scope for increasing investment effectiveness, and exploitation of this scope could do a great deal to ease the strain of the basic consumption/investment/defence macro-economic balance. The mini-reform reiterates the stress of recent policies by trying to attack the problems of *raspylenie* and poor finishing. 'Completed project' is to be the key indicator for production and financial planning, and for incentives. Experimental running of this kind of approach in Belorussia has yielded good, if not outstanding, results, and the big question is whether the system can be extended throughout an industry that varies enormously in terms of technological level and type of work. What the mini-reform does not appear to do is to back up planning reform at the *construction* stage with planning reform at the *design* stage. Attempts since 1965 to make design organisations more sensitive to clients' needs and to the need for the highest technological standards have not been successful, and the authorities seem to have given up on this one for the time being. Once again, then, there is a question mark over the degree of integration of the separate elements in the mini-reform.

*   *   *

It looks, then, as if the possibility of a radical and clearly-directed initiative on the planning system must still await a change in the political leadership. But we are only talking of *possibilities*, for the kind of political stability produced by accommodation of apparatchik vested interest and shop-floor complacency must continue to have strong attractions for a régime and society that has good enough reason to fear instability. On the other hand, extrapolation of existing trends can only mean a continued downward trend in growth rates, an ever tighter macro-economic balance and continued failure to 'intensify' the economy, except in patches. Consideration of likely energy trends suggests that 3 per cent is the maximum growth rate that the Soviets can hope for in the next decade or so.[101] Growth rates of 2–3 per cent may, indeed, be 'normal' high rates throughout the industrial world in the future, but they leave little room for manoeuvre to an economy that still cannot guarantee that even a low growth rate represents quality growth and that is still at an early stage in the consumption revolution. There is no immediate prospect for a dramatic improvement in the living standards of the Soviet worker, and the price of a Shchekino-based revolution in labour productivity could be very high, at least for some workers. Soviet experience suggests no magic formula whereby high productivity, high earnings, relaxed working conditions and total job security can be combined. Surely such a formula can be found, but the search will require a sustained and deeply considered pragmatism such as has not characterised Soviet policy on planning up to now.

NOTES

1. O. Lange, 'Role of planning in Socialist economy', in O. Lange (ed.), *Problems of Political Economy of Socialism* (New Delhi: People's Publishing House, 1962) p. 18.
2. See A. Helgeson, *Perevod vs. Perekhod: Prospects for a Soviet Population Distribution Policy*, paper read at the annual conference of the British National Association for Soviet and East European Studies, Fitzwilliam College, Cambridge, 24–6 March 1979, p. 17.
3. 'A esli vniknut', in *Pravda*, 15 November 1968, p. 2.
4. See Helgeson, op. cit., p. 19; D. A. Dyker, *The Soviet Economy* (London: Crosby Lockwood Staples, 1976) pp. 99–100.
5. See Dyker, op. cit., p. 100.
6. Helgeson, op. cit., p. 18.
7. Ibid., p. 20.
8. I. Komarov, 'Zarplata stroitelya', *Ekonomicheskaya gazeta*, No. 12 (1979) 9.
9. Dyker, op. cit., p. 108.
10. See G. Mil'ner and E. Gilinskaya, 'Mezhraionnoe regulirovanie urovnya zhizni naseleniya', *Planovoe khozyaistvo*, No. 1 (1975).
11. See Helgeson, op. cit., p. 11.
12. Ibid., pp. 16–17.
13. See V. Andriyanov, 'Problemy kadrov dal'nego vostoka; 2. pereselenets', *Komsomol'skaya pravda*, 24 July 1971, p. 2.
14. Helgeson, op. cit., p. 13a.
15. Ibid., p. 22.
16. 'Trebuyutsya spetsialisty', *Komsomol'skaya pravda*, 6 September 1979, p. 2.
17. A. Larionov, 'Sluzhba truda', *Komsomol'skaya pravda*, 20 July 1971, p. 2.
18. See Helgeson, op. cit., pp. 26–7.

19. A. Nove, *An Economic History of the USSR* (London: Allen Lane, The Penguin Press, 1969) pp. 191 and 225.
20. M. Feshbach and S. Rapawy, 'Soviet population and manpower trends and policies', in *Soviet Economy in a New Perspective* (Joint Economic Committee, US Congress, 1976) p. 128.
21. Ibid., p. 132.
22. 'O meropriyatiyakh po material'nomu stimulirovaniyu raboty pensionerov v narodnom khozyaistve', *Ekonomicheskaya gazeta*, No. 41 (1979) 3.
23. Dyker, op. cit., p. 39.
24. For a detailed discussion, see ibid., chapter 3.
25. The phrase was invented by Alec Nove. See his *The Soviet Economy*, 3rd ed. (London: Allen and Unwin, 1968) p. 308.
26. See A. Hirschman, *The Strategy of Economic Development* (New Haven: Yale University Press, 1958).
27. See E. Devons, *Planning in Practice* (London: Cambridge University Press, 1950).
28. All figures derived from OECD National Accounts statistics.
29. See, for example, Dyker, op. cit.; A. Nove, *The Soviet Economic System* (London: Allen and Unwin, 1977).
30. *Economic Survey of Europe in 1977*, Part I (New York: United Nations, 1978) p. 77, footnote 8.
31. See G. Alekseev, 'Effekt novatorstva', *Pravda*, 13 September 1976, p. 2.
32. See I. Birman, 'From the achieved level', *Soviet Studies*, xxx, No. 2 (April 1978).
33. See D. A. Dyker, *Decentralisation and the Command Principle – Some Lessons from Soviet Experience*, paper read at the Annual Convention of the American Association for the Advancement of Slavic Studies, New Haven, 10–13 October 1979.
34. See L. Urbanek, 'Some difficulties in implementing the economic reforms in Czechoslovakia', *Soviet Studies*, xiv, No. 4 (April 1968).
35. Reported by I. Shatunovskii in *Pravda*, 18 December 1968.
36. See D. Roy, 'Quota restriction and goldbricking in a machine shop', in T. Lupton, *Payment Systems* (London: Penguin, 1972).
37. See ibid., and T. Lupton, 'On the shop floor: output and earnings', in the same collection.
38. Yu. Krasnopol'skii, 'Obyazatel'stva dlya otcheta', *Trud*, 13 September 1979, p. 4.
39. See National Board for Prices and Incomes, Report No. 65, *Payment by Results Systems* (London, 1968) cmnd. 3627, p. 20.
40. J. W. Gillula and D. L. Bond, 'Development of regional input – output analysis in the Soviet Union', in V. G. Treml (ed.), *Studies in Soviet Input – Output Analysis* (New York and London: Praeger, 1977) p. 296.
41. V. Poltorygin, 'Napryazhennyi plan predpriyatiya i khozyaistvennaya reforma', in M. Z. Bor and V. Poltorygin (eds), *Planirovanie i khozyaistvennaya reforma* (Moscow: *Mysl'*, 1969) p. 39.
42. N. Savichev, 'Pochem nynche minuta', *Pravda*, 21 October 1979, p. 2.
43. See R. Gareev, 'V bor'be za ritmichnost' proizvodstva', *Ekonomicheskaya gazeta*, No. 39 (1977) p. 8.

44. P. J. D. Wiles, 'A note on Soviet unemployment on US definitions', *Soviet Studies*, xxiii, No. 4 (April 1972).
45. 'Bol'she produktsii s men'shei chislennost'yu rabotnikov', *Ekonomicheskaya gazeta*, No. 10 (1970).
46. S. Shkurko, 'Voprosy stimulirovaniya proizvoditel' nosti truda', *Planovoe khozyaistvo*, No. 7 (1971) 10.
47. A. Mirgaleev, 'Shchekinskii metod i ego perspektivy', *Voprosy ekonomiki*, No. 10 (1977) 105.
48. P. Sharov, 'Shchekinskii opyt: dal'neishii etap', *Ekonomicheskaya gazeta*, No. 13 (1976) 6.
49. A. Agenbegyan, 'Chelovecheskii faktor', *Izvestiya*, 1 April 1975, p. 2.
50. See A. Burik, 'Stimulirovanie za schet ekonomii fonda zarplata', *Ekonomika sel'skogo khozyaistva*, No. 12 (1974).
51. N. Utkin, 'Kak "Sekonomili" kombinat', *Pravda*, 9 January 1975, p. 2.
52. 'Proizvodstvo udobrenii', *Ekonomicheskaya gazeta*, No. 9 (1975) 2.
53. Sharov, op. cit.
54. Mirgaleev, op. cit., pp. 104–5.
55. *Economic Survey of Europe in 1977* (see note 30), pp. 134–6.
56. 'Brigadnyi khozraschet', *Pravda*, 21 February 1978, p. 1.
57. See G. Silkin and M. Marakin, 'Potok est'. A "nepreryvka"?', *Ekonomicheskaya gazeta*, No. 17 (1978) 9; 'Pozabyli o podryade', *Ekonomicheskaya gazeta*, No. 48 (1978) 14.
58. See, for example, source cited under note 56.
59. See V. Dolzhnykh and V. Bezdeleev, 'Dva kryla stroiki', *Pravda*, 8 March 1978, p. 2.
60. See V. Kachurin, 'K novinke—po starinke', *Komsomol'skaya pravda*, 22 September 1979, p. 2.
61. See A. Nestik, 'U sosedei i doma', *Pravda*, 9 March 1978, p. 2.
62. Mirgaleev, op. cit.
63. See Helgeson, op. cit.
64. Larionov, op. cit.
65. V. Chichkin, 'Rekomenduyet byuro po trudoustroistvu', *Ekonomicheskaya gazeta*, No. 46 (1975).
66. *Radyans'ka Ukraina*, 15 August 1973, p. 3, as abstracted in *ABSEES*, January 1974, p. 45.
67. See N. Limonov, 'Ishchi u sebya doma', *Sotsialisticheskaya industriya*, 14 November 1974, p. 2.
68. See Agenbegyan, op. cit.
69. Z. Skarupo, 'Sokrashchenie tekuchesti i uluchshenie ispol'zovaniya rabochei sily', *Planovoe khozyaistvo*, No. 6 (1977) 119.
70. Chichkin, op. cit.
71. S. White, 'The USSR: Patterns of autocracy and industrialism', in A. Brown and J. Gray (eds), *Political Culture and Political Change in Communist States*, 2nd ed. (London: Macmillan, 1979) p. 55.
72. L. Danilov and V. Korchagin, 'Sovershenstvovanie upravleniya trudovymi resursami', *Planovoe khozyaistvo*, No. 11 (1976) 24.
73. See G. Lisichkin, 'Demokratiya i trudovoi kollektiv', *Komsomol'skaya pravda*, 8 August 1974, p. 2.
74. See N. Aleksandrova, 'V komandirovke', *Zhurnalist*, No. 11 (1974).

75. See R. Conquest (ed.), *Industrial Workers in the USSR* (London: Bodley Head, 1967) pp. 34–5.
76. See A. Solomakhin, 'Ukrali voskresen'e', *Pravda*, 14 January 1969, p. 2.
77. G. Yasinskii, 'Prokurorskii nadzor po delam o khishcheniyakh sotsialisticheskogo imushchestva', *Sotsialisticheskoe zakonodatel' stvo*, No. 10 (1973) 19.
78. G. Tarnavskii, Obespechenie zakonnosti v dogovornykh otnosheniyakh kolkhozov', *Sotsialisticheskoe zakonodatel'stvo*, No. 7 (1973) 26.
79. See V. Loginov, 'Premiya – ne podarhka', *Pravda*, 6 April 1975, p. 2.
80. D. Akhvlediani, 'Mertvye dushi', *Zarya vostoka*, 28 March 1975, p. 3.
81. Yu. Sakharov and N. Petrov, 'Leningradskii eksperiment', Part 3, *Pravda*, 14 May 1969, p. 2.
82. A. Matveev and R. Ismagilov, 'Vspomogatel'nye proizvodstva: problemy spetsializatsii', *Planovoe khozyaistvo*, No. 3 (1976) 75.
83. See R. Portes, *The Control of Inflation – Lessons from Eastern European Experience*, seminar paper presented at the Centre for Environmental Studies, London, 30 January 1976.
84. *Economic Survey of Europe in 1976*, Part II, (New York: United Nations, 1977) p. 116.
85. See Solomakhin, op. cit.
86. A. Nove, 'How the Russians balance their books to disguise the effects of inflation', *The Times*, 30 October 1974, p. 14.
87. See Dyker, *Decentralisation and the Command Principle – Some Lessons from Soviet Experience.* (See note 33.)
88. See V. Zangurashvili, '"Tolkachi" *Ponevole ekonomicheskaya gazeta*, No. 10 (1979) 13; 'Snabzheniyu – opytnye kadry', *Pravda*, 30 June 1979, p. 1.
89. Portes, op. cit., p. 13.
90. See Roy, op. cit.
91. Nowhere more obviously than in the investment and construction sector. See *Economic Survey of Europe in 1977*, Part I (New York: United Nations, 1978) pp. 134–7.
92. The *postanovlenie* was published in *Pravda*, 29 July 1979, pp. 1–2.
93. A. Kondratenko and V. Churasov, 'Razvivaya shchekinskii metod', *Ekonomicheskaya gazeta*, No. 26 (1979) 7.
94. 'Khozyaistvennyi mekhanizm i trud', *Ekonomicheskaya gazeta*, No. 37 (1979) 5.
95. V. Kozhemyanko and A. Panchenko, 'Uskorenie tempov', *Pravda*, 11 September 1974, p. 2.
96. See G. Boiko, 'V zavisimosti ot tempov rosta', *Ekonomicheskaya gazeta*, No. 22 (1975) 3.
97. See M. Dalton, 'The industrial "rate-buster": a characterisation', in Lupton (ed), op. cit.
98. See N. Nagibin and I. Ryazhskikh, 'Eshche raz ob aksaiskom metode', *Pravda*, 18 January 1975, p. 2.
99. I. Kirillov and R. Povileiko, 'Chelovecheskii faktor', *Pravda*, 19 October 1979, p. 2.
100. Decree published in *Ekonomicheskaya gazeta*, No. 3 (1980) 4.
101. See L. Dienes and T. Shabad, *The Soviet Energy System*, (New York: John Wiley, 1979) pp. 256–7.

4 Eye-Witness to Failure

Murray Seeger

Of all the secrets buried deep within the labyrinth of the Soviet Union, few are so closely guarded as those concerning the status of workers. The 'working class' is constantly extolled in the controlled press and its 'leading role' in directing the society towards that elusive, shimmering mirage of pure communism is reiterated at frequent intervals.

The foreign correspondent assigned to Moscow produces meagre results, however, when he strikes out to explore the actual living and working conditions of individual workers. Although he is told over and over again about the important position of trade unions in the Soviet system, the foreigner rarely meets any of their officers. Visits to factories are rare; those finally agreed to are carefully controlled and managed like a Bolshoi Theatre production of *Swan Lake*. The visitors meet the factory manager and the secretary of the Communist Party. Occasionally, outstanding 'shock' workers are introduced, but 'union' officials are conspicuous by their absence. It is the party that speaks for the workers at such times with its select cadres setting the examples which others are expected to follow.

Of course, the party and government media proclaim daily the dogmas of Soviet life – the absence of unemployment, complete equality of the sexes and the regular achievements of individual workers and brigades in surpassing output quotas. What is missing is any suggestion that ordinary workers have any influence on the vital questions of their working conditions. Who determines wage rates, working hours, production quotas, safety and environmental standards? Who investigates grievances? Who speaks for the workers?

The answer to all the questions is that it is the party that resolves all conflicts, makes all plans and anticipates all problems through its 'scientific' approach to economic issues. When the official press discusses the role of the party, it emphasises that its ranks are made up of a majority of 'workers'. The press fails to disclose that those described as 'workers' are, more often than not, persons in authority far removed from the workbench.

Foreign correspondents are almost never allowed to talk with ranking Communist Party officials, but do occasionally meet with provincial officials or cadre leaders in factories or on farms. These people, however, are so highly disciplined and indoctrinated that they will rarely answer substantive questions about either their work or about the status of workers. In addition, the Soviet press rarely provides reliable information of the routine type concerning workers' problems. Only general 'average' figures are given for wages. Little is printed about workers' attitudes towards their jobs or working conditions.

What little is printed about factory operations concentrates on managerial bungling – the inevitable stories about raw materials left to rot in open storage areas, continued production of shoddy products and failure to maintain important machinery. Some such stories, the papers claim, result from workers' letters to the editor, a tacit admission that there is no alternative means of airing grievances. Workers are criticised for drinking too much and malingering. But any complaints they have about working conditions are channelled away from where outsiders might see them.

We know by gossip that there have been occasional strikes in Soviet factories, just as there have been riots over persistent shortages of meat. We know from former prisoners' testimony of the substantial contributions made to the economy by penal camp inmates, including the manufacture of souvenir 'Mischa' bear dolls designed for the 1980 Olympic Games tourists. But valid information about general working conditions is perhaps second only to military information on the list of secrets maintained by the Soviet Union.

When the workers do protest about some management decision which they do not like, the rare public revelation of the incident tells us a lot about the official position of wage-earners in relation to the *vlast* (authority). A recent example of this surfaced in January 1979 in the official Azerbaijan republican newspaper, *Bakinsky rabochii.*

The bus-drivers of Baku, the oil-producing capital city, resisted a decision made by the city party committee to change the way they collected passengers' fares. For years, the newspaper said, the bus system had not worked well and the authorities had made a proper decision to change the method of collecting fares. Also:

Preparatory work for the switch to the new system was, however, not carried out, and its introduction was accompanied by serious

shortcomings. All this led not to an improvement but to a deterioration in the work of the city's transport and brought to light grave
errors in party educational work in transport collectives and a low
consciousness and self-seeking tendencies among a substantial section
of the city's transport workers . . .

After the city's motor transport switched to the new conditions of
work, a large number of drivers, including communists, handed in
their notice to the vehicle depots with the aim of frustrating this
progressive measure . . .

The leaders of the Ministry of Road Transport showed their
helplessness in combating the disorganizers, failed to rally the healthy
forces in the labour collectives and to direct their efforts against the
unworthy, and have still not taken effective measures to bring about a
radical improvement in the situation on the city's transport.

In any Western country, the newspaper report would have called the
incident in Baku a strike. But the Soviet-style report could not use such a
word and could only refer to the protesters as 'unworthy' elements in the
workforce and suggest they were more powerful than the 'healthy' ones.
Even more interesting was the parenthetical admission that 'communists', the nominal paragons in the workforce, joined the walkout.
Such rare, veiled admissions of labour unrest and protest suggest the
presence of much deeper undercurrents of worker unhappiness and
disillusionment.

The subject of worker happiness and satisfaction with his conditions
of employment and general social position is important for more than
simply satisfying curiosity. After all, it is the failure of the Soviet Union
to meet its targets for raising productivity that is a major reason why the
country is experiencing a steadily declining rate of economic growth.
The centrally-planned system has functioned without taking proper
account of workers' incentives and grievances. Revolutionary zeal has
long since faded from the Soviet workers' bosom, but nothing has
replaced it.

For many years, the party could attack those accused of complaining
and criticising of still being imbued with bourgeois ideas and capitalist
materialism. Now, with two full generations indoctrinated with
Marxism – Leninism, it is difficult for the authorities to make such
accusations against trouble-makers without admitting that their entire
education and ideological training programme is a failure. Now, the
Kremlin tries to attack complainers for falling victim to foreign ideas

that somehow filter through the ideological barriers.

Instead of making substantial improvements in working conditions and incentives, the Soviet planners rely heavily on the hoary methods of exhortation. Such tired, sloganeering techniques are no longer effective – workers who are outside the privileged party ranks refer to communists as 'they' and 'them'; those who have power and use it against those without power.

My first experience with this phenomenon of hiding the true conditions of workers came early in my thirty-one months as a correspondent in Moscow. Since I had previously written economic and labour news from New York City and Washington, I was especially curious to learn what I could about the same topics in Moscow. I found, one day, among the pile of translations and abstracts supplied on subscription by the *Novosti Agency* a report of a study on industrial accidents.

I telephoned *Novosti* to ask for a full copy of the report and was told they would look for it. Since *Novosti* charges hard currency for all its services, I assumed they would give me a copy if I were willing to pay an atrociously high price for it. Instead, my contact at the agency called back to say that they had only one edition of the study in the building and were unable to let me have it. I asked for a copy to be made – at my expense – but the official said that was not possible.

This experience was added to many other frustrations such as lack of contact with responsible officials, denials of permission to travel and petty harassment. This was 1973, when *detente* between the Nixon White House and Brezhnev Kremlin was in its fullest bloom. Why, we asked, have not working conditions for journalists been improved in light of this better diplomatic atmosphere between our countries?

At first, the official pleaded for understanding of the Soviet situation. 'I have lived and worked in London, ' he admitted. 'I know some of the problems you face. I couldn't believe the amount of information provided to me as a journalist there. We just have not developed an information system in our country.'

The travel sector also was under-developed, he continued: it was a shortage of accommodation suitable for foreigners that often prevented officials from allowing us to travel out of Moscow. 'Even I,' he said, 'had to sleep on the floor in a hotel during my recent visit to the Donbas.'

In a later meeting with a smaller delegation of correspondents, however, the official became more specific. There could be no relaxation of restrictions against foreign journalists under existing official policies.

'We view foreign correspondents as agents of the enemy ideology and there is no peaceful co-existence for ideology,' he declared.

It was later that we discovered with what authority the official spoke because he became the centre of a minor international incident early in 1980. Vsevolod Sofinsky left the Foreign Ministry to become Ambassador to New Zealand from where he was expelled by the government of Prime Minister Robert Muldoon. The New Zealanders said they had hard evidence that Sofinsky had personally given Kremlin money to the small pro-Soviet Socialist Unity Party and that he was a long-time officer in the KGB. No wonder he had been given the job of dealing with the Western reporters in Moscow and was so well-versed in the ideological definition which pertained to us.

Ugly as Sofinsky's statement sounded to our non-Marxist – Leninist ears, we then knew where we stood. The revealing of 'economic information' by Soviet citizens to foreigners is a specific offence, so that attempting to report news on such simple things as wages, prices, working hours, factory output, accidents, quotas and supply situations was more than a challenge – it entailed legal risks.

Even a massive secretive society like the Soviet Union, however, reveals a great deal about itself at the same time as it is trying to hide its dirty linen and to present a false front to the outside world. The resident correspondent who walks the Moscow streets, reads the press thoroughly, travels as widely as possible and talks to as many witnesses – Soviet and foreign – as possible learns a great deal.

Occasionally, the correspondent will even find obvious examples of lying and exaggeration in the higher ranks of the Soviet press system itself. Several of us found, for instance, a blatant example of faking a photograph of an official occasion, apparently to shore up the reputation of a Politburo member. The occasion was Lenin's birthday when the centre of Moscow was closed off to outsiders for a few hours so that the Kremlin leaders could safely venture into Red Square to stand outside the revolutionary leader's mausoleum. The major newspapers the next day showed that most of the Politburo members were there, lined up behind Brezhnev, who had placed a wreath at the tomb. In the local party paper, *Evening Moscow*, however, the editors had clumsily pasted a head photograph of the city's party boss, Viktor Grishin, close behind Brezhnev in the Kremlin pecking order. The paste-up was especially clumsy since the editors were unable to provide Grishin with feet, and the other printed photographs and stories suggested he was not at the ceremony at all.

The editors of *Evening Moscow* repeated their efforts in May 1979 when they chopped out the likeness of Andrei Kirilenko from the traditional photograph of the Politburo standing on the Lenin tomb to review the May Day parade. The action had the effect of moving Grishin one step closer to Brezhnev on the ladder of power, at least for the evening newspaper readers. The following day's edition of *Moskovskaya pravda*, also published by city communists, restored Kirilenko to the position that the television audience and parade witnesses remembered.

This faking was easily caught out, but other printed lies were more difficult to catch, except when one official organ blew the whistle on another as '*Journalist*' did in early 1973. The subject was an article in *Trud*, the daily newspaper of the All-Union Central Council of Trade Unions, which in October 1972 had printed a typical glowing account of life in a remote fishing village on Sakhalin Island, a territory also claimed by Japan.

'The Nekrasovka of today is drawn with asphalt ribbons of streets with stone parallelipipeds (six-sided prisms) of houses and shops,' the labour paper said. Not only was the village a seeming paradise, but the workers of the 'Red Dawn' fishing collective were also apparently in seventh heaven. The *Trud* correspondent said he watched them haul in more than 15 tons of fish in two boats.

Investigation showed, however, that the article was filled with 'basic absurdities', *Journalist* commented.

'Where the asphalt ribbons are concerned, the author has evidently exaggerated,' a fishing-boat captain wrote. 'It is a pity, but for the time being there is no asphalt in our Nekrasovka. And there is still only one small shop for two settlements, the new and old Nekrasovka separated by a distance of one and a half kilometers. The houses of both settlements resemble parallelipipeds only to one with a rich imagination.'

As for the big haul of fish, that too was a strange story. The collective did not catch more than three tons during the whole season, only 10 per cent of its quota, the captain said. There were no salmon, the fish of the region, running when the *Trud* man visited. Yekaterina Mikheyeva, the Party Agitation and Propaganda chief in the regional headquarters at Okha, told *Journalist*: 'We have no asphalt, even in Okha . . . I am surprised that such material could be printed'.

The incident suggested a behind-the-scenes tug-of-war between contending forces trying to keep the official press from losing all credibility. The *Trud* article, of course, referred to a very small, remote village and not a major industrial complex or central economic issue. The corrective was a light tap on the wrist to suggest that there were authorities interested in disciplining the press, but such criticism was never directed at major policy articles. Still, the official press occasionally parted the curtains slightly on scenes ordinarily blocked from view. One example was the unique article in *Izvestia* in early 1974 which reported on the findings of a survey taken among workers at a locomotive works in Voroshilovgrad in 1973.

Two-thirds of the workers polled said that they were 'not satisfied' with their wages, while five years before a similar question was answered in the same way by 54 per cent. In that five-year period, it was known that the government had slowed down the rate of annual wage increases. In 1973 alone, profits in all state enterprises rose by 12 per cent, productivity went up by a claimed 6 per cent, while wages rose by only 3.7 per cent, on average.

'The difference in opinion about salaries can be explained first of all by the increase in demand, especially for expensive, hard-to-find products,' the *Izvestia* analysts claimed.

In both 1968 and 1973, 71 per cent of the workers said that their working equipment was not good. Health conditions in the plant were objected to by 70 per cent of those polled in 1973, compared with 65 per cent in 1968. Only 43 per cent of the workers approved the production quota they were supposed to fulfil that year and only a third were content with the plant's total efficiency.

'The equipment is out-dated,' workers said, according to the paper. 'The plant needs basic reconstruction. New technology is introduced too slowly'.

The pollsters found that 78 per cent of the workers did not know a new reform programme had been introduced to overhaul the management system at the plant, and many other similar enterprises. What they did know was that they had not fulfilled their 1972 output quota and were therefore deprived of 'the 13th month' pay cheque, the usual reward for achieving quotas. '

These few studies have to be compared with regular statements about general manpower problems in the country, particularly discussions of turnover rates and apparent labour shortages. In Western terms, the Soviet Union suffers from over-employment, using too many people to deal with too little work. Soviet planners talk of manpower shortages and admit that one big problem is the high turnover, particularly in industries where working conditions are unsafe, equipment old-fashioned, the jobs arduous and the surroundings primitive.

Despite the strict controls on individuals' movements, the internal passports and domicile registration rules, workers simply vote with their feet when conditions get intolerable. They will walk away from a lousy job and talk their way into a new one. The bosses will help them to fix their papers if they need the workers. Other workers simply report to a health clinic and ask for sick-leave. By coughing and complaining, an individual can easily get a three-day sick pass which opens the way for a long drinking bout. A regular feature in the Soviet press is the article about all the people who fill the streets of Moscow and other cities when statistically nearly everyone is in a job.

Invariably, the reporters find a high proportion of those interviewed are on sick-leave or have simply taken a 'walk-about' through one excuse or another. A labour researcher said in an article in the *Literaturnaya gazeta* in November 1978 that unauthorised absenteeism was officially set at three days a year for each member of the workforce. But he said that the true estimate of under-utilisation of workers was over 10 per cent. In factory visits I made, I invariably found signs on bulletin boards criticising workers by name for excessive absenteeism. One sad-looking fellow had his picture posted in a textile mill alongside quotations from the letter he had written to his boss to describe his absence because of illness. The boss added that the letter was a lie, that the man had simply been on an extended drinking bout.

The ubiquitous quota system is probably the source of more complaints than any other single element in the Soviet worker's life. While the central planners build their overall targets for the five-year plans on the assumption of achieved production targets, managers and workers play the game of 'beating the quotas'.

Foreign residents of Moscow learned when stores had not met their sales targets by noticing which ones stayed open for extra days at the end of the month. They could also tell when restaurants had achieved their quotas by the degree of difficulty encountered in trying to obtain a meal. One could always recognise mealtime in the best Moscow restaurants because that was the hour when the doors were locked.

In its simplest form, the quota system required service workers to produce so much revenue for specific periods. A month was usually the touchstone – if the quota was not going to be made, the restaurant or hair saloon or taxi driver would work extra hours or serve more customers than normal. If the quota was in the bag, then service was slowed down. The idea was to make the quota with a slight excess. In that way the workers would get their extra month's pay without working too hard. To exceed quotas by too much was to make sure that the next year's quota would be raised substantially.

Factories had their quotas denominated in rubles or volume terms.

With the month closing, and the norm unachieved, the workers could count on 'voluntary overtime' to make up the losses. The phenomenon was called 'storming'.

'We work on our days off at the end of every month and in addition the working team stays for overtime work at the end of the working day,' plant workers from Kostroma wrote to *Trud*. 'All of us get 30 hours of overtime and more during a month which is not registered in any documents'.

A husband in Balebeyevo complained that his wife lost her days off because her 'factory is underfulfilling its plan'. The extra work was neither paid for in cash nor in commensurate time off. Those who refused the extra work were denied their annual bonuses.

In another letter, a foreman said that his motor car parts factory in Kazan turned out 12 to 22 per cent of its production in the first third of a month, 24 per cent in the second third and 63 per cent in the final third. 'Some workers have been putting in about five extra hours a day on the last two or three days, which far exceeds the amount permitted by the labour laws,' he told *Izvestia*. 'Records on the overtime worked by each employee are not kept by the plant – although the law requires that this and other information on overtime be reported to the local [party] committee, thus ensuring that the legal limit on overtime is observed.'

The Soviet laws ban forced overtime. But just like the state constitution, the gap between the written word guaranteeing democratic freedoms and the exercise of those freedoms is wide indeed. The official quotas have the force of law when they are put into effect by the octopus-like central planning agency, Gosplan. Workers have no say in setting the quotas but are required to meet, or beat, them. The party and the unions are expected to take the lead in making sure that the quotas are met and turn a blind eye to the methods which managers use in order to achieve that patriotic goal. At the plant level, it is the party members – a small minority among the workforce – who are expected to be the first in line for the overtime and Sunday work.

In their turn, the party members ask for special rewards for undertaking such 'storming' chores since they are paid the same as other workers. The incentives for party members include possible promotion to full-time party work, which is well-paid and guarantees lifetime security, and such other rewards as first consideration for trips to factory or ministry holiday resorts, rest homes and access to their housing blocks.

'Storming', of course, is terribly expensive in real economic terms. Running machinery overtime without maintenance speeds its deterioration; crash work lowers quality, and dragooning workers against their will demoralises their spirit and causes deep antagonisms which cannot be fully expressed.

'By making workers work overtime or on Sundays, managers commit a gross violation of labour laws and cause damage to the enterprise,' *Trud* scolded. Another paper aimed at party youth, *Komsomolskaya pravda*, told of the manager at a naval repair station in Volgograd who organised an expensive storming weekend. He cancelled two days off and asked his force to 'struggle for the honour of the enterprise'.

'He promised to pay 45 rubles each in addition to their salaries for three days' rush work and to supply their meals on the account of the enterprise,' the paper said. Some of the workers left the plant while some of those who showed up turned to vodka to assuage their frustrations. The result was that one team made a 'technical error' in a ship and got into a fist-fight with another team. It was what one could call a 'lost weekend'.

In the key housing industry, the crucial period is December and the last day of the month should be called 'disaster day', the important weekly newspaper, *Literaturnaya gazeta*, organ of the Writers' Union, said.

'The builders try to catch up with the closing year on December 30 and since the day is too short, they try to stretch it with searchlights,' the paper said. In Leningrad in one December, the builders finished 104 houses, 67 on the last two days. The next month found only two houses finished. The house committee which must approve the buildings closed their eyes to obvious defects in order to report quotas fulfilled. In January, the housing inspectors took a holiday and the construction workers returned to finish their jobs.

Workers do not have to feel guilty about cheating on quotas since the game is played at every level in the Soviet economy. At the top, Gosplan sometimes reduces quotas midway through a planning period and never again refers to the original targets. Fulfilment of the reduced target is announced with as much fanfare as if the original quota had been met. Other institutions participate with the same enthusiasm. *Pravda*, the national Communist Party paper, once discussed a night school at Ob which was geared specifically to help workers to improve their education after working hours.

Inspector after inspector came to the school, interviewed the director and looked at her books. They heard the class bells ring and heard the usual commotion as classes changed. Chairs were scraped, voices raised; the bells rang, and classes resumed. 'Each inspector left the school convinced that everything was all right,' *Pravda* said. 'But immediately after the man left, a small performance ended. Bells were not needed any more as there was no one to ring them for except teachers.'

One resolute inspector finally went beyond the director's office and found the school empty except for the teachers and the director. 'She had to fulfil her plan for educating the local working youth at any price. So that was one more case of exaggerating figures,' *Pravda* concluded.

The Soviet factory worker suffers most under this system of regular lying and dissembling. He has few opportunities to protect himself from the abuses of forced overtime and no extra pay, while service workers have managed to develop ingenious schemes to bend the quota system to their favour. Many of the factories in European Russia are antiquated, the buildings in poor repair and the fixtures and equipment primitive. Nearly all are surrounded by high walls surmounted with barbed wire which supports the frequent official complaints about worker thievery.

My first experience with this scene came early in 1972 when an Italian television journalist urged me to go with him to see the mammoth ZIL automobile factory on the east side of Moscow. In this ugly region of the city, an area where no foreigners live and few visit, he had been filming to show the contrast with the environment under which Italians worked in the big industrial belts around Milan and Turin. Italian-Fiat was then building a complete auto factory for the Soviet Union in an area along the Kama River of Central Russia where foreign journalists were not allowed to travel.

Although the ZIL factory was the home of the mammoth, hand-made limousines used only by top-level party officials, the workers coming out at the end of their shift looked as if they had been employed at a nineteenth-century mill in the industrial British Midlands. They apparently had no facilities for cleaning up and their shoes and work clothes were ragged. They jammed the tram and bus stops waiting for the crowded, dirty old vehicles that would take them to their homes, mostly tall, prefabricated cement flats lined up row upon row in typical Soviet style. Later, when Italian journalists were finally allowed to visit the new central Russian city of Togliatti, named after a famous Italian communist leader, and the factory making the Soviet version of the Fiat car (Zhiguli or Lada), one of the visiting Italian workers showed his disgust at working conditions by eating his Communist Party card in the presence of the visiting official delegation.

Service workers can compensate for some of their grievances by resorting to what is known as *na levo* (on the left) or illegal work. Among the most adept at this are the construction workers who turn up at newly-opened housing projects to greet the new occupants. A journalist in Kharkov reported what he found when he went to one of those buildings slapped together to meet the year-end deadline.

'The linoleum is laid badly, wallpaper comes off the walls, the ceiling leaks with the rain. Not a single door or window closes properly. The bath is unstable, white paint falls off the ceiling; the electrical and sanitation systems are out of order.' A pensioner wrote to *Pravda*: 'We cannot be happy because the door glass is broken, the sink is cracked and the floor is so badly painted that we had to do it again.'

Just as the newcomers finish the survey of their recently-acquired disaster, 'suspicious-looking men come to such houses in the evening and promise to do everything necessary in a short time,' *Pravda* said: 'They know very well what is missing in each apartment.' 'We worked here and so we know what is unfinished and where the necessary things are hidden,' a workman told one resident.

These enterprising men are called *shabashniki* (finishers), and officials estimated in the early 1970s that they did about fourteen million dollars' worth of illegal business a year in Moscow alone. Some of these workers had organised themselves into private firms to devote full-time to make up for the gaps in the official construction industry.

Western economists have estimated that the *na-levo* economy is at least 25 per cent as large as the official Soviet gross national product and perhaps as much as 50 per cent. Foreigners living in Moscow, and the Soviet citizens they meet, would favour the higher estimate because of the frequent, regular encounters they had with *na levo*. The cheapest thing was to keep bottles of vodka handy to buy immediate services not obtainable by regular channels. Otherwise, cash was the answer for the taxi driver who didn't want to turn on his meter, the hairdresser who didn't want to turn in a slip to show she had served a customer, and the clerk in the second-hand or antique shop who would hold back some special item for you.

Doctors and teachers engaged in the system to provide better services for the Soviet elite class of professionals, intellectuals and higher party brass who had plenty of cash to spend. The best doctors rarely saw the usual run of patients in the public clinics because they operated big private practices. School teachers, who worked only a half-day in state classrooms, sought tutors' jobs with well-to-do families in order to prepare youngsters for the state examinations that determined entry into the prized universities and institutes.

The cleverest *na levo* entrepreneurs were probably those in the Republics of Georgia and Armenia. Early in my period in Moscow, the authorities arrested two Georgian millionaires who were operating a complete illegal, private factory to make raincoats. Each day, one of them spent as manager of a state factory that was able to meet its quotas in a morning's operation. The workforce was then transported by taxis to another factory where the product was a coat better styled and better made than the official output. The raw material, equipment and factory building itself had all been purloined from official channels. The coats were sold in a wide area outside and inside Georgia by travelling salesmen, who managed to place them in state stores by letting the managers have a cut of the selling price.

Typically, the businessmen were not informed on by their workers, the taxi drivers or anyone else who knew of the operation. One of the entrepreneurs was caught trying to cash a forged lottery ticket and investigators went on to unravel his operations and living style, which included two homes. In nearby Armenia, we found a wide selection of wide, colourful men's ties on sale, unlike any product from a state tie factory. These were also the product of private operators. When they were caught, it was discovered that they had used an ambulance from the Yerevan Red Cross to deliver their products.

The few official factory visits I was allowed to make were confined to operations carefully selected and prepared for outside scrutiny. At a shirt factory in Moldavia, for instance, the paint on the floor and in a men's room was not yet dry when we arrived. Fresh lime had been packed around the plumbing and then painted over to cover the obvious faulty connections.

In that factory and at a large woollen mill at Ivanovo, east of Moscow, the workforce consisted predominantly of women who were dressed in clean, new uniforms. The Ivanovo mill, which made cloth for military uniforms, awarded its outstanding workers with red bandanas to denote that they had achieved their output quota the previous month. When they fell behind, these 'heroes of labour' had to resort to ordinary blue bandanas.

We saw few men in either factory, although most of the managers and party bosses were men. When we were invited for a 'typical' lunch at the workers' canteen in Moldavia, an American colleague and I noted with suspicion that a platter of small steaks was resting on top of the steam table. Our companions, all from Eastern Europe communist papers, took the steaks while my friend and I asked for the soup which was in one of the regular deep pots sunk into the steam table. When we lined up to get utensils, my colleague and I were rewarded for our prescience. There were no knives supplied in the dining room so that our companions ended up eating their steaks off their forks or with their fingers. We enjoyed the soup and were sure that we had the normal workers' lunch while the others had the Potemkin-like visitors' special.

Ivanovo, a traditional textile centre since the earliest days of industrialisation under the Tsars, was clearly what Soviet planners concede are 'female cities' which have developed around 'feminine industries'. One of the few countries in the world where there are more women in the workforce than men, the Soviet Union constantly struggles with the sociological and economic problems this fact causes.

The women are guaranteed, on paper, equal rights with men. On the other hand, they are channelled into certain work sectors and systematically kept out of others. They are so essential to the economy that the state cannot decide what its policy towards birth control and sexual rights should be.

On the one hand, the state wants the Slavic women, especially in the European areas, to have more children to counter the rapid rise in the non-European, largely Moslem populations of the Asian republics and to fill job demands in the older industrial regions. On the other hand, the planners need the women at their jobs and cannot afford to have them raising the big families that were traditional in pre-industrial Russia. The state, therefore, pays bonuses for babies and has no general programme for modern birth control. Yet, abortions are cheap and available and divorce is easy and quick. Over and over again we met Russian women aiming to have one child with or without the benefit of a resident husband or father. And we knew women who had undergone twenty to thirty abortions.

With forty-nine textile mills, an industry where the workforce is more than 70 per cent feminine, Ivanovo looked like a bachelor's paradise. Young girls brought to the town to learn how to operate the mills' machinery strolled in ranks down the grubby main street every night. They filled the dining room of the best hotel where the town's only live band played dance music. There was a movie house in the town and the bigger mills had singing groups and gymnasiums. A dance studio offered lessons but otherwise Ivanovo had little to offer in the way of social distractions. Off the main street, the lanes were deep with mud in the classic fashion of Russian provincial towns. The atmosphere was reminiscent of turn-of-the-century New England and Theodore Dreiser's novel, *An American Tragedy*.

At the Communist Party headquarters, Ivanovo officials said the ratio was 132 women for every 100 men, which may have included the young soldiers at a nearby training base. Some mill towns have as many as 167 women to 100 men.

'When you hear there are 132 women for every 100 men, it doesn't sound as bad as the problem really is for some of us,' a young engineer said. 'There are proportionately a much higher number of girls in their early 20s than men the same age.

'What can we do to find husbands? Go to Moscow on weekends and hope for the best when we go on vacation to other parts of the country. A bright good-looking guy doesn't remain a bachelor very long around here. What is left over isn't worth fighting over.'

The situation of such feminine-dominated towns is that there is a regular turnover as frustrated husband-seekers leave along with the newly married who find there are few good jobs for the husbands. 'Very often a major bread winner in a family is a wife because there are considerably fewer highly-qualified and well-paid men's occupations,' a writer for *Komsomolskaya pravda* said of another mill town nearby. 'Every third girl stays there without hope of getting married.'

'It is very difficult to create a family in such a city,' *Trud*, the labour daily, admitted. 'That means that childbirth is lower there. The population is getting rapidly older than in other cities and the number of unwed mothers is growing. All that results in migration.

'Women, mostly younger ones, leave for other cities at the first convenient opportunity . . . Girls are invited from other regions and are taught the jobs of weavers, but they do not stay at the factory long because of the unfavourable demographic situation.'

The situation I witnessed has grown progressively worse so that in 1979 the birth rate was so low that the growth in population was less than 1 per cent. The number of articles discussing the role of women increased and the usual ambivalence of official spokesmen reiterated — on one hand, women were praised for carrying a work burden 20 per cent greater than men and, on the other, were criticised for losing their finer feminine qualities. A 1979 article in *Literaturnaya gazeta* said alcoholism among women was rising faster than among men, an ugly indicator of social dissatisfaction and personality frustration.

The rise in illegitimacy attributed to the growth of largely female economic strata and other reasons has been dramatic, although it is little discussed in public. One study at Belorussia State University found that the frequency of illegitimate births had leaped from 24.4 for every 1000 single women (15 to 39 years) in 1959 to 62.5 in 1970. A commentator in *Literaturnaya gazeta* said the study reflected 'the situation in many places in the Soviet Union'. (The illegitimacy rate in the US in 1968 was 24.1 per 1000 unmarried women 15 to 44 years old.)

While the women in the model plant were busy and industrious, the managers seemed to have ignored fundamental safety rules. The women we saw operating large machines with foot controls wore only sandals with no protection for their bare toes. A union safety inspector in the West would have halted production in a minute until the workers were better equipped.

With no statistics on industrial accidents published, it is difficult to determine how serious the problem of on-the-job safety is. It is clear then that there were many accidents, just to judge from street observation of the risks construction workers took regularly and the lack of safety equipment and rules we noticed on our trips. Occasionally, as in 1972, there is an accident so great that the Kremlin issues a general condolence message to victims' families and promises an official investigation. The 1972 accident was an explosion in a new Minsk radio factory which caused many deaths. Later, some factory officials and designers of the facility were sent to jail for cutting corners on general design and the installation of the ventilating system. A few weeks after the big explosion was announced in *Pravda*, a foreign visitor asked a Minsk taxi driver to take him to the site. The driver said he didn't know anything about the accident, a strong suggestion that the local security force had given him strict instructions.

The coalmining industry has been notorious for its lack of safety and has also been singled out for failing to meet production quotas. Pay and benefits for miners have been raised higher than any other class of workers except those in the far north and Siberia. In 1978, Nikolai Grinko wrote in *Trud* that, after 1977, the number of mining accidents increased along with work-associated illnesses, and he blamed poor management and enforced 'storming' to meet quotas.

A major explosion in the Voronezh region was announced in 1979, but no specific number of deaths was acknowledged. Of course, a commission was named to investigate. In that same year, the managers of a mine at Voroshilovgrad offered demobilised soldiers a total of 6000 rubles in incentives to join the work force. The average wage there was reported as 350–60 rubles a month, more than twice the industrial average for that year of 165 rubles, or the equivalent of 250 dollars at the arbitrary Soviet exchange rate.

One of the leaders of the Association of Free Trade Unions, Vladimir Klebanov, who was a miner, asserted that twelve to fifteen workers were killed every year at Bazhanova where he had worked. Because output targets were 'unrealistically high', men often had to dig coal twelve hours a day instead of the normal six. Injuries under such conditions made 600 to 700 men a year idle, Klebanov told Western journalists before the Soviet authorities committed him to a psychiatric hospital.

In 1977, a team of Western experts who visited coalmines in the Donetsk region found that the danger level for methane gas there was 2 per cent compared with the American rule of 1.15 per cent. A visitor who entered a mine tested the air and found levels of methane as high as 5.5 per cent, above the level for potential explosions. The foreigners also found safety equipment in use which they considered to be fifteen to thirty years out-of-date.

A planning official admitted in an article in *Socialist Labour*, printed in January 1977, that 'a particularly high proportion of workers are engaged in manual labour in the coalmines, in the timber industry and in the food industry'. Problems of safety in the mines have probably received more open discussion in the Soviet press than other industrial safety problems.

In August 1975 and December 1978, Chairman Leonid Melnikov wrote in the pages of *Trud* of mine managers who overruled the warnings of his USSR Committee for Supervision of Safe Working Practices in Industry and for Mine Supervision. He told in the earlier article of a roof fall at Vorkuta, where 'shoring-up in a gallery was carried out haphazardly despite a threatening situation'. He also told of a methane explosion in a mine where men were working despite a ban imposed by safety inspectors. Injuries are highest among young miners, Melnikov added, 'because they are still sending into the coal seams people who are not properly trained and have not been informed adequately about safety measures'.

The later article charged Ukrainian officials with 'underestimating the importance of improving working conditions where miners have to work in high temperatures. In the mines of Donetsk Oblast only seven out of fifteen permanent cooling plants are functioning and many mobile air conditioners are out of action. And this despite the fact that, at the most conservative estimate, permanent plants should be installed without delay at another 16 mines.' The safety problem will only get worse in that area because digging goes deeper and deeper. In 1980, the experts forecast the operation of fifty to fifty-nine deep mines in the Donetsk, with the number soon rising to eighty.

The Soviet labour problem relates both to the amount of economic remuneration and to the buying power of wages. By Western standards, wages are abysmally low. But it is also true that there is little for the worker to buy with what he has. It is this second factor which probably makes it so difficult for Soviet planners to entice workers to the remote, underdeveloped regions of the country where labour shortages are critical. The former – the small cash wage – is mostly to blame for making urban workers so clearly dissatisfied with their lot. A combination of both factors drives young men and women off the farms and leaves them largely to the older generation to operate. In my two and a half years in the Soviet Union, I visited two of the areas, Murmansk and Siberia, where big bonuses are paid to attract workers. The chief driller at an oil well outside Nizhnevartovsk, supervising a crew of twenty, told us he was paid 1200 rubles a month, nine times the country's average wage for 1973. The lowest crew member got 480 rubles, or 630 dollars at the rate of exchange then in effect. The men worked four days straight, had a day off, and then worked four more.

The men had been promised housing before they arrived and got three months' extra pay for going to the region 360 miles south of the Arctic Circle where temperatures ranged from 50 degrees below zero in winter to 80 in summer. As they worked, the men accumulated bonuses which they could pick up later. Many of the crew we met claimed to own automobiles, a major symbol of prosperity and special privilege in the country where the waiting list for a cash-paid new car was three years or longer. The cars were left many miles to the south of the oil region, however, since there were few local roads on which to drive them. The workers said they spent much of their money buying apartments at special resort areas around the Black Sea and travelling from western Russia to the working zone.

Still, despite the benefits, the planners have trouble getting workers to move to Siberia. The officials who guided us on a brief tour of the oil fields would not say what the balance between those leaving and those arriving was, but other studies showed it was a negative balance. Although five Western journalists were taken on the rare trip to the oil fields in early 1974 with high-level escorts from the *Novosti News Agency*, we were told on arrival in Tyumen that instead of staying five days we would stay 24 hours. Because we dragged our feet and because transport in that region is so difficult and crude, we stayed some hours longer but never did see Tyumen, the oil capital. We were also never told why the trip was cancelled. It was simply a matter of local authorities exercising their power for their own reasons.

Soon after we returned to Moscow, however, we found that a high-level investigative group had been to the same region and had sharply criticised the planners and builders of the new towns there. The six investigators representing the party and government claimed that regional developers had spent too much money and effort on developing oil and gas wells and not enough on delivering the promised housing and comforts for workers.

Writing in the fourth year of the planning period, *Pravda* said that 'fulfilment of the programme has seriously lagged. About 40 per cent of the residence houses scheduled in the plan were built during the last three years. Construction of buildings for social and cultural purposes is even slower. The quality of building work is far from high. Often it happens that the corners are freezing through in a newly-built house, heaters have to be added and third panes of glass put into windows.'

The article went on to criticise the builders for setting up the same ugly, prefabricated, badly-fitted cement rectangles in Siberia 'as one can see in Krasnodar Territory or the Crimea'. There was no extra insulation on the tall flat side of the buildings which caught the northern winds and no effort was made to use the structures to break the winds. Walking through the area on a cold, star-filled night, a colleague and I saw that in nearly every apartment rugs or newspapers had been hung over the windows to cut down the icy blasts which left frost on all the glass.

In nearby Surgut, where we saw a new housing area for workers in a power plant, there was only a hole in the ground to show the location of a projected food store. The housewives travelled 'quite a distance' to buy their basic groceries, one man admitted. There were as many as five persons living in single dormitory rooms. From their windows, string bags of food dangled in the absence of domestic refrigeration. There was little clean drinking water and virtually no social centres to provide amusement for after-working hours.

'It happens that a house has been built, but there is neither water nor heating and other conveniences in yet,' *Pravda* went on. 'It also happens that houses have been built and people moved in, but the construction of cultural and social centres then starts with ground digging and engineering that could have been done in a single process.'

The *Pravda* criticism sounded much different from the glowing tales of economic and social development we were given by local officials. Earlier, in 1973, an engineer and architect working in the show-place scientific centre at Novosibirsk, Alexander Landinsky, levelled his own charges.

'More people leave Siberia than arrive there,' he said. 'The problem looks even more serious when we consider the fact that the majority of those who leave Siberia are people capable of working. . . . A vicious circle is created.' Builders would not go to Siberia because there was no housing for their workers and there were no houses because there were no people – no one wanted to be the first.

'If one asks why capital allocations are not completely used, the first answer will be because of the shortage of people everywhere, at building sites, at machine-building plants, at oil and gas wells, at timber mills,' Landinsky continued. 'Cities are being built slowly and badly. The consequences are evident: cadres of industrial enterprises are getting thinner in number, a great migration starts.' His article was carried by *Literaturnaya gazeta.*

Although Siberia has long been seen as the resource treasure house of the future, just waiting to be unlocked, the government found that in the 1960s a half-million more people left Siberia than settled there. The big bonuses were not enough and the social plan was faulty. Instead of building elite camps in the wildest areas for the temporary use of rotating work crews, as big oil companies have done in northern Alaska and Canada, the Soviet planners have tried to build complete new cities in Siberia. They used the same blueprints as in the ugly prefabricated suburbs which surround every major Soviet city and have been extended to large state and communal farms.

The workers, having no voice in the development process, stay only long enough to collect a pile of rubles and then leave. In a typical reaction to that phenomenon, the regime turned to party discipline as the alternative to a more humanistic approach. The high-priority construction project of the 'BAM' railway line from north of Lake Baikal to the Pacific was made an enterprise of the Young Communists (*Komsomol*) just as the earlier, massive hydro-electric project at Bratsk was.

In this way, young party members who want to make a career in the apparatus enhance their chances for getting ahead. We found, for instance, that in the oil-drilling crew at Nizhevartovsk, all twenty men were members of the party or the *Komsomol.* Usually, in any work brigade, the number of party members is between 10 and 20 per cent.

The lower-level party officials groused that they have to take too much responsibility for the rewards they get. 'Communists have more duties than rights,' one official in Moldavia told me. 'The task of the party is to activate the workers,' an official of the Moldavian Academy of Sciences added, during a 1973 visit. 'The party does not give orders. Members are the people in the front line. It is up to them to decide which problems are to be solved for the benefit of the republic and the people. Our members are spread all through the ranks, beginning with a chauffeur and going to the chairman of the academy.'

Asked if there were ever any conflicts between members of the academy and the party, another official said, no, their interests were identical. 'Not a single problem can be solved without the participation of the party organisation. The party secretary is an educated man.'

Another party official described the functions of his *apparatchniki* as making sure the terms of the five-year plan law were fulfilled. They are 'trouble shooters', he said.

'In Beltsy [Moldavia], we have three new factories that must be finished by the end of the five-year-plan [1975],' a party secretary said. 'They are a candy factory, a small clothing factory and a milk plant. To make sure those projects get done on time, we assigned one man from the party to each one to oversee everything.'

Another party boss in an electronics factory in Kishenev reiterated the same theme – the party's role was to make sure the plan was completed on time. 'The best workers are the communists,' he said. His next biggest job was 'ideological training', particularly of young communists.

The party leaders were very cautious about discussing their functions because they knew best the penalties for talking out of turn with Western journalists. Still, on factory visits, the party secretary was invariably on hand, sitting silently on one side, listening to what the factory managers told us. There was never a union representative present – unions were paper organisations while the party was iron and steel.

In a clothing factory, an official described how the communists in the workforce met regularly among themselves to discuss problems. The party leaders harangued the members to 'show an example' to the other workers by raising their output and making the extra effort required to fulfil the plan. They were also expected to report on any grousing heard from the non-party members and to be prepared with the official answers to any political questions. The entire workforce was called to meetings to hear pep talks on fulfilling the plan and explanations for government or party actions.

The interest in such meetings is low and if workers were not required to attend they probably wouldn't go. Regardless of the 'spirit of internationalism' espoused by the party lecturers, the workers in the Soviet Union, as in every other country, are chiefly interested in their own welfare.

Communists employed at routine jobs complained that they were not properly rewarded for taking the lead in working harder or longer than their fellows. Morale among the cadres was raised by giving the party members in good standing preference for taking their holidays at the resorts which many ministries and enterprises maintain in the Black Sea region. If the employer had housing under his control, party members were rewarded by getting priority for open flats. The city committees which control most housing were also supposed to give communists preference. In Moscow, foreigners were witnesses to another manner of rewarding loyal party members, especially in the lower ranks, for outstanding service. Before holidays, and especially near New Year which doubles as Christmas for atheists, a flood of Soviet workers would hit the special store set aside for foreigners to buy prime goods with their hard currency. The loyal workers were given rations of the special coupons they needed to buy high-quality vodka, imported wine and chocolates – they seemed rarely to buy groceries – not available in state stores. Higher party officials did not have to grub around in the foreigners' store – they had their own special stores for privileged shopping.

The workers of the Soviet Union know that they are poorly paid and complain that there is little to buy with what cash income they earn. When they hear about their country sending millions overseas to support revolutionaries in Africa, Asia or Latin America, they argue that it is money that could be better spent at home.

Living in Moscow at the time when Egypt expelled its Soviet military advisers, we were fascinated to see Russians react to the news. The Muscovites had not known how many people the Kremlin had sent to Egypt. More and more Soviet citizens have radios which are able to pick up international broadcasts that contradict the domestic party propaganda lines. The party has been warned several times by President Brezhnev that it must improve its ideological campaigns.

'Every day we have political information meetings for 14 minutes in the mornings before classes begin,' a party official at an agricultural training school told me. 'We want our students to be able to understand everything going on in the world from the correct point of view. They can listen to radio stations from all over the world. We have to deal with many sides of events.'

The ideological training included persistent warnings against 'imperialist encirclement' and efforts to 'reverse the gains of the revolution'. The party theorists insisted that military and self-defence planning be carried out down to the level of pre-teenage school children.

Young boys learned in school how to handle rifles and the entire student body in our neighbourhood was turned out every year for an exercise to 'defeat the imperialist invaders'. The foreign youngsters in the school were told that the day was a holiday and that they need not come to classes, but on the following day the young Russians asked where they had been. 'We defeated you yesterday,' one young Russian said with a smile. The youngsters then told the foreigners of the day-long mission of playing war in a park area and using tactics of World War Two partisans to beat back the imperialists.

The war, of course, is kept in front of Soviet citizens all the time in movies, television, radio and printed media. Vigilance is the watchword – vigilance against the enemies of the revolution, the revanchists who want to reverse the war result, and the multiple forces that want to destroy the policy of *détente* with the West. This strident, persistent campaign helps to rationalise the low salaries paid to workers and the continued low standard of living which every Soviet citizen is familiar with. While the campaign is largely ignored by most of the population, which has heard it for too long, it does raise the question among them: 'Who won the war?'

The Muscovites by no means represent the Soviet Union, but it was from them that we heard this question. At a hockey game, for instance, the Russians next to me asked if I were from the GDR – meaning East Germany. When I said no, that I was an American, they expressed surprise and then went into a discussion of how well dressed the Germans whom they saw were. The same comment was repeated to me about other citizens of Soviet Bloc countries who are the foreigners most Muscovites are likely to see. When the few privileged Soviet citizens who are allowed to travel to East Europe come home they, too, are impressed by the better standard of living they have seen. My own observation is that every East Bloc country is now giving its citizens a better standard of living than the Soviet Union, with the exception of Romania and, possibly, Bulgaria. And, even so, I am convinced Bulgarians eat better than Russians.

In Moscow, Soviet citizens told us that this was true to a large extent because the Kremlin was paying for all the defence of the East. The grousing sounded very reminiscent of what some Americans say about their own European allies.

Defence, of course, requires the compulsory drafting of all Soviet young men for two years' military service, unless they are enrolled in special, high-priority institutes, including those which train diplomats and intelligence officers. This constant draining off of young men is also one reason for the clear shortage of males in some economic sectors, especially agriculture. Historically, the Soviet Union has had an imbalance of population between the sexes because war, revolution and political purges killed a disproportionate number of men. In the post-war era, however, normal birth patterns have prevailed. Still, the outside observer in Moscow asks: 'Where are the men?'

They were not painting houses and buildings–that work was done by women. The mail was delivered by women, who were also the clerks in the post office and the stores. The crews who shovelled snow on the ground were mostly women, but men drove the trucks and operated the other clearing machines. The same division of labour applied to patching holes in the streets–the women shovelled and raked the hot asphalt while the men drove the trucks and road-rollers.

On the farms, the situation was similar–the field crews we saw were mostly women, while men drove the trucks and tractors. The common trend found the boys from the countryside drafted almost completely since they had fewer chances to enter the privileged institutes. Once in the army, the boys did not return to the lonely, hard life of the farm: they stayed in the city. If the girls from the country were fortunate enough to be enrolled in a training course which gave them a marketable skill, they too fled the farms. The boys who did return home after army duty soon left when they found no marriageable girls.

'My sons are grown up and are good workers now, but I am deeply concerned with some of my grandsons and with their attitudes towards their responsibilities,' a farmer in the Tambov region wrote to *Pravda* in early 1974. 'One of them told me that times were too different for them to continue digging manure.'

The farm standard of living at that time was officially admitted to be half of the urban standard, which was the lowest for any industrial country. Part of the problem was that Soviet agriculture was so notably inefficient that it required more than 20 per cent of the country's population to produce its poor results. The urban–rural split in the Soviet Union in the early 1970s was the same as that of pre-World War Two USA.

A study printed by the magazine *Novy mir* in 1974 said that the net loss of rural population was 1.6 million persons. The average age of the person leaving the farms was 24 while the average arrival was 36 years old. In the study of a Ukrainian village, *Pravda* said, 'during the last two years not a single school leaver or demobilised soldier stayed in the village'. In two years, the Ukraine trained almost 3 million farm-machine operators, but $2\frac{1}{2}$ million of them – the best-paid workers on farms – left for the city.

The men apparently were working in the heaviest industries as well as in the many layers of security–from traffic policeman to secret agent in Washington. Women still worked in such heavy tasks as railroad maintenance and coalmining; they were 84 per cent of the textile industry workforce, as in Ivanovo; 67 per cent in shoemaking and 40 per cent of machine building. They were, in fact, 46 per cent of all industrial workers and 51 per cent of the total workforce. In addition, they filled 70 per cent of teachers' jobs and 72 per cent of medical doctors–and nearly 100 per cent of the doctors in the neighbourhood ambulances.

Men predominated in the ranks of the party professionals and, as the pyramid narrowed towards the top, men held exclusive sway. Only one woman in modern times has served in the Politburo–Ekaterina Furtseva–who was demoted by the successors to her sponsor, Nikita Khrushchev. Despite their crucial role in society, no woman has been in the higher ranks of party or government for many years.

Women comprise less than 25 per cent of party membership. In 1979, only eight women were among the 287 full-time members of the vital party Central Committee. The press is filled with articles on the theme 'woman's work is never done'. One of the most recent, in *Literaturnaya gazeta* in January 1979, said that the average Soviet working woman spent over five hours a day on domestic chores, six days a week. The figure had dropped only half an hour since 1923. The magazine *EKO*, the year before, said that only 15 per cent of a woman's housework was mechanised, compared with 80 per cent in the US. The *EKO* comparison emphasised that any gains a woman made with more modern household appliances in the half-century of communism had been more than wiped out by the loss of time in the essentials of shopping and finding services. In 1923, when much of the retail business was still in private hands, shopping took an average of twelve minutes a day. The 1978 average was nearly two hours a day, much of the time standing in long queues or going to the shops looking for essentials in short supply, or travelling long distances to the few private peasants' markets which supply many food necessities. 'Domestic chores, as if someone has cast a spell on them, continue to take up about 30 hours of working women's time a week,' *EKO* said.

The acknowledgement by Soviet planners that they face a manpower shortage is an admission that they have not been able to increase productivity to any level close to that of the major non-communist industrial societies. There was a surplus of manpower in Central Asia, where there were few jobs, and a scarcity of manpower in the European regions, which are most heavily developed.

To an outside observer, of course, the problem appears to be not a shortage of actual working hands, but a disgraceful misuse of the hands available. The men who are available do not work very hard and the labour they exert produces meagre results because of the inefficiencies inherent in central planning and the backward nature of the country's technology.

One young Soviet Jew told me just before he emigrated to Israel that 'the Soviet Union is the greatest society in the world for malingering. No one has to work here. You just keep your head down and show up where you are supposed to be and you can survive at a low standard of living. Most people are satisfied with that.'

One solution for the manpower imbalance would be a massive shift of workers from Central Asia to European Russia, but the planners are unlikely to take such a step. The Kremlin does not want to risk the danger of internal unrest by bringing thousands of darker-skinned Moslem men and women into the Slavic areas where ethnic differences are keenly felt. And the Asians would resent being moved from their homelands.

The Soviets have done little to train the Central Asian nationalities, and efforts to develop industries in that huge region have been modest. In a visit to Uzbekistan, we found that many Russians and Ukrainians had been moved there to attend a recently-opened university. Local natives were attending also, but they resented the fact that they had rarely been allowed to attend older, high-level institutions in the Western republics and had to give up places in their new school to Slavs.

Workers, especially young communists, were recruited from both Uzbekistan and Kirgistan, to help carry out an ambitious project announced in 1974 to develop the 'non-black earth' region of the Russian Republic. When this was announced, we were told in Moscow that the project would be comparable to Khrushchev's effort to develop agriculture in the 'virgin lands' of Central Asia and Western Siberia. By 1979, however, reports in Uzbek newspapers suggested that the programme was less than a success. A large number of the names mentioned of participants in the programme were Slavic, not Uzbek or Kirgiz, and the Uzbek newspapers said that many young people left the project sites to come home before their jobs were done. *Komsomolets Uzbekistana*, in September 1978, wrote of the disillusionment of young people, who said that they had found the promises of pay, work and living conditions unfulfilled. Talking of the project managers in Tashkent, a labour foreman in Novgorod said 'for some reason they are sending general labourers or concrete pourers although we aren't working with concrete'.

In their efforts to fill manpower gaps, Soviet planners in the late 1960s started a programme to attract pensioners back to work. 'Under the conditions of a growing labour force deficit in the rapidly developing economy of the Soviet Union, employment of pensioners is becoming particularly important,' two Soviet researchers said in a paper presented at the International Congress of Gerontologists held in Kiev in 1972. 'It will allow not only to utilise more fully the experience, skills and habits of the pensioners but also partly to decrease the state expenditures for paying out pensions at the expense of additional production.'

The planners were disturbed because retirement even at very low pensions was very attractive to Soviet men and women. The study showed that while 83 per cent of men from fifty to fifty-nine were working, only 53 per cent continued after passing the eligible pension age of sixty. At the rate of exchange then in effect, the 1972 average Soviet wage was the equivalent of $154 a month and the average pension $100. Many pensions, and wages, were below those figures, however. The women delivering our mail, for instance, were paid less than half of what was the announced average wage and many pensioners complained in letters to newspapers that their incomes were less than the equivalent of $70 a month.

While in Western industrial countries it is common for workers to resist early retirement, Soviet workers seemed to have retirement as a goal. The early, guaranteed pension is one of the inducements for young people to enter such high-prestige professions as the circus, ballet and sports. A colleague and I chatted with a pretty young trapeze artist one May Day in Moscow and asked what led her into a circus school. 'You can retire and get a pension after only twenty years,' she answered quickly. We met many older pensioners squeezing a few extra rubles out of the system by working as coat checkers in restaurants and public buildings.

The drive to re-enlist pensioners into the workforce has intensified as the number of older persons increases in proportion to the total population, the birth rate falls and the demand for labour increases. In October 1979, the Central Committee issued a new decree in a long series on the subject which increased the number of persons eligible for special benefits for staying on the job and raising some of the cash rewards.

From 1968 to 1978, the number of persons receiving old-age pensions rose from 19 to 31 million, but the minimum pension had not risen from 45 rubles a month, where it was set in 1956. 'In 1956, the maximum old-age pension exceeded the average wage by more than 50 per cent,' the magazine *EKO* said in May 1978. 'Now, the average wage has outstripped the average pension by 150 per cent and is ahead of the maximum old-age pension.' The minimum pension can also be compared with the unofficial estimate that the subsistence income in the Soviet Union at that time was 50 rubles a month.

The series of decrees on pensioners includes contradictions and complications but, in general, allows many workers to earn a total of 300 rubles a month in both wage and pension. Some workers were given incentive bonuses of 10 rubles a month for each year worked past retirement age in order to get their pay closer to the maximum. Some workers in high-priority areas such as coalminers and bookkeepers—who can watch for thievery—were allowed to keep both wages and pensions in full.

The impressions and conclusions a foreign correspondent makes after a tour in the Soviet Union are based on an unusual accumulation of evidence. Unlike most other foreign posts, Moscow offers practically no direct contact with news sources, whether with individuals or with official material. The most successful journalist has to have a substantial knowledge of the Soviet system and society before entering the country. Then, after his arrival, he must be prepared for continual interference and harassment that makes the gathering of routine information difficult and sometimes hazardous. The harassment level is raised and lowered, depending on general international political conditions and the correspondents' manner of working. Those journalists who get out of their offices to walk the streets of Moscow, to meet as many Soviet citizens as they can, and to travel as far and often as they can, collect a remarkable amount of information despite all the Kremlin's efforts to shield the truth from them. These active journalists also draw the most attention from the massive internal security apparatus of the KGB.

In recent years, American journalists have led the way for all free correspondents to spend more time trying to find out how Soviet citizens really live; how the system actually works in human terms. There has been a de-emphasis on Kremlinology as such and an increased interest in human stories. This change in style has confused the Kremlin even more than usual about the goals of Western journalism and made the leaders even more apprehensive of its impact. At one time, the Soviet authority could ignore most of what was printed in the West about their failings and excesses. But now they must react to what the major Western organs publish and broadcast because a large portion of the output reaches a Soviet audience and even more gets to readers and listeners in Eastern Europe. The third audience of great concern to Moscow—the Third World, the underdeveloped world, the non-aligned world—receives a substantial portion of its information about the Soviet Union from the Western press.

Moscow and many of the Third World countries share an interest in trying to inhibit the work of Western journalists. They believe that the correspondents whom they cannot control will focus on the failings of the aged managers in the Kremlin and the younger leaders of the Third World.

In my own case, I was often harassed in ways ranging from silly to aggravating: I was blocked from travelling many times and refused many requests for interviews and information from official sources. The reason for this treatment, I believe, was because I tried very hard to examine especially the functioning of the centrally-planned, Marxist–Leninist economy in terms of its effects on individuals. One of my conclusions was summarised in a 1974 article which carried the headline: 'Russian Workers Shortchanged in Economic Growth.'

The year before, the *Gosplan* had raised the official minimum wage from the equivalent of $77 to $90 a month and claimed the official average was $174. But the average included big variations from industry to industry and region to region. The far north, far east and Siberia got extra benefits, and the workers in heavy industry (*A* category) were paid more than those in the consumer sector (*B* category).

In order to get more output from workers, the planners reduced the portion of wage increases granted automatically and put more emphasis on incentive bonuses for exceeding quotas.

'In the current five-year plan, only about half of the wage increases will derive from the introduction of the new basic wages, salaries and other conditions of pay, while the other half will be received by workers and office employees in proportion to their improved production performance,' an official announcement said.

'The living standards of the wage and salary earners are being further improved and at the same time the incentive role of wages, the use of wages as one of the economic levers in the planned economy, is being enhanced.'

In other words, if the individual enterprises failed to meet their production targets for whatever reason, the workers would get smaller wage increases than they had received in earlier years and could expect no '13th wage' so important to them. The enterprises would not earn the extra money used by them to build workers' homes and vacation resorts and other typical fringe benefits.

The trade unions had the right to 'discuss' such a fundamental change in the compensation system, but not to engage in collective bargaining about it. Just like the production targets themselves, the compensation system came down from the top, from that huge bureaucratic jungle of

Gosplan and the Central Committee of the Communist Party.

Since overall growth rates have been declining steadily through most of the last decade and productivity gains have been consistently below target, the workers' share of economic rewards is also declining. The official profits of state enterprises have risen at rates two and four times as fast as wage rates; even the slow productivity increases were greater than the rises in worker compensation.

The planners rationalise the low rate of wage increases by claiming there is no inflation in the Soviet economy. Certain prices – of bread in particular – are kept steady as symbols of this claim. The workers know better because they see that the prices they pay for many goods have risen, often under the guise of 'new models' or 'higher quality'. Since model changes make a product eligible for a higher price, enterprises move the buttons on coats or paint items a different colour to qualify. Enterprises will also over-produce the higher priced items in an inventory of goods because that makes it easier to achieve production targets based on value. The same dodge is used by the makers of cement sections used for pre-fabricated housing – since targets there are based on weight, they keep pushing out massive, low-quality blocks that crack easily, but fulfil quotas.

Workers probably do not sense how badly they are cheated in the Soviet system because there is so little for them to spend their meagre wages on. If they received more money, there would still be little to buy in official stores. Their wives do patronise the few peasants' markets and bid up the prices on the goods available there which are of greater variety and better quality than what the state stores provide. And the workers spend a disproportionate amount of money on vodka, brandy and wine, maintaining the country's reputation as a centre of alcoholic abuse.

The end result is a collection of sullen, disillusioned, unproductive workers who have little say in economic decisions and who have no outlet for their grievances. The party which claimed to represent them and guarantee them a privileged position in society has failed them. No other institution has been permitted to challenge the party for authority. It is easy to see why the regime reacted so quickly and so brutally to repress the tentative efforts by a few workers to organise independent trade unions. If the party had succeeded in delivering justice to Soviet workers over the last half-century it would not have to fear the challenge of any other citizens' organisations. But the party and the system have failed its original constituents.

5 The Role of the Trade Unions

Joseph Godson

The communist view, as enunciated by Lenin and his successors, of the nature of trade unions and their relation to the state changes radically once a communist regime comes into power. Prior to a take-over, communists inside the trade union movement strive unceasingly and by all means available to generate hostility to the capitalist state. Once in power, with the state now supposedly on the side of the workers, the relationship is totally changed. This apparently signifies the trade unions' almost total surrender of their position as independent institutions to promote and defend the workers' interests and welfare.

Indeed, the concept of trade unions as an independent organisation permanently dedicated to protecting its members' welfare and suspicious of state or management paternalism, is alien to theorists of trade union activity in the Soviet Union or, for that matter, in any other communist country.

The functions attributed in communist countries to trade union organisations are so different from those in the West as to raise the question, whether they may, in the words of the International Confederation of Free Trade Unions, be properly described as 'trade unions'.[1] These bodies, according to the ICFTU,

> do not perform the main function of trade unions in the accepted sense of the word – defence of the rights, the standard of living and the working conditions of the workers. Instead, they are used by the state machinery as yet another organ of labour supervision, of enforcement of labour discipline and, above all, of driving the worker relentlessly to greater and greater exertions.

The justification for this changed role of unions in a communist state is relatively straightforward. According to T. Nikolayeva, a Secretary of the Soviet All-Union Central Council of Trade Unions (AUCCTU), 'when the working class took power, there appeared a qualitatively new content of trade union activities, a cardinal change in their tasks, their role and place in the State system, in their functions and forms of work'.[2] It is also argued officially that 'The position of the trade unions changes basically with the victory of the Socialist revolution. From an organisation of an oppressed class they turn into an organisation of the ruling class and become one of the major institutions of Socialist democracy.'[3]

In theory, then, since the trade unions represent the working class, and since the working class is said to hold state power and owns the means of production and means of exchange, any trade union criticism of, or opposition, to the state or management would be tantamount to the working class fighting against itself. Unions in a communist state are thus asked to view any type of disruptive industrial action such as strikes or work stoppages not only as harmful to the national interest, but also as totally illogical and therefore intolerable.

Consequently, while the communist approach to trade union activities in non-communist countries subordinates the defence of workers' interests to the political struggle against the state system, the approach to unionism in communist countries demands 'responsible' conduct, making the rights of members and unions subordinate to the development of industrial production and maintenance of the state system. The definition of a trade union most frequently cited in communist countries in this connection is the one by Lenin that it is 'a school of administration, a school of economic management, a school of communism'.[4] Leonid Brezhnev added to this doctrinal corpus, in his address to the 16th Congress of the Soviet Union on 21 March 1977, as follows:

The Soviet trade unions have been, and remain, a school of communism in which people learn to live and work in communist style. A new spiritual type of man is moulded in this school. It cultivates the lofty qualities of worker-internationalists. It cultivates loyalty to the unfolding slogan, 'Workers of all countries, unite.' As time passes and the situation changes, new tasks are always arising, but the road indicated by Lenin remains the only true and correct one.

This was reiterated by the party's Central Committee in its list of slogans for 1 May 1979. Slogan 17 reads:

Soviet trade unions! Participate actively in the administration of State and public affairs, in the solving of political, economic and socio-cultural problems! Improve socialist competition and the movement for a communist attitude to work! Long live the Soviet trade unions, schools of communism.

As part of their campaign to develop relations with non-communist European trade unions and to play a larger role in international European trade union activities, spokesmen for the Soviet Union often claim that their own unions are independent organisations, comparable to their counterparts in the West. But the evidence disproves the claim.

Thus I. L. Portnoi and N. Y. Fedyukov, in an attempt to refute 'bourgeois myths' about the relationship of Soviet trade unions and the Communist Party of the Soviet Union (CPSU), quoted Lenin's classic description of the trade unions as 'the transmission belts from the Communist Party to the masses' and described party leadership as 'a guarantee of success in the work of our unions'.[5] A more extensive definition was provided by historian G. Sharapov in *Trud* on 24 August 1973:

The trade unions are formally non-party organisations. However, sharing the same social basis as the Communist party and working under its direct leadership, they are developing as essentially communist . . . Their activity is directed towards fulfilling the purposes and tasks determined by the Party. The trade unions act as supports and conveyors of the Party's policy to the masses, as one of the links connecting the Party to the whole mass of workers, and direct their energy and effort towards the successful implementation of the grand tasks laid down in the new historical situation by the 24th CPSU Congress.

The message sent by the last congress of Soviet trade unions to the Central Committee of the Party (CPSU) defines in unmistakable terms their complete subordination to the party authority as follows: "The Congress expresses a sincere gratitude to the Leninist Central Committee of the Party and the Politburo of the CPSU for the constant attention and care concerning the largest social organisation of the workers".

A characteristic feature of the activity of trade union organisations is their ceaselessly deepening concern with the problems of the economy of production and their creative implementation of the drive towards higher efficiency and quality of work everywhere.

In the name of 113,000,000 trade union members, the Congress assures the Leninist Central Committee of the Communist Party of the Soviet Union and its Politburo headed by the General Secretary, Comrade Leonid Ilich Brezhnev, that the trade unions of the USSR will always be reliable supporters of the Party and its active helpers in the struggle for the implementations of the grandiose plans set up by the XXIVth Congress of the CPSU.[6]

In the Soviet trade unions, according to Portnoi and Fedyukov, 'the Party expresses its guiding influence . . . through the communists working in them. It is constantly reinforcing the leading trade union bodies by well-trained and authoritative functionaries, and controls their work.'

This party 'reinforcement' is particularly evident at the highest levels. While in Western Europe prominence in trade union activities may lead to prominence in a political party, in the Soviet Union loyal service in the administration seems to be seen as a qualification for trade union leadership.

The bases upon which Soviet trade union structure is built are:

(1) The principle of democratic centralism which theoretically means that all union organs from bottom to top are elected by union members and are accountable to them and that the lower organs of a union are subordinate to higher ones. The operative principle here is that which binds lower organs to accept the decisions of higher organs and the fact that all union activities are controlled by the party from within, through party groups within all trade union bodies and meetings as well as through the recommendation or appointment of party members to responsible positions.
(2) The production principle, which means that all persons working in the same enterprise belong to the same union.

In practice, this machinery has afforded neither independence nor democracy.

The supreme organ of the trade unions is the All-Union Congress (which elects the AUCCTU). Statutorily bound to meet every four years, the Congress met only twice between 1932 and 1954 – in 1949 and 1954. The President of the AUCCTU has always been a party man, with little or no experience of trade union work (except for Mikhail Tomsky, who was dismissed in 1929) and appointed at the will of the party. This was true of Nikolai M. Shvernik, Vassili Kuznetsov, Victor Grishin, A. N. Shelepin (a former head of the KGB), and the present head (since 23 November 1976) Alexei Shibaev. Born into a peasant family in February 1915, Shibaev started work at the age of 15 in the Krasnoe Sormovo works in Gorki, becoming a draughtsman and later a designer before entering the physical-mathematical department of Gorki University, from which he graduated in 1940. In 1947, he became director of a large industrial plant in the Rostov province, later moving to a similar post near Saratov. Mr Shibaev was not a member of AUCCTU before becoming its president and had no trade union background whatsoever.

According to a recent study, every trade union body 'is infiltrated by the Party in an organised way'.[7] All the party members in a trade union, the report states, 'have the duty to constitute a Party group which is subordinated to the Party organ of the same level'. Thus,

the communist members of the AUCCTU or of the Central Committee of one of the national trade unions are subordinated to the Central Committee of the Party (that is, to the competent department of the secretariat of the Central Committee); those who assume trade union responsibilities at the regional level, to the regional committee of the Party, and so on . . . The operation of the Party groups is kept secret from the non-Communist members of the trade union body which that group steers and manipulates.

The role of the party groups is defined by current Communist Party rules as follows:

68. At the congresses, conferences and meetings called by Soviet, trade union, co-operative and other mass organisations of the toilers, as well as in the elected bodies of those organisations, wherever at least three Party members are present, Party groups are organised. The task of these groups is to strengthen in every respect the influence of the Party and to implement its policy among those who are not members of the Party, to strengthen the Party (discipline) and governmental discipline, to fight bureaucratism and to verify the implementation of the Party and governmental instructions.

69. The Party groups are subordinated to the corresponding Party organs: to the Central Committee of the Communist Party of the

Union Republic, to the regional, the oblast, the district, the city, [and] the area committee of the Party.

For all the issues the Party groups have the duty to follow strictly and rigidly the decisions of the Party organs which lead them.

Despite the suggestion that industrial action to protect workers' interests is unnecessary in a communist country since the working class is now in power, it is admitted, from time to time, that injustice and mismanagement do occur in such fields as industrial safety, conditions of work, employment of women and adolescents, unfair dismissals and so on. But these are described by Soviet officials and their organs as exceptional and it is asserted that the law is supposed to give sufficient protection, with trade union officials acting to invoke the labour legislation where necessary – a duty, it is said, not always carried out.

While local trade union committees have some powers to enforce observance of legislation on working conditions, questions of basic wages and salaries, however, are decided nationally within the framework of the government's overall economic plans. Nominally, the AUCCTU has a say in formulating wage rates under the five-year plan, in practice though its powers to influence final decisions are very limited, to say the least.

The wages system in industry is based on pay differentials or grades, which reflect firstly the degree of skill required in the job, but may also be used as a means to further national economic policies by attracting workers to certain priority industries or to unpopular areas. Since 1957, the number of pay scales has been drastically reduced. A worker's pay depends primarily on his grading within the pay-scale for his particular industry. And the actual size of his weekly pay-packet will vary in relation to his fulfilment of the production norm for his job and the overall performance of the enterprise in which he is employed. Increased automation has meant a fall in the number of workers on piece-rates, but still about half of all Soviet industrial workers are estimated to remain on the piece-rate system.

In theory, trade unions are said to have considerable powers to influence wages and norms but, in practice, their role is consultative, with wages being set at levels considered economically viable by the party and the state planning committees.

The official legal position of trade unions in wage negotiations was described by A. P. Volkov, Chairman of the State Committee for Labour and Wages in the USSR Council of Ministers, as follows:

The new statute on the rights of factory and office trade union committees approved by the Decree of the Presidium of the USSR Supreme Soviet of September 27, 1971, is clear evidence of the increasing role of the trade unions in adjusting labour relations. At present not a single essential question of the organisation of labour and pay is decided by the management without the participation of the factory or office trade union committee.

Production quotas . . . and the norms for the number of factory and office workers on the staff are introduced and revised in agreement with the given factory or office TU committee . . . the trade unions have to strive for the introduction of progressive, technically grounded production quotas and promote the correct implementation of the existing labour remuneration system.[8]

It is evident, however, that since the aim is to create 'scientifically' based norms and wages determined by the 'national interest' as determined by the state planners, the trade unions can have little scope for objection to government or party decisions. In any event, their part in negotiations is seen as a privilege granted by the state, which in effect means the party, rather than as a right to advance the needs of their members.

In addition to norm-fulfilment, the size of the worker's wages may vary according to whether or not he or she receives bonus payments. These incentives were part of the economic reforms introduced in 1965, which allowed enterprises to keep a larger proportion of profits and redistribute them through bonuses and welfare funds. Moral incentives, the traditional means of securing greater effort from the work force, are given in the Fundamentals of Labour Legislation introduced in 1971. Under Article 5 of the 'Statute of the Rights of Factory and Office Trade Union Committees' (decree of 27 September 1971), trade union committees are theoretically empowered to decide upon the distribution of bonuses and, according to a Moscow radio report, the 'trade union organisations have been recommended to make wider use of their powers to grant benefits, better living conditions and advancement in work to workers who achieve particularly good results'.

In practice, however, the activity of the unions 'is centred mainly not on the interests of their members but on furthering production and helping management to fulfil its production plans, even when that entails, as it often does, bringing all sorts of pressure to bear on the workers'.[9] The fact that the trade unions or factory committees are from time to time encouraged to advocate measures that are claimed to benefit workers does by no means indicate 'a significant departure from past Soviet theory and practice', as suggested by a recent article on Soviet trade unions.[10]

Indeed, the 'central task' of the trade unions, as defined in the Preamble of their by-laws, is explained as follows:

> The central task of the trade unions is to mobilize the masses for the attainment of our principal economic goal – the creation of the material and technical basis of communism, for the further strengthening of the Soviet Union's economic and defence power, for ensuring a steady rise in the people's material and cultural standards.
>
> The Soviet trade unions direct their activities towards securing a further and powerful advance in all branches of the economy, fulfilment and overfulfilment of economic plans, promotion of technical progress and an uninterrupted rise in labour productivity and in the effectiveness of social production, towards the lowering of labour input, rational utilization and economy of raw materials and material resources, the improvement of the quality of the products, a better use of the production funds and of investment capital. Trade unions jointly with the organs of management organize socialist emulation among workers, collective farmers, engineers and technicians and office employees, they organize the movement for a communist attitude towards work, the mass technical creativity of the toilers, they help the workers, the collective farmers and the white-collar workers to improve their productivity, their skills and their economic and juridical knowledge, they conduct propaganda regarding production and technique, spread the experience of front-rank workers and innovators of production, promote the introduction of advanced technologies and scientific achievements in industry, agriculture and other branches of the national economy.

To fulfil the 'central task', a series of disciplinary measures to which every member can be subjected is explicitly provided for in the trade union by-laws, most if not all of which would never be tolerated in the Western countries.

An indication of the reaction of workers to the so-called central task and its implementation on a local level is illustrated by an open letter recently received in the West which was written by a group of workers from a Togliatti dairy products combine. The document exposes with striking clarity the myth that under growing pressure the Soviet trade unions, especially on the shop floor, have begun to evolve towards a defence of the interests of their members.[11] It describes, first of all, how the process whereby the chairman of the trade union committee at the combine is elected. Some years ago, the outgoing chairman was replaced by a single unopposed candidate – the choice of the director of the combine. 'All that was required of us was to raise our hands as a sign of approval. And we, accustomed to our position as robots, did just that, as one man'. The director stole goods from the factory, swindled and in the end was removed. Rumour had it that there was a trial, but if there was it was kept secret and all that was known for certain was that he was moved to a different enterprise, leaving the chairman of the trade union committee still in place.

However, the change of director produced no change of management patterns. With the connivance of the director and the factory party committee, the trade union chairman kept on taking bribes for the allocation of apartments and places in the creche and kindergarten. And

we, who 'elected' her, do not have the right to demand from the chairman an account of how she worked in her trade union position. We only have the right to be silent.

You may ask why did we not write to the newspapers? The answer is that we do not have any newspapers – they belong not to the people but to the authorities. Here is an example: last autumn the administration of our combine was very unjust in its distribution of prizes. A group of workers from factory No. 1 (the combine has two factories) appealed to the trade union committee but the chairman sided with the director and refused to support the workers. It was not published and the workers achieved nothing. That is another of the ways in which we are taught to observe the great silence.

The point, the authors of the letter insist, is not so much that they have had a bad trade union chairman who is not accountable to them, as that any trade union chairman would behave in the same way bearing in mind that he or she is chosen by the director and the party office. On the other hand, the director himself is appointed by the town party committee as is the combine's party organiser. The result is that everyone invested with power has been designated by the town party committee. But the town party committee and the workers have, as a rule and naturally so, different objectives. Thus the principal duty of the trade unions, as laid down by the party at national and local levels, continues to be the encouragement of harder work, increased productivity and labour discipline. On the positive side, they are expected to take an active part in campaigns for 'socialist emulation' and socialist competition which has replaced Stakhanovism of the 1930s. While overtime as such is restricted by law, it is more often than not used to fulfil plan targets, and sometimes paid for out of bonus funds. According to a pre-congress report on the 15th Soviet Trade Union Congress,

> there is still a great deal of formalism and conventionalism in the organisation of emulation. The democratic principles of emulation are violated and at times formal, low targets are undertaken . . . There are shortcomings in the practice of providing incentives for the winners of socialist emulation. At times the funds for incentives to leading workers are used to pay for overtime and separate jobs done.[12]

The invidious position of the unions towards their members, exacerbated by their collusion with management in such abuses, is also the result of their responsibility for maintaining labour discipline. Thus Shelepin, in his 1972 trade union congress report, exhorted the unions to play a still greater part in labour discipline:

> It is our commitment to step up the struggle for the strengthening of labour and production discipline. In his speech today Leonid Ilyich Brezhnev said that everyone must know that idlers and slackers, job-switchers and bad workmen will receive no indulgence or leniency and that nothing will protect them from the wrath of their comrades. The rights and opportunities of the trade unions for this are great and they must be used to a substantially improved degree.[13]

Yet, in a somewhat rare admission almost seven years later, we are told that labour discipline in Belorussia, which presumably is not untypical in the USSR, leaves much to be desired. Lost working time in 1978 amounted to 987,600 man days and, because of absenteeism, enterprises lost millions of roubles of production; 10–12 per cent of enterprises annually failed to fulfil the planned growth in productivity. Moreover, surveys confirmed that on average between 30 and 40 per cent of tasks assigned are either not fulfilled on time or not fulfilled at all.[14]

Although there is no admitted unemployment in the Soviet Union, some exists, and since October 1930, when unemployment was officially said to have been abolished, Soviet law has made no provision for unemployment benefits. In fact, the average period of unemployment for those changing jobs is twenty-eight days. Labour legislation only allows for two weeks' average earnings to be paid to workers who are made redundant, but the redundant worker could lose his annual paid leave as well as his annual bonus (which depend on length of service).

In addition, the Soviet worker may be penalised for idle-standing, even if this is no fault of his own. Shoddy workmanship is also penalised. Where a worker is entirely responsible, his pay for a particular item is reduced, or not paid at all if it is completely useless. Where a worker is not directly responsible (for example, because he has been supplied with defective components), his pay may be reduced by up to a third.

While dismissals for any reason must have the agreement of the trade union committee, in practice this agreement is either not sought by the management or is treated as a mere formality. Thus the following words, as reported in *Soviet Justice*, no.19, 1979, by a trade union official in the Omsk region reveal the typical state of affairs as follows:

> Conclusions drawn from the practice of the Courts (i.e. in the Omsk region) have once again confirmed that some economic managers are still permitting sackings of workers and employees with crude infringements of labour legislation and with poor supervision on the part of trade union committees . . . There are still cases when a management's report on the sacking of a worker is examined without the necessary quorum of (trade union) committee members after the dismissal order has been issued.

A worker who feels he has been wrongly dismissed may, under Soviet law, appeal to the People's Court which can, and frequently does, reinstate him. Indeed, according to the *Bulletin of the USSR Supreme Court* (No. 6, 1968), 51.7 per cent of workers claiming unfair dismissal, presumably with the consent of the trade union committees, won reinstatement through the courts. The most telling aspect is the light it throws on the concern of the trade unions to keep on the right side of management. A deputy Soviet Procurator General commented on the situation as follows:

> Sometimes, trade union committees, not wishing to spoil relations with management, give agreement to the dismissal of workers and employees without checking the circumstances of the case, the validity and lawfulness of interceding with management. As a result people are illegally dismissed and subsequently reinstated by the Courts. People waste time, energy and nerves for nothing . . . .[15]

One of the reasons for this state of affairs, according to *Trud* of 11 May 1969, 'is lack of publicity about cases of illegal dismissal. Usually nothing is said about them outside the courtroom where the case is tried. Riders are usually expressed only about management personnel, whilst the members of the trade union committees which have abetted them escape unpunished.' On 9 June 1973, the same paper asked: 'Why is it that some local trade union committees at times forget about their direct duty to defend the workers' interests?'

While, occasionally, Soviet press comment approaches criticism of the system, a more characteristic official reaction is to try to cure the disease by making the symptoms go away, blaming the courts for accepting so many pleas of unjustified dismissal. Whatever the explanation, it would appear therefore that the facts do not completely square with the claim that 'it has become virtually impossible to dismiss a Soviet industrial worker for other than political reasons'.[16]

Absenteeism and drunkenness are probably the most common motives for dismissal. According to the Soviet Fundamentals of Labour Legislation, 'the obligation for an employee to observe labour discipline is of cardinal importance' and he is also obliged to take care of 'socialist property', to work honestly and conscientiously, to execute the management's instruction with precision and at the proper time, to raise the productivity of labour, to improve the quality of output, and to observe technological discipline, labour protection requirements and industrial hygiene. Violation of these rules can be punished by admonition, reprimand, transfer to a lower-paid job or lower-ranking post for a term of up to three months and eventually, 'if an employee fails systematically to cope with his duties or if he is absent without valid reasons, the management is entitled to dismiss him'.[17] When that happens the Soviet 'parasitism' law – originally designed to control the activities of tramps and gypsies – may come into effect, whereby any person who is unemployed for more than four months in a year is liable to two years' imprisonment. The Soviet worker, in fact, has not only the right to work but also, often overlooked, a positive obligation to do so. Under no circumstances (except in cases of illness, accidents or on achieving pensionable age) does he have the right to the withdrawal of labour.

Besides their main duties of helping to increase production, maintaining labour discipline and enforcing the provisions of the labour laws, the trade unions have also been given extensive responsibilities in housing, health and social welfare. These responsibilities, usually dealt with in non-communist countries by government ministries, serve to incorporate them further in the bureaucratic machinery and the party, and to isolate them from ordinary workers.

In justification of the system, P. T. Pimenov, an AUCCTU Secretary, wrote:

> In the Soviet Union the trade unions exercise full control over social insurance and run a broad network of health resorts and holiday homes. The tendency of transferring to the trade unions some of the functions that are performed by the State in other countries can be seen in the matter of protecting the legitimate interests of the factory and office workers in socialist society.[18]

However, such a system can only be of benefit to the workers if the trade unions are really independent, and not merely accepting responsibility for the work of government departments in an attempt to find a role to replace the basic one of defending the interests of their members.

Thus, Masherov, First Secretary of the Belorussian Communist Party Central Committee, told the 23rd Congress of the Belorussian trade unions:

> Working conditions are still poor at many enterprises. The situation as regards industrial safety is still bad, and regulations on hours of work are not being observed in many localities. Both enterprise managements and trade union leaders must be strictly answerable for infringements of labour legislation.[19]

Western visitors who have toured Soviet factories and job sites agree almost unanimously that the most elementary safeguards are often ignored. A contributing factor may be increasing pressure from top Soviet officials to raise output at a time when the economy is showing unmistakable signs of slowing down. With the pressure on to produce, those responsible, that is, management and the trade unions, are apparently closing their eyes to unsafe or unhealthy conditions.

On paper, the Soviet trade unions have extraordinary powers to stop safety and health abuses. In every plant there is a labour protection commission that has the power to shut down the plant. The problem is that trade unions act more as an arm of the party than as a representative of the workers. And when worker interests conflict with those of the party, the party's directives come first. The question is not only whether the Soviet trade unions have a role to play in protecting their members' interests and ensuring proper working conditions, but also whether they are able to do so within a system which requires their complicity with management in enforcing discipline and raising productivity. It is this, as much as their subservience to the party, which challenges their claim to independence. Because of their integration in the administrative structure, Soviet trade union officials at all levels are encouraged to see their function as a bureaucratic one rather than as 'watchdogs' against attempts to sacrifice the workers' needs and dignity to the economic demands of the state.

Soviet law does not provide for the right to strike for the reason that 'the workers have every possibility of obtaining satisfaction in other ways – through production meetings and through the governmental and legislative authorities whose membership consists of workers' representatives'.[20] Work 'guaranteed' by the Constitution is regarded as an obligation and moral duty. The Russian Republic Labour Code (operative since 1 April 1972) states that 'workers and employees are obliged to work honestly and conscientiously, to observe labour discipline [and] carry out managements' instructions accurately and in good time' (Article 127). In addition, strikers automatically lay themselves open to prosecution under criminal statutes governing anti-Soviet agitation, Nevertheless, strikes have taken place, notably at Temir Tau in 1959 and Novocherkassk in 1962. These were suppressed by troops, as were serious riots in Dneprodzerzhinsk, a centre of heavy industry in southern Ukraine, in June 1972.[21] In all these cases, including so-called 'Italian strikes', in which workers turn up at the factory but in practice do not work, the events resulted in dismissals, arrests and jail sentences for anti-Soviet activities and hooliganism, indicating clearly that the non-recognition of the right to strike means that strikers or strike leaders are subject to various degrees of punishment.

This is, of course, in violation of Article 8 of the International Covenant on Economic Social and Cultural Rights, which proclaims the right of everyone to form a trade union and join a trade union of his choice; the right of trade unions to function freely; and the right to strike. What is more, it is contrary to the charter of the communist-controlled World Federation of Trade Unions which declares that 'every worker has the unrestricted right to come out on strike, whatever his work'. Nevertheless, according to a Soviet government order of 5 May 1961, those responsible for 'unauthorised interruption of work' may be deported and subjected to forced labour for a period of two to five years.

While deportation as such is usually an administrative measure, the authorities can, if they deem it advisable, act under the RSFSR penal Code's Article 190 which states as follows:

> Organisation of, as well as active participation in, group actions grossly infringing public order or entailing manifest disobedience to legal orders of the representatives of power or having resulted in disturbance of the work of transport (or) of state (or) social institutions or enterprises – is punished by deprivation of liberty for up to three years, or by corrective labour for up to one year, or by a fine of up to one hundred roubles.

The 'alienation' of workers in repetitive and de-humanising jobs is as important in the Soviet Union as in industrial societies in the West, though awareness of it tends to be blunted at higher levels by glorification of 'heroism' of industrial work and by lip-service to the belief that the working class is the leading force in a communist society. While trade unions in free societies have a major role to play in solving this problem, either by helping to evolve new systems of production or at least by ensuring proper respect for the human needs of industrial workers, such a role cannot be undertaken by a state-controlled organisation which sees its functions as purely administrative and which tends to adopt the management view of its members as simply elements in a productive process. A somewhat surprisingly sharp criticism inherent in this situation was expressed by Mario Dido, socialist secretary of the communist-controlled Italian General Confederation of Labour (CGIL), after he returned from a visit to Togliattigrad in the Soviet Union where a Fiat motor plant had just been built:

> The question we asked ourselves is whether, at a time when the USSR and other Socialist countries are beginning to adopt work-organisation systems of the Western type, they do not stand in need of completely autonomous trade union organisations, capable of expressing even through open conflict, the needs of the workers; and whether, in the absence of this form of dialectic and pluralism, there is not the risk of creating an unbalanced and therefore in the long run socially dangerous situation.[22]

Similar questioning heretical thoughts were expressed in *Comment*, the British Communist Party's fortnightly. Writing in its issue of 3 March 1979, Roy Lockett, reporting on a visit by a journalists' delegation in the Soviet Union, states:

An issue which inevitably fascinates the British trade unionist is that of conflict between management and union. Nurtured in the tradition of free collective bargaining, disputes and their resolution are central to the experience of the British official. The Soviet Union is a complex, urban, industrial society. Its wages system, reliance on incentives, piecework and bonus rates would seem a fertile field for argument and conflict.

But no official whom his delegation met indicated that industrial action of any kind ever took place. This was very difficult to believe, Lockett says, and he adds that informally it was suggested to the group that industrial action is widely known to take place, but how widely and in which sectors, the visitors could not discover.

Collective agreements between trade unions and employers, which had some reality in the 1920s, were a victim of the five-year plans and ceased to be concluded from 1937 until 1947.[23]

Reintroduced by Stalin in 1947, collective agreements have nothing to do with wage rates – basic in Western countries – which are decided centrally by the government. The government has argued in substance that owing to the very nature of the organisation of its economy there is no opposition of interest as between management and the workers but

an identity of tasks which devolve on the management of a socialist undertaking as representative of the socialist state, which itself is the expression of the general interests of the whole of the workers, and those which devolve on the trade union committee as representative of the interests of the collective of workers and employees in the undertaking in question.[24]

According to the Soviet government, this identity of tasks explains why the object of collective agreements in the USSR is to ensure the execution and surpassing of production plans, 'a condition for the progressive improvement of the workers' standard of living'.

On the basis of its study, the ILO Governing Body's Committee on Freedom of Association concluded that,

while collective agreements in the USSR contain provisions relating to wages and other conditions of employment, these provisions are based on indices fixed by the State Plan from which the parties cannot deviate. In other words, the determination of basic wages and fundamental conditions of employment is outside the scope of regulation by collective agreement.

Since the economic reform of 1965, some attempts have been made, mostly cosmetically, to lend greater importance to the collective agreement. A new definition of the collective agreement was promulgated in 1966 which provided for the inclusion of clauses on plan fulfilment, improving the use of funds and materials, norm-setting and labour productivity, socialist emulation and the training of cadres. Agreements must also contain 'concrete normative provisions on labour and wages worked out by managements and union committees within the rights accorded them'. But the rights 'accorded' them, it is to be remembered, are fixed by the State Plan from which the parties cannot deviate and which lie outside the scope of regulation by collective agreement.

The wages system as a whole is based on grades in which pay differentials are used to further the government's economic policy and on a norm or output quota. To increase productivity, the system is bolstered by bonus payments and, conversely, by fines, and tied to so-called socialist competition where the rewards are material and honorific.

Norms, assessed by state management, have been paid in various ways over the years. The tendency has been to revise them upwards based on the increased power of the machine, rationalisation and the experience of workers engaged in socialist competition.

The piece-rate system based on norms has, from a government point of view, two great advantages. First, it destroys collective feeling among the work force since every worker is paid according to what he or she alone produces. Secondly, the norms bear no relation to 'the true time taken to make a piece', according to Miklos Haraszti, a young Hungarian Marxist. The rate-fixers, Haraszti states, 'cannot but set a production time which demands a super-human effort, since the whole point of norms is to hold wages to a level fixed in advance'.[25]

The real meaning of piece-rates, he maintains, lies in the constant increase in production. This means that workers have to work harder to earn less. Indeed, a 30 per cent reduction in piece-rates was one of the causes that sparked off the strike in Novocherkassk, mentioned above.

At the 17th Soviet Trade Union Congress, Shelepin, the then head of AUCCTU, complained that 'administrative and trade union organisations have serious shortcomings in the work of setting work norms and wages, show little initiative in working out and introducing scientifically based norms and normatives, and the improvement of the system of wages and bonuses is insufficiently actively pursued . . . '.[26]

Recent trends in wages policy do not abolish the system, although they are said to alleviate the lot of the poorest worker by the introduction of a minimum wage. But the minimum wage is no guarantee of a regular income as it is paid to the worker only if labour norms have been met. If the worker fails to meet the set norms through some fault of his own, he cannot be considered conscientious and his wage may fall below the official minimum.

Trying to relate Soviet wages to Western standards is extremely difficult. Keith Bush, chief of research for the US Congress-financed Radio Liberty which broadcasts to the Soviet Union, estimated in January 1979 that the officially-stated Moscow average monthly take-home wage for industrial workers related in this way to US, British, French and West German levels: USSR, $243.43; US, $798.94; Germany, $978.11; France, $854.87; Great Britain, $612.79. The numbers reflect the weak position of the dollar in currency conversions and the few deductions taken from the Soviet worker's pay which was assumed to be 165.64 rubles a month.

Even more difficult, but more meaningful when it is done with proper sophistication, is a comparison of what wages will actually buy in terms of consumer goods. With the help of friends in Washington, Munich, Paris, London and Moscow, Bush estimates the working time required for the average individual to buy items from the same 'shoppers' basket'. In 1979, the total basket required 12.5 hours of work time to buy in Washington; 12.6 in Munich; 18.1 in Paris; 21.4 in London; and 42.3 in Moscow. The figures showed that the Soviet worker had made a substantial gain in spending 28.5 per cent less time in 1979 than in 1976 to buy the same items, but each of the other workers had reduced the time output even more. The Soviet worker had one big advantage – he spent only 12.5 hours to pay his rent – half what the London worker spent and a quarter of the Washingtonian. But the Russian spent eight times as many hours working to buy a colour television or a small car than his American counterpart and four times as much as a British worker. Even a litre of vodka, which cost the Muscovite 380 minutes of work time, cost the Washingtonian only 52 minutes and the Londoner 132. The full study by Bush, the latest of his periodic surveys of retail prices and wages, is given in the Supplement at the end of the book.

So-called socialist competition and emulation are basically means of raising productivity both by individual and collective effort and by means of improving techniques. The results attained are intended to be emulated by all workers and are applied in the assessment of norms as well. To foster socialist competition is the duty of Soviet trade unions, according to their statutes.

The 1976–80 Five Year Plan, approved by the 25th Party Congress, lists among the trade unions' tasks the development of 'socialist competition' and of a communist attitude to work and the steady raising of productivity. Improvement of working conditions and strict control over the observance of labour legislation occupy last place. The effect is to create a labour aristocracy and thus disrupt working-class solidarity.

Trade union membership is theoretically voluntary but, in 1972, 97.5 per cent of the employed were trade union members. Soviet trade unions are industrial and cover the entire country. They are organised in much the same way as the party – in factory committees, town committees, regional committees and so on up to the AUCCTU. 'The power of the centre is practically unlimited, and the standing provisions about the responsibility of the trade union officials to their electorate are disregarded.'[27] The leaders are in fact appointed by the government. In the enterprise, the factory committee is chosen by the management, not by the workers. The main task of the union, as indicated earlier, seems to be not to defend the workers' interests, but to discipline them and make sure they fulfil the plan.[28] For example, the collective agreement for the Zapozozhtal Iron and Steel Workers (1975) begins: 'In order to ensure the fulfilment of the plan ahead of time . . . '; and goes on,

> the management and the trade union undertake: to examine every infringement of labour discipline (absenteeism, lateness, breakdown of equipment, production of faulty goods, etc.) and breach of public order at meetings of trade union groups and shop trade union committees. Disciplinary measures shall be applied by the management in concert with the trade union organisation.[29]

The trade union's secondary task, which it carries out through various commissions, is to organise social insurance, cultural and educational activities, housing, holidays and so on. 'But these, whatever the official theory may be, they have performed as subsidiaries of the State administration, not as autonomous social bodies or working class organs in the accepted sense.'[30]

The Soviet trade unions are completely centralised and the national industrial unions are not free to decide any matters of general policy, since the AUCCTU alone is competent to do so.[31] The republican, regional or district council of trade unions 'directs the activity of trade union organisations [functioning] on the territory of the republic, region or district, checks the activity of trade union committees [committees of single industrial unions], hears reports on their work' (Article 39 of the by-laws). And, as a general rule, 'lower trade union bodies are subordinate to the higher ones' (Article 13d).

Moreover, the primary union bodies are shaped in such a way as to prevent the members from forming groups of any strength. It is apparently not safe enough, in view of the regime,

> to entrust the leadership of the union members in every factory to a works committee, or even to set up a committee in every important workshop; most of the union activity on the factory level is supposed to be carried out in groups of about twenty members, each led by its own officers. Consequently, meetings of all the union members in a workshop are very rare and those of the whole factory occur only very exceptionally. The atomisation is very effective. It prevents the crystallisation of any coherent collective opinion.[32]

At ILO discussions in Geneva and in the forums abroad, Soviet representatives have repeatedly claimed that workers in the USSR are free to establish any trade union they please. This is hardly likely according to an ILO Mission study in 1960, in view of the principles enunciated in Article 17 of the Rules of the Trade Unions that 'all persons employed in the same factory or office belong to the same union'.

This judgment has been fully confirmed when the Soviet authorities crushed in brutal fashion two recent attempts by Soviet workers to form genuine trade unions.

To start with, the Soviet constitution says: 'In accordance with the aims of building communism citizens of the USSR have the right to associate in public organisations that promote their political activity and initiative and satisfaction of their various interests.'

Accordingly, trade unions are given the right to nominate candidates to the Supreme Soviet and frequently call shop-floor meetings, where attendance is compulsory, at which party policies are explained and poor workers publicly reprimanded. In practice, this political activity means little to the average worker who regards the meetings as a dull obligation; and the elections are a foregone conclusion.

But what the constitution does not seem to envisage is the setting up of any rival to the existing official unions. It therefore came as a rude shock to the Soviet authorities at the end of 1977 when a number of dissatisfied workers, led by a former coalmine foreman Vladimir Klebanov, who had been dismissed from their jobs, got together to form an independent union free of state control – the Association of Free Trade Unions (AFTU). The need for Soviet workers to go outside the formal structure of trade union, state and party administrations arose because of the formal hierarchy's inability or unwillingness adequately to respond to the need of its citizens. In their appeal to the ILO and Western trade unions, the AFTU pleaded:

> On the one hand, the Party and government call upon citizens to correct violations whenever they occur – in industry and in the life of the state and society. On the other hand, the authorities react with special brutality to those who respond to propaganda appeals by strictly observing the regulations and speaking out in the interests of the enterprise. All our attempts to get justice from government authorities have been in vain. As individuals we have appealed to the central organs of Soviet power; the Central Committee of the CPSU; the Presidium of the Supreme Soviet; the council of Ministers of the USSR; and the All-Union Central Council of Trade Unions. They do not reply to us.

By the end of March 1978, the AFTU had been virtually neutralised through harassment, arrest or detention in psychiatric hospitals. To continue the work, a second group – the Free Interprofessional Association of Workers (SMOT) – was announced in Moscow on 28 October 1978. Its purposes were outlined as

> the defence of its members in cases of the violation of their rights in various spheres of their daily activities: economic, social, cultural, spiritual, religious, domestic, and political. This defence is to be carried out by all possible means within the framework of the constitution and international agreements signed by the Soviet government. Furthermore, SMOT intends to look into the legal bases of the complaints of workers; to ensure that these complaints are brought to the notice of relevant organisation; to facilitate a quick solution to workers' complaints; and, in cases of negative results, to publicise them widely before the Soviet and international public. In order to give stronger assistance to workers who are not members of SMOT a working commission is also being organised.

In May 1979, the ILO's Committee of Experts on the Application of

Convention and Recommendations, acting on protests lodged by the International Confederation of Free Trade Unions (ICFTU) and the World Confederation of Labour (WCL), presented their findings on Soviet compliance with ILO Convention 87 (Freedom of Association and Protection of the Right to Organise, 1948). Referring to Article 2 of the Convention, the committee having 'noted' the relevant provisions of the Labour Code of the RSFSR (Sections 7 and 230) and the 1971 Regulations on the Rights of Factory or Local Trade Union Committees, recommended that the Soviet government should amend existing legislation in order to provide for the right of workers to establish organisations of their own choosing.

Under Article 6 of the Soviet constitution, the Communist Party is said to be 'the leading guiding force of Soviet society and the nucleus of its political system and of all state and public organisations'. Taking this into account, the ILO Committee made the following further observations about Soviet compliance with Article 3 of Convention 87:

> The term public organisation as used in this provision seems to cover workers' organisations. If so, the Committee can only observe that the law [in this case, the Constitution of the State] establishes a link between the Communist Party and the workers' organisations, in which the leading role falls as of right and permanently to the Party. Thus, even if the policy of this Party is carried out through workers' organisations in accordance with procedures laid down in their rules, the legal system does not seem to accord these organisations the full right to organise the activities and formulate their programmes, as provided by Article 3 of the Convention.

In November 1979, the ILO Committee of Experts again found the information requested of the Soviet government inadequate and urged the Governing Body to press for confirmation that workers in Russia can form unions in a 'climate of full security', and independent from existing unions, the government and the party, and that Soviet legislation be amended in order 'to recognise clearly the right of workers to establish if they so wish an organisation outside the factory, works and local trade union committees'.

In June 1980 the Soviet Union also came in for new criticism of its penal code provisions on unproductive work. The ILO, at its annual conference, adopted a committee report saying that the provisions were too broad and might be contrary to the convention prohibiting forced labour. The committee report voiced concern that discussion of the penal code clause, which has been going on for several years, was lasting too long without coming to a conclusion. It urged the Soviet government to do all it could to clarify the situation.

While the ILO recommendations represented a serious loss of prestige for the Soviet Union, the prospects for any foreseeable changes in the role and functions of the official trade unions in the USSR appear doomed. Basically, their function remains and will continue to be

> the promotion of the further development of the national economy through the successful fulfilment of the Five Year Plan . . . Trade union participation in the formulation and implementation of economic and industrial policies has always been formally assured, but, in actual fact, this participation is precluded by the narrow role assigned the trade unions in the administrative implementation of decisions made and not in the decision-making-process itself.[33]

Nor is there any visible prospect of forming independent unions, free of state and party control. The Russians do not allow any organisation to be established unless it has the prior approval of the party. Any hope of establishing an association of workers for free collective action that goes against this principle is, for the immediate future at least, totally unrealistic. Soviet authorities have systematically repressed all forms of protest and, as indicated in the recent experience with the AFTU and SMOT, they respond especially fast and strongly against anyone able to reach a potentially wide constituency for possible opposition to the entrenched authority.

NOTES

1. Trade Union Rights in the USSR, ILO's Studies and Reports, New Series, No. 49 (1959) p. 10.
2. 'V. I. Lenin on the role of trade unions in building communism', *Trud*, organ of the Soviet All-Union Central Council of Trade Unions, 13 January 1970.
3. From a report of a conference on the role of trade unions, *Trud*, 1 December 1971.
4. *Complete Collected Works*, vol. 42, p. 203.
5. 'Bourgeois Myths About the Interrelations of the CPSU and the Trade Unions', *Voprosy istorii KPSS*, No. 11 (1972).
6. *Trud*, 26 March 1977.

7. Paul Barton, 'Trade Unions in the U.S.S.R.', AFL-CIO *Free Trade Union News*, 26 September 1979, p. 3.
8. Interview in *Trud*, 6 November 1971.
9. Paul Barton, op. cit.
10. Blair A. Ruble, 'The Changes in Soviet Trade Unions', *The New Leader*, 23 April 1979.
11. *Soviet Analyst*, 8 August 1979.
12. *Sovetskiye profsoyuzy*, No. 4 (1972).
13. Moscow Radio, 21 March 1972.
14. Minsk Radio, 11 October 1979.
15. A. Pankratov, *Trud*, 12 December 1973.
16. Blair A. Ruble, 'Full Employment Legislation in the U.S.S.R.', *Comparative Labor Law*, vol. 2, No. 3 (1977).
17. *Kommunist*, No. 2 (1971), article on Fundamentals of Labour Legislation.
18. 'Trade Unions and Communist Construction', *Rabochi klass i sovremenny mir*, No. 1 (1973).
19. Minsk Radio, 3 March 1972.
20. ILO's Studies and Reports, op. cit.
21. In June 1980 there were Western press reports from Moscow that one- to two-day work stoppages took place at the giant Togliatti and Gorki automobile plants and a four-hour stoppage occurred at the Kama lorry plant in Naberzhniie Chelnii. The Gorki and Kama actions were said to be directed against inadequate food supplies. The appearance of almost daily denials in the Soviet press and radio from 18 to 24 June suggested considerable sensitivity of the Soviet authorities to these reports. On 21 June *Pravda* and *Izvestia* both reaffirmed the standard Soviet line on the absence of reasons for strikes in the USSR. As *Pravda* put it: 'The gentlemen who have raised the ballyhoo have evidently forgotten that, unlike their social system, we do not have employer bosses and hired workers breaking their backs for them. And, therefore, antagonistic relations do not exist. The workers themselves are the plant's bosses.'
22. *L'Expresso*, Rome, 26 September 1971.
23. Robert Conquest, *Industrial Workers in the U.S.S.R.* (London: Bodley Head, 1967).
24. ILO's Studies and Reports, op. cit.
25. Miklos Haraszti, *A Worker in a Worker's State* (trans. M. Wright) (Penguin Books, Ltd., 1977) p. 40.
26. *Pravda*, 28 February 1968.
27. Isaac Deutscher, *Soviet Trade Unions* (London: Oxford University Press, 1950) p. 127.
28. Viktor Haynes and Olga Semyonova, *Workers Against the Gulag* (London, 1979) p. 13.
29. Quoted in M. Costello, *Workers' Participation in the Soviet Union* (Moscow: Novosti Press Agency, 1977) p. 17.
30. Deutscher, op. cit., pp. 135–6.
31. Paul Barton, op. cit., p. 14.
32. Ibid.
33. Radio Liberty, 304/79, The Independent Trade Union Movement in the Soviet Union, by John C. Michael, 11 October 1979.

6 Schooling and Inequalities

Murray Yanowitch

The substantial extension of schooling in the Soviet Union is undoubtedly an impressive achievement of the regime and an important
factor contributing to the country's comparatively impressive long-run
economic growth performance. But like 'progress' in other areas of
Soviet life, the increased educational attainment of the population has
generated its own social tensions and problems. In particular, the
advance towards 'universal' secondary education has made it necessary
to moderate the traditionally ambitious occupational plans of secondary school graduates, and to confront such issues as social inequality in
access to higher education and the problem of work discontent among
'overeducated' workers in routine jobs. A brief examination of the
structure of the Soviet educational system and of recent changes in the
relative importance of its components will set the stage for our
discussion of these problem areas.

THE STRUCTURE OF SOVIET EDUCATION

The completion of the eighth grade of the general-education school in
the Soviet Union signifies the attainment of an 'incomplete' secondary
education (an 'elementary' or 'primary' education corresponds to
grades one to three). By the late 1970s the 'obligatory' minimum of eight
years of schooling had become wellnigh universal for school-age
youngsters (with the number completing the eighth grade in 1978
standing at some 95 per cent of those entering the first grade eight years
earlier).[1] The main stress in Soviet educational policy in recent years has
been to make a 'complete' secondary education 'universal'. The
principal channels through which Soviet youngsters can complete their
secondary education – upon finishing the eighth grade – are the
following:

(1) Continuation of schooling in the ninth grade of the ten-year general-education school. Enrolment in daytime classes of these schools (followed by graduation from the tenth grade) is the path traditionally taken by those aspiring to a higher education. Although most tenth-grade graduates have not gained admission to a higher educational institution (*VUZ*) in recent years, a large majority of *VUZ* candidates are drawn from this group. Hence youngsters with comparatively ambitious occupational plans (or whose parents have ambitious plans for them) are likely to continue their secondary education in these schools.

(2) Admission to a specialized secondary school (*tekhnikum*). For those enrolling in a *tekhnikum* after completion of the tenth grade, the course of study is one to two years, leading normally to semi-professional occupational status (technician, accountant, agronomist, nurse). For those enrolling after the eighth grade, the course of study is three to four years and encompasses a 'complete' secondary education as well as training in one of the semiprofessional areas cited above. The *tekhnikum* is the main channel of access to the lower levels of the 'specialist' or intelligentsia stratum, although an increasing proportion of its graduates in recent years have moved into skilled workers' occupations. The *tekhnikum*, in any case, is a much less likely path to higher education than the general-education school.

(3) Enrolment in a vocational – technical school (*proftekhuchilishche*) providing training for semi-skilled and skilled workers' occupations. Prior to 1969, the course of study was 12 to 18 months and graduates were not considered to have attained a 'complete' secondary education. Beginning in 1969, an increasing number of these schools have shifted to a three-year course of study which seeks to combine a 'complete' general – secondary education and vocational training in a worker's trade. Graduation from one of these 'secondary vocational – technical schools' is the least likely route to a higher education.

In the late 1970s, more than 90 per cent of the youngsters finishing the eighth grade continued their schooling in one of these 'upper-level' forms of secondary education.[2] An approximate picture of the relative importance of the various channels of post-eighth-grade schooling is given in Table 6.1. Although these figures apply only to the Russian Republic (RSFSR), they may be taken as broadly representative of trends in schooling in the country as a whole. The principal form of upper-level secondary schooling throughout the 1970s remained the daytime general-education school. At the end of the decade, some 60 per cent or more of eighth-grade graduates continued their education through this channel. The proportion of youngsters entering the least 'ambitious' form of upper-level secondary education – the secondary vocational – technical schools – increased substantially over the decade (from about 1 per cent in 1970 to 14 per cent in 1977), but apparently not at the expense of the general-education school. In 1980, the secondary vocational – technical schools were planned to absorb some 21–3 per cent of eighth-grade graduates. In the light of the discussion which follows, however, it is worth stressing that the general-education school was to remain the principal vehicle for making a 'complete' secondary education 'universal' among Soviet youth.[3]

TABLE 6.1 *Flow of eighth-grade graduates into 'upper' levels of secondary education, by type of schooling (in %), RSFSR*

'Upper' levels of secondary education	Proportion of eighth-grade graduates entering 'upper' levels of secondary education (%)			
	1970	1973	1975	1977
9th grade of general-education school:				
daytime	55.4	54	58.1	61
evening	n.a.	n.a.	18.4	n.a.
Secondary specialized school	n.a.	11.6	10.9	n.a.
Secondary vocational–technical school	1.4	6.4	10.1	14

SOURCES
1970: *Narodnoe obrazovanie*, No. 8 (1976) 9; No. 7 (1978) 4.
1973: Akademiia nauk SSSR, Institut sotsiologicheskikh issledovanii, *Sotsial'naia struktura razvitogo sotsialisticheskogo obshchestva v SSSR* (Moscow, 1976) pp. 186–7.
1975: Calculated from *Narodnoe obrazovanie*, No. 9 (1976) 2.
1977: *Narodnoe obrazovanie*, No. 7 (1978) 4, 6. This source cites 'almost 61 %' as admissions to ninth-grade classes. We assume this figure applies to daytime classes.

THE PROBLEM OF REDUCING ASPIRATIONS

As noted earlier, the comparatively successful attempt to 'universalize' secondary education among Soviet youth has created new problems, or at the very least intensified some old ones. We may consider first the need to deflate the unrealistic occupational aspirations fostered by the extension of secondary education.

When the campaign to 'universalize' a secondary education was in its early stages in the 1960s, a number of studies appeared which, at least implicitly, seemed to question the wisdom of the campaign. Some of these studies showed, for example, that for youngsters who entered workers' occupations, the extension of schooling beyond the seventh or eighth grades of the general-education school contributed less to their productive performance on the job than a comparable period of work experience.[4] Whatever the full explanation for the apparently low economic 'yield' of post-eighth-grade schooling, part of the problem was that the youngsters who had attained a complete (ten-year) secondary schooling, or were close to it, and who found themselves employed in a worker's occupation, must have regarded their current employment as a temporary state of affairs. The reason was simply that the completion of a secondary education had traditionally been associated with subsequent admission to a *VUZ* and thus the promise of eventual attainment of intelligentsia social status. This situation has changed markedly in the last two decades.

The traditional view of the upper grades of secondary school as preparation for *VUZ* admission developed during a period when the attainment of a ten-year general education was confined to a small proportion of Soviet youth. In the immediate prewar years, less than 10 per cent of the corresponding age group could expect this much schooling, and this was apparently still the case in the early 1950s. By the late 1950s, Soviet sources claim, the proportion of youngsters graduating from daytime general–secondary schools had reached 29 per cent and, by the early 1970s, 49 per cent.[5] While Soviet sources report conflicting information on the proportion of youth completing a secondary education,[6] there is little doubt that this proportion increased substantially over the decades of the 1960s and 1970s. If all forms of upper-level secondary schooling are considered, and if Soviet claims are anywhere near the truth, perhaps some four-fifths or more of Soviet youth were completing a secondary education in the late 1970s.[7]

But from the standpoint of the problem we are considering here, the important fact is that admissions to higher education increased comparatively slowly, so that the proportion of secondary school graduates who could realistically expect to go on to a *VUZ* declined sharply (see Table 6.2). In the early 1950s, distinctly more than half of

TABLE 6.2   *Number of students admitted to daytime study in higher educational institutions (VUZy) in % of number of graduates of general–secondary school*

	Daytime VUZ admissions	
Years	In % of daytime secondary school graduates	In % of total secondary school graduates
1950–63	77	61
1960–63	57	32 .
1970–73	24	19
1975	22	17
1976	21	16
1977	20	15

SOURCES   Calculated from figures in: S. L. Seniavskii and V. B. Tel'pukhovskii, *Rabochii klass SSSR (1938–1965)* (Moscow, 1971) p. 153; Tsentral'noe statisticheskoe upravlenie SSSR, *Narodnoe khoziaistvo SSSR v 1974g.* (Moscow, 1975) p. 693; *Narodnoe obrazovanie, nauka i kultura v SSSR* (Moscow, 1977) pp. 93, 247; *Narodnoe khoziaistvo SSSR v 1977g.* (Moscow, 1978) pp. 490, 501.

the small contingent of secondary school graduates were able to continue full-time study at a *VUZ*. Some 25 years later, fewer than one in five had such prospects.

The resulting process of transforming – more accurately, 'deflating' – the customary educational and career expectations of this group of Soviet youth was by no means a painless one. Nor does it seem to have been, in the usual sense of the term, a 'planned' process. Perhaps the most frequently conducted type of social research in the Soviet Union in the 1960s was the study of young people's 'career plans' (or 'vocational orientations'). Almost invariably the results showed that a substantial majority of youngsters reaching the graduating classes of secondary schools planned to continue a full-time schooling, usually at a *VUZ*, as a means of attaining 'specialists' occupational and social status.[8] Most were destined to be disappointed and were forced to seek employment in workers' occupations (moreover without prior vocational training) as competition heightened for the relatively small number of *VUZ* vacancies. Contemporary Soviet discussions of this process did not hesitate to stress its demoralizing impact on a section of Soviet youth. The 'shattering' of career plans was accompanied by the growth of 'attitudes of scepticism, a weakening of belief in ideals . . . '. Youngsters 'roamed' from one lower-level job to another, jobs which they regarded as 'temporary evils' which had to be borne pending ultimate admission to a *VUZ* – which usually failed to materialize.[9]

There is no need to exaggerate the Soviet problem of 'disaffected youth', but it does seem clear that the continuing orientation of secondary school graduates to *VUZ* entry when objective circumstances no longer justified it must have been of some concern to authorities entrusted with maintaining the morale of Soviet youth. By the mid-1970s, however, the tone of Soviet discussions of young people's 'career plans' suggested some easing of the difficulties associated with the transition from secondary school. A process that we might loosely call 'consciousness-lowering' had apparently begun to take effect. The more recent surveys of graduating students' educational plans now showed a marked decline in the proportion looking ahead to *VUZ* admission after graduation. One of the sociologists most active in conducting these studies, F. R. Filippov, summed up his findings as follows: in the period 1973–5, about 46 per cent of the youngsters surveyed were 'inclined' to seek admission to higher education, compared with some 80–90 per cent in the mid-1960s. These figures certainly lent support to Filippov's contention that 'the career plans of graduating students are moving into greater conformity with the objective requirements of Soviet society', and that the new situation also had the welcome consequence of reducing the 'tensions' and 'conflict situations' that had prevailed earlier.[10] It does seem reasonable that with fewer trying to gain admission to higher education, fewer could be disappointed by failure.

The main factors contributing to the declining expectations of secondary school graduates seem fairly obvious. Perhaps most important was simply the gradual adaptation of youngsters to the new reality, the fact that the normal 'fate' of most such graduates had become entry into working-class, or at best semiprofessional, occupations. Hence it made good sense for increasing numbers of young people to prepare for this eventuality by enrolling in the types of educational institutions explicitly geared to such occupations (the vocational – technical or secondary specialized schools). The transformation of many vocational – technical schools into full-fledged secondary schools was undoubtedly an attempt to make these institutions more attractive alternatives to the general-education schools with their traditional orientation towards preparing their graduates for *VUZ* admission. Although graduates of secondary vocational – technical schools are eligible to apply for *VUZ* admission, they rarely do so. Thus the expansion of these institutions has been part of the process of adapting Soviet youngsters to the limited career prospects of secondary school graduates. Indeed, it is more than a bit surprising that the secondary vocational – technical schools have not yet replaced the general-education schools as the principal vehicles for 'universalizing' a secondary education. Our suspicion is that this reflects the continuing (but weakening) resistance of students, their parents and the 'educational establishment' to abandoning the traditional college-preparatory role of upper-level secondary schooling.

Recent years have also seen vastly increased efforts to use vocational guidance activities in secondary schools, explicitly to steer youngsters into workers' trades.[11] It is difficult to appraise the effectiveness of such efforts (one may doubt, in particular, the effectiveness of the recent turn to celebrating 'workers' dynasties'), but they must be seen as one aspect of the 'cooling-off' process we have been describing.

However, the apparent success attained in moderating the over-ambitious educational and career plans of secondary school graduates has had its problematic features as well. Some observers have noted that the decline in *VUZ* applications (from 269 per 100 vacancies in 1970 to 245 per 100 vacancies in 1977 – for daytime study) has been accompanied by 'a reduction in the authority and importance of general education and partly of higher education' in the thinking of some youth.[12] Could it be that efforts to reduce young people's aspirations have overshot their mark? In addition, it has become clear that these efforts have been more successful in their impact on working-class children than on youth from intelligentsia families. As F. R. Filippov put it:

> . . . the higher school, while retaining its rather high prestige, is at the same time becoming gradually 'equalized' with other forms of vocational education in the consciousness of youth. Among children of workers and collective farmers (especially among the former) this is proceeding more rapidly than among the children of employees (*sluzhashchikh*) and specialists because of the traditionally high evaluation by the latter of the occupations and social 'positions' requiring higher education.[13]

Although this could hardly come as a surprise (it certainly seems easier to persuade workers' children to accept workers' occupations than to convince intelligentsia children that this would be a desirable future for them), it could not help but be a matter of concern in a situation in which youth of working-class background are already under-represented in higher education. But this brings us to another issue.

EDUCATION AND SOCIAL INEQUALITY

There is no particular difficulty in 'unearthing' evidence of social inequality in Soviet schooling. Soviet sociological and educational literature is replete with such evidence. Indeed, the issue of social inequality has probably been explicitly discussed more frequently in connection with the educational system than in any other context. But simply to display some of the abundant evidence of such inequality does not seem a useful exercise. Like educational systems in Western industrialized societies, the Soviet system simultaneously reproduces prevailing class inequalities and provides mobility opportunities for large numbers of working-class and peasant youth. The more serious Soviet discussions are fully aware of this dual (or 'contradictory') function of the educational system. These discussions have reflected an on-going tension between 'egalitarian' and 'efficiency' (or 'meritocratic') orientations in Soviet education. The important point is to recognize that both of these elements are integral parts of the ideology and functioning of Soviet education and to avoid simplistic characterizations of the system as either 'egalitarian' or 'elitist'.

Educational controversies have provided some opportunity – however limited – for both orientations to receive public expression. The 'egalitarian' emphasis has appeared in the form of opposition to 'early specialization', insistence on a 'common' secondary education for all youngsters, and arguments for extending 'social regulation' of college admissions (preferential admissions for particular social groups). The 'efficiency' (or 'meritocratic') standpoint has stressed the desirability of special opportunities for 'gifted' children, the need for 'differentiated' secondary schooling geared to the economy's occupational requirements and reliance on competitive entrance examinations as the principal method of selecting *VUZ* students.[14] In our view, these controversies and the conflicting positions expressed in them have their counterparts in the actual operation of the educational system, a system which in some ways transmits class inequalities across generations and, in other ways, limits them. The discussion which follows is intended to provide a few illustrations of this point.

One of the Soviet Union's leading sociologists has characterized his country's educational system in the following terms (which seem readily applicable elsewhere):

> From a sociological standpoint the educational system is a totality of escalators of differing length, each of which unloads youngsters at different 'stations', at different levels of the occupational pyramid. Each of these has its own opportunities for freedom of choice and its own limitations. At these 'stations' there are also transfer points from one escalator to another. But these transfer points cannot always be utilized to an equal degree, and they always require effort, abilities, will, and time. That is why the finish depends upon the start, which to a large extent pre-determines not only the choice of occupation but social position and mode of life.[15]

If, as Shubkin suggests, 'the finish depends upon the start', there is good reason why Soviet concern with the issue of social inequality should emerge at the very initial stage of schooling; indeed, at the stage of preschooling. It should come as no surprise that Soviet studies have found that children from different social groups enter the first grade with different levels of preparation for formal schooling. Of course, this is just what one would expect in a culturally diverse society in which children are reared in families that differ markedly in educational, occupational and income levels. But these studies have also have found that children's unequal readiness for formal schooling is related to differences in the extent to which families rely on (or have access to) kindergarten training. Moreover, 'there is a direct correlation between the level of education of parents and the percentage of children receiving preschool training in kindergartens'.[16] Since families with relatively high levels of education are likely to be engaged in professional and managerial occupations, while those with lower levels are almost certainly in working-class and peasant employments (particularly the latter), the intergenerational transmission of class inequalities obviously manifests itself in the earliest grades of schooling.

However, there seems to be no extensive separation of youngsters into distinct 'streams' until the eighth grade. An 'incomplete' secondary education, it will be recalled, has become almost universal. Hence the classification of eighth-grade pupils by the social standing of their parents is essentially the same as that of youngsters entering the first grade. But the completion of the eighth grade marks an important turning point (in Shubkin's words – a 'station' on an escalator at which transfers to other escalators become available). The differential impact of social origins on children's futures comes distinctly into view at this stage. In what form does social inequality appear and how is the issue posed in Soviet public discourse? (We restrict our discussion mainly to 'class inequalities', ignoring significant urban – rural and male – female differences in schooling patterns.)

One of the persistent features of Soviet studies of the 'career plans' of eighth-grade youngsters is the finding that working-class (and peasant) children have less ambitious educational expectations than the children of 'employees' (the latter category includes professionals of all kinds as well as lower-level nonmanual employees). Thus a larger proportion of employees' children normally look ahead to entry to ninth-grade classes of general-education schools, while a larger proportion of working-class children plan to enter vocational – technical and secondary specialized schools. The choice among educational paths at this point is to some extent a choice of anticipated positions in the country's social structure. The decision to enter the ninth grade is essentially a decision eventually to apply for *VUZ* admission and thus to follow the route to intelligentsia status.[17] The other choices point to working-class or semiprofessional occupations. One consequence of the unequally ambitious plans of working-class and intelligentsia children (admittedly it might be more appropriate to refer to the plans of parents) is the distinct change that occurs in the class backgrounds of youngsters enrolled in the eighth and tenth grades of general-education schools. Table 6.3 illustrates the decline in the working-class component of the student body (and the rise in the relative share of nonmanual strata) as youngsters move into the graduating classes of general-education schools. In eighth-grade classes of regions like Moscow and Sverdlovsk, children of working-class background in the early 1970s were some two-thirds or more of the student population. In tenth-grade classes (the main source of *VUZ* applicants), their share of pupil enrolment fell to something in the neighbourhood of one-half. Children of nonmanual strata, on the other hand, increased from less than 30 per cent to more than 40 per cent of pupil enrolment as youngsters moved from the eighth to the tenth grade. The other side of this picture is the overwhelmingly proletarian component of youngsters enrolled in urban vocational – technical schools. Where studies of the social composition of these students have been conducted, they reveal that some 90 per cent are normally of working-class social origin. The secondary specialized schools occupy an intermediate position in this respect; the share of working-class

TABLE 6.3 *Distribution of eighth- and tenth-grade students of general-education schools by parental occupational status, Moscow and Sverdlovsk regions, 1973/4*
(%)

| Parental occupational status | Distribution of students (%) | | | |
| | Moscow | | Sverdlovsk | |
	8th grade	10th grade	8th grade	10th grade
Workers	66.2	49.0	70.5	58.5
Collective farmers	3.6	3.7	0.7	0.3
Specialist[a] and other nonmanual employees	28.3	45.6	28.8	41.2
Undetermined	1.9	1.7	–	–
Total	**100.0**	**100.0**	**100.0**	**100.0**

[a] This category includes individuals employed in jobs normally requiring a higher or secondary specialized education.

SOURCES
Moscow: G. A. Slesarev, *Demograficheskie protsessy i sotsial' naia struktura sotsialisticheskogo obshchestva* (Moscow, 1978) p. 137.
Sverdlovsk: Filippov, 1, p. 41.

children here is usually smaller than in vocational – technical schools, but larger than in general-education schools.[18]

The meaning of this pattern is clear. As youngsters leave the eighth grade and move on to upper levels of secondary schooling, large numbers of working-class children abandon the route that leads to a higher education and settle for those channels that promise the relatively early acquisition of vocational skills. Children from upper-strata families are much more likely to continue on the path that leads to a higher education and are rarely found in schools that train youngsters for workers' trades.

But we should not exaggerate the impact of class background on educational opportunities at this point. The Soviet system is certainly not one which rigidly 'tracks' children of differing social origins into distinct educational and career paths upon completion of the eighth grade. It is, rather, a system in which class inequalities among adults in the society at large reappear – at least in broad terms – in the structure of schooling, the aspirations of youngsters and the composition of the student body at various levels. Although the share of workers' children declines as youngsters move 'upward' in the general-education system,

Table 6.3 (and other material at our disposal)[19] suggests that such children remain a substantial, if underrepresented, part of the pool of potential *VUZ* students. Indeed, it is precisely the extension of general-secondary schooling to large numbers of working-class youth in recent years, followed by their failure to gain admission to a *VUZ* (or even to try for such admission), that has become the source of new tensions.

How is the issue of social inequality in schooling patterns posed in Soviet public discourse? First, we should stress that no particular effort seems to be made to conceal the existence of systematic differences in the social origins of youngsters at different levels of schooling and in different types of educational institutions. It is true, of course, that the advantaged position of the most privileged groups is somewhat obscured by 'collapsing' into the 'employees' social origins category the children of such diverse groups as factory managers and lower-level clerical staffs. (There may be some 'employees" children in vocational–technical schools, studying alongside their working-class colleagues; the offspring of 'specialists' will undoubtedly be difficult to locate here.) But the kinds of inequalities which are disclosed, the kinds we have summarized thus far, are clearly regarded as a problem in need of rectification. The problem is rooted in the fact that some features of 'social-class differentiation continue to exist and to be partly reproduced', and that the educational system, in addition to promoting a 'socially homogeneous society', must also promote the country's rapid economic development by providing specialized and extended schooling for its most 'capable' youth.[20]

These flourishes of ideological rhetoric should not obscure the genuine interplay of both 'egalitarian' and 'efficiency' orientations in public discussions of the school system and in its actual operation. One element of the system we have not yet considered may serve as an illustration. We refer to the so-called 'specialized schools' (not to be confused with the secondary specialized schools described earlier). These may be regarded as a Soviet version of 'elite' college–preparatory schools.[21] They are intended for the most 'capable' youngsters, who are selected through competitive examinations, and provide intensive training in subjects like mathematics, computer technology, physics, chemistry, biology and foreign languages, along with a general–secondary education. Some are organized as adjuncts of the country's more prestigious universities and thus can draw on a university faculty for teaching and curriculum design. Although the number of such schools is not known, they seem to have multiplied considerably since the early 1960s when Novosibirsk University established the first of the specialized Physics–Mathematics Schools. In 1973–4, there were 254 of these specialized schools (not counting foreign language schools) in the Russian Republic. In some areas these schools apparently account for a sizeable proportion of the youngsters admitted to *VUZy*. In the Estonian Republic, for example, more than a quarter of the students entering higher education in 1974 were drawn from specialized schools and classes with 'enriched programmes of study' in the regular secondary schools.

Soviet discussions have revealed considerable uncertainty about the advisability of extending this form of the search for 'talent'. Some of the reactions have been openly hostile. Whatever the full range of problems associated with specialized schools, one of the most troublesome concerns the social composition of their students. Children of intelligentsia parents, or at least of nonmanual social origins ('employees'), usually comprise the majority of students in specialized schools.

One of the participants in these discussions has posed the issue as follows:

> On the one hand the advantages of these schools are indisputable: they raise the quality of training of incoming *VUZ* students. On the other hand, specialized schools increase the inequality of opportunity for admission to a *VUZ* (and for subsequent social advancement) between graduates of these schools and graduates of regular secondary schools.[22]

The specialized schools are a 'socially differentiating' element in a secondary school system which is already a highly differentiated one. Given the social composition of their students, the costly resources used in training them (university facilities and faculty) and their high rate of entry to *VUZy*, these institutions clearly add another 'layer' to the already existing class inequalities in access to advanced schooling. Although some critics of these schools have directed their fire against 'excessively early specialization' and argued for the principle of 'a single general-education school',[23] it is the issue of social inequality that underlies the discussion. Defenders of specialized schools recognize this and, in their counterarguments, have stressed the success of some of these schools in recruiting working-class and peasant students. One such example concerns the Mathematics–Physics School associated with Novosibirsk University, perhaps the most celebrated of the specialized schools. Some 60 per cent of its students 'in recent years' have come from families in which parents had no more than a secondary education, implying that they were clearly not of intelligentsia social origins.[24] Most of the Soviet literature on this subject, however, suggests that this case is probably exceptional. A more typical case is probably that of the specialized school in the Urals industrial centre of Nizhnyi Tagil, which recorded only 14.5 per cent of its tenth-grade students in 1971–2 as workers' children; the vast majority of its students were the children of specialists and other nonmanual strata, although these groups comprised no more than 25 per cent of the city's population.[25] Our impression is that supporters of these schools are on the defensive and that the schools themselves are under strong pressure to increase their complement of lower-strata children. But the principle of providing a separate and 'enriched' education for selected groups of 'talented' youngsters seems to be accepted for the moment as a necessary adaptation to the era of 'scientific–technological revolutions'.

The issue of social inequality in access to education has tended to focus on higher educational institutions in recent years. With most youngsters now completing a secondary education in some form, and thus becoming at least theoretically eligible for college admission, much attention has centred on the selection process and the resulting social composition of *VUZ* students – the future intelligentsia. Whatever the 'practical' grounds for interest in this issue, there are ideological considerations involved here as well. Soviet educators explicitly reject the view that 'natural talents' or 'abilities' are unequally distributed across class lines. Hence any evidence of significant disproportions between the social origins of *VUZ* students (the most 'capable' youngsters) and the relative importance of different strata in the population at large is necessarily an indicator of the continuing impact of 'class forces' on the distribution of opportunities for the young generation. Moreover, a society which unceasingly proclaims the 'leading role of the working class' in the construction of a new social order must generate certain expectations about the extent to which the offspring of this class will contribute to the formation of a new intelligentsia. Clearly, there are good reasons for the recent heightened interest in the issue of the social composition of the *VUZ* student body.

We have seen that as youngsters progress through the upper levels of secondary school the proportion of students of manual social origins declines in those institutions that prepare youngsters for *VUZ* admission (Table 6.3). But even at the critical juncture of graduation from general–secondary school, a process of 'self-selection' apparently operates to reduce still further the relative share of working-class youngsters among those competing for *VUZ* entry. Table 6.4 may serve as an illustration. While workers' children comprised almost half of the students in the graduating classes of Moscow's general–secondary schools in 1973, their relative share among those planning to apply for daytime college study fell to one-third, (with the share of nonmanual groups moving in the opposite direction). Soviet studies of the plans of graduating secondary school students invariably show a smaller proportion of working-class than of intelligentsia youngsters planning to apply for *VUZ* admission. Whether they are discouraged by their relatively poor academic performance in secondary school, or by their family's need for additional breadwinners (parents' plans for their children's futures reveal the same pattern of social differentiation as their children's plans), or by the trauma associated with the high probability of failure in the intense competition, workers' children are more likely than their fellow-graduates from intelligentsia families to drop out of the running even before *VUZ* entrance examinations.

TABLE 6.4 *Distribution of tenth-grade students and those planning to apply for daytime college admission, by occupational status of parents, Moscow region, 1973 (%)*

Parental occupational status	Distribution of students (%)	
	10th grade students, total	10th graders planning college application
Workers	49.0	33.2
Collective farmers	3.7	1.0
Specialists and other nonmanual employees	45.6	65.3
Undetermined	1.7	0.5
Total	**100.0**	**100.0**

SOURCE G. A. Slesarev, p. 137.

The cumulative effect of social inequalities at successive critical junctures of the school system (the first, eighth and tenth grades), climaxed by the superior performance of upper-strata children on college entrance examinations,[26] has produced a *VUZ* student population in which working-class and peasant youth are clearly underrepresented. How marked is this underrepresentation? Our answer can be only a rough approximation. But the question is an important one since it bears on the issue of the extent to which the offspring of the country's 'leading class' and peasantry fill the more privileged positions in the occupational hierarchy.

In the early 1970s, the relative importance of the principal groups in the country's 'class structure' was as follows (as percentage of total employment):

workers	60.5
collective farmers	13.5
employees (total)	26.0
specialists	16.0
nonspecialist employees	10.0[27]

Thus manual strata (workers and collective farmers) made up almost three-quarters of the employed population. The remaining one-quarter was officially classified as engaged in 'mental work' ('employees') and comprised two subcategories: specialists (16 per cent), the Soviet version of the intelligentsia, and a smaller group of lower-level nonmanual employees (10 per cent). How do these proportions compare with the social composition of the *VUZ* student body?

The results of a 1973 study of *VUZ* students conducted by the Academy of Science's Institute of Sociological Research in a half-dozen 'centres of higher education' are shown in Table 6.5. Perhaps most striking is the fact that in each of the six *VUZ* centres, youngsters of nonmanual social origins were the largest single group in the student body, and in five of the six areas their relative share exceeded that of workers' and peasants' children combined. The combined share of manual-strata children came to some 40 per cent of the total student population (we ignore here the uncomfortably large proportion of youngsters whose social origins were 'undetermined'), little more than one-half the relative importance of workers and collective farmers in the employed population as a whole.

We cannot determine, of course, how representative the student body in these six *VUZ* centres was of the country's total student population, although these results are cited in the Soviet literature in a manner that suggests they are not untypical. But there are at least two respects in which the figures in Table 6.5 understate the advantaged position of upper-strata children in access to full-time *VUZ* education. First, the 'employees' category, accounting for 45 per cent of the student body, undoubtedly consisted overwhelmingly of 'specialists', that is, those employed in upper-level nonmanual positions. Thus the share of

TABLE 6.5   *Social origins of first-year daytime students in higher educational institutions, 1973 (%)*

			Social Positions of Fathers of Students (in %)		
	Workers	Collective farmers	Specialists and other nonmanual employees	Pensioners, military personnel and position undetermined	Total
Moscow	24.1	3.4	56.7	15.8	100.0
Sverdlovsk	36.5	3.6	43.4	16.5	100.0
Novosibirsk	34.3	6.6	43.4	15.7	100.0
Odessa	32.4	9.6	44.3	13.8	100.1
Voronezh	29.0	13.4	36.6	18.0	97.0
Tallin	32.4	9.5	44.3	13.8	100.0
Total, all regions	**31.2**	**8.4**	**44.8**	**15.6**	**100.0**

SOURCE   G. A. Slesarev, p. 138.

students of intelligentsia social origins was certainly more than double the relative importance of this group in the population as a whole (16 per cent). Second, and more important, the figures in Table 6.5 apply only to first-year *VUZ* students. By the time youngsters reach *VUZ* graduating classes, the social composition of the student body becomes even less 'representative': the share of workers' children declines and that of nonmanual strata increases. In the six *VUZ* centres shown in Table 6.5, the proportion of all students in graduating classes drawn from workers' families was 26.2 per cent; from collective farmers' families, 9.7 per cent; and from nonmanual strata (specialists and other 'employees'), 61.5 per cent.[28] (The residual 2.6 per cent, presumably, were the children of pensioners, military personnel or of 'undetermined origin'). Thus workers' and peasants' children, coming from social groups that comprised some three-quarters of the employed population, accounted for little more than one-third of the students in daytime graduating classes of higher educational institutions.

Some caution is necessary, however, to avoid overstating the 'elitist' nature of the institutions which train the future intelligentsia. The social composition of evening and correspondence students (more than one-third of recent *VUZ* graduates) is clearly of a more proletarian nature than that of daytime students. Moreover, the secondary specialized schools which train 'middle-level specialists' (or semiprofessionals) are attended by a predominantly working-class student body. But a class-divided society – East or West, 'socialist' or 'capitalist' – seems to reserve its preferred channels of access to the higher levels of its occupational hierarchy to a disproportionately large share of the offspring of its more privileged families. Or put somewhat differently and perhaps more directly, workers' and peasants' children are substantially underrepresented in institutions that provide the most direct route to professional and managerial positions.

It cannot be said that Soviet authorities have been indifferent to this underrepresentation of manual strata among *VUZ* students. Indeed, there is probably no more frequently repeated refrain in the Soviet literature on this problem than the need 'to bring the social composition of the higher schools into greater conformity with the social structure of our society'. A variety of measures of 'social regulation of *VUZ* admission' have been implemented which, directly or indirectly, accord some degree of preferential treatment to youth of working-class and peasant social origins.[29] That is, their opportunities for admission depend on factors other than their performance in competitive entrance examinations and their secondary school academic records. Thus rural youth, most of whom are from collective-farmers' and state farmworkers' families, receive additional 'points' in the competition for entry to teacher training institutes, medical schools and agricultural *VUZy*. The objective here clearly is to recruit students who are likely to remain in rural areas upon graduation. During the late 1960s and at least part of the 1970s (it is not clear if this is still in effect), applicants for *VUZ* admission who had received some work experience after secondary-school graduation were treated as a separate 'line' of admissions (with its own entrance examinations) distinct from that of youngsters who applied immediately upon graduation. Since the former group was more likely to include youngsters of manual social origins than the latter, this procedure permitted the admission of more working-class youth than would have entered if all applicants had been subject to the same testing procedures.

But the most important recent measure of 'social regulation' of college entrants has been the establishment, beginning in 1969, of *VUZ* 'preparatory departments'. The purpose is to provide college-preparatory instruction, using *VUZ* premises and faculty, for youngsters who have been employed for at least one year as workers or collective farmers ('demobilized military personnel' are also eligible) and who have already received their secondary school diploma. The course of study for full-time 'preparatory students' is eight months; for those who combine employment with attendance, ten months. Most students receive stipends. Those who pass 'graduation' exams upon completion of the course of study are then admitted to higher educational institutions without the need to take the regular *VUZ* entrance examinations. These 'preparatory departments' are explicitly intended to 'improve the social composition' of the *VUZ* student body.[30] Although working-class or peasant 'social origin' (that is, parents) is not a condition for admission, previous employment in the 'social position' of worker or collective farmer is required. While intelligentsia children who 'pick up' a year of work experience may sometimes be admitted, these preparatory departments are clearly intended to be, and in reality usually are, mainly working-class institutions.

In recent years, some 90,000–100,000 'graduates' of these college-preparatory institutions have entered *VUZy* annually, most of them apparently being admitted to full-time study. This means that perhaps some 15 per cent of all entering daytime students – drawn mainly from workers' and peasants' families – have gained access to a higher education without having to pass the regular *VUZ* entrance examinations. This is not an insignificant measure of 'social regulation' of *VUZ* student composition.

Recent Soviet claims of increases in the share of workers' and peasants' children in the total college population undoubtedly reflect the expansion of the 'special' measures just described. Some Soviet sources claim that by 1975, youngsters of manual social origins came to roughly one-half of the total student body.[31] (These sources, incidentally, do not make the important distinction between full-time students, who un-doubtedly are a less 'representative' group, and all students combined, nor between graduating and entering students.) Allowing for possible exaggerations, it does seem likely that the social composition of *VUZ* students at the end of the 1970s was more 'representative' than at the beginning of the decade. But there is also little doubt that such students, especially those in full-time attendance, continued to be dispropor-tionately recruited from nonmanual families. Soviet authorities are proceeding cautiously in this area, trying to moderate 'social disproportions' in student composition but avoiding hasty and disrup-tive changes in admissions procedures. Thus, entry to *VUZ* preparatory departments for the near future is to be confined to no more than 20 per cent of total daytime *VUZ* admissions.

The tension between 'egalitarian' pressures and short-run 'efficiency' considerations which we noted earlier also appears in public discussions of the troublesome issue of social inequality in access to higher education. Some writers, ever ready to justify existing inequalities, stress the importance of admission to higher education of the 'best prepared' youngsters as a necessary means of 'accelerating the development of the productive forces' and thus the transition towards greater social equality in the future ('utilizing the remnants of social inequality as a lever to advance to social equality').[32] Others stress the importance of encouraging aspirations for a higher education among working-class and peasant youth, and of increasing their recruitment to *VUZ* 'preparatory departments'.[33] Actual policy runs the uneasy course of trying to reconcile both these approaches.

What participants in these discussions cannot seriously consider – at least openly – is that as long as the privileges of a distinct professional stratum of 'specialists' (or 'intelligentsia' or 'managers' or whatever label one finds appropriate for the privileged) remain unquestioned, and children are reared in families with markedly unequal material and cultural resources, the problem of social inequality in access to advanced schooling will remain unresolved.

EDUCATION AND WORK ATTITUDES

Our final illustration of the way in which the extension of schooling has created new problems or exacerbated old ones concerns the impact of increased education on workers' attitudes towards their jobs. We refer here mainly to those youngsters who, after graduation from secondary school, fail to gain admission to higher education (or fail to apply for such admission) and are thus forced in most cases to enter workers' trades. The subject of work attitudes and, more particularly, of work discontent in the Soviet Union is a large one which deserves a separate study. Our comments here are intended only to introduce the topic and to illustrate an additional context in which new social tensions associated with increased schooling have emerged.

It would be a gross oversimplification, of course, to attribute Soviet problems of work discontent, chronically unsatisfactory labour discipline and excessive labour turnover simply to the phenomenon of 'overeducated' (or 'undereducated') workers. But the connection between job dissatisfaction and 'surplus education' among workers has been a principal theme in a score of Soviet studies of work attitudes. Perhaps the first Soviet investigators to call attention to this problem were the industrial sociologists Iadov and Zdravomyslov in their excellent study of young Leningrad workers' job attitudes in the mid-1960s. One of their principal findings was that the 'richness of content of work', the 'creative opportunities' offered by the job, was the most important single factor determining the attitude of the worker towards his job. 'We can assert that for the young worker the most important factor determining the general level of satisfaction in work is the content of labour, and only then comes the magnitude of wages and the opportunities for advancement on the job.'[34] Without seeking to negate the role of 'material incentives' (that is, wage differentials), the authors stressed that if the question concerned the relative importance of money wages versus job content, the answer was unambiguous. Differences in the degree of work satisfaction experienced by workers in low-skilled manual jobs and in skilled 'high-content' (or 'creative') jobs were substantially greater than differences in the average wage levels of these groups.

But the importance of job content as a determinant of work satisfaction was precisely the problem. Even in the early 1960s (when their survey was conducted), the authors claimed, the proportion of workers with relatively high educational and cultural levels exceeded the proportion of 'high-content', creative-type jobs. Moreover, the 'disproportion' between the relatively small number of satisfying jobs and the work aspirations created by rising educational levels would probably increase with the extension of secondary education. In short, Iadov and Zdravomyslov warned, work discontent could become a more serious problem unless measures were taken to 'compensate' workers for the gap between their 'low-content' jobs and their need for 'creative work' fostered by increased education.

In one form or another, the same problem was posed and documented in a series of studies published in the 1970s. One of the most direct formulations of the issue appeared in the writings of N. Aitov, who had conducted his studies in machine-building plants in the late 1960s. Aitov's findings showed that, in this industry, a seventh-grade education was 'the average level necessary for a worker under existing conditions of technological development'. Those with a tenth-grade education generally showed lower levels of productive performance (as measured by their degree of fulfilment of output norms) and lower levels of job satisfaction than workers with less schooling. Aitov formulated the problem ('the contradiction between the educational level of workers and the content of their work') as follows:

More than a quarter of the workers in machine-building have a tenth-grade educational level or more. At school they studied the binomial theorem, genetics, the history of literature. The school gave them a certain conception of the intellectual content of work. But at the factory in most cases they have to perform elementary work on a conveyor. Obviously this cannot have a positive effect on their attitude toward work.[35]

The existence of a significant proportion of workers with a tenth-grade education who express the view that 'our education is more than the job requires' has continued to be one of the common themes in more recent Soviet discussions of labour problems. Table 6.6 illustrates the kind of evidence invoked in these discussions to illustrate the problem of 'mismatch' between workers' educational levels and their job content (in this case, some 36 per cent of the workers with ten years of schooling felt that their schooling was excessive in relation to their work requirements). In the late 1970s, the country's leading sociologists commonly referred to the 'underutilized educational potential of the young generation' as a principal source of job dissatisfaction among young workers.[36] We cannot determine, of course, on the basis of this brief review of the Soviet literature, how widespread is the existence of work discontent in the Soviet Union or to what extent it is linked to the

TABLE 6.6   *Degree of conformity between workers' educational levels and job requirements, meat-packing plant in Kazakhstan, early 1970s (%)*

Workers' response to question: Does your educational level correspond to your job?	Educational level of workers			
	4th–6th grades	7th–8th grades	9th grade	10th grade or more
Yes, the two correspond	72.3	68.5	65.3	55.4
My education is more than job requires	2.8	15.0	23.4	36.4
My education is less than job requires	6.7	3.4	3.0	3.3
My education is less, but my experience offsets the lack	18.2	13.1	8.3	4.9
Total	**100.0**	**100.0**	**100.0**	**100.0**

SOURCE   Akademiia nauk Kazakhskoi SSR, *Upravlenie sotsial'nym razvitiem proizvodstvennykh kollektivov* (Alma Ata, 1975) p. 80.

'mismatch' between educational levels and job content. However, if the problem was a real one when it was initially raised by industrial sociologists in the late 1960s, it is unlikely to have become less pressing since then. Indeed, the opposite is probably the case. Certainly workers' educational levels, especially those of young workers, have risen since the late 1960s with the campaign to 'universalize' a complete (ten-year) secondary education. By the late 1970s, Soviet sources claim, a majority of young workers (in this case, those below the age of 25) employed in 'almost all' sectors of the economy had completed a ten-year education.[37] (We have already noted that secondary school graduation for most youngsters is now followed by entry into the labour force, in workers' trades, rather than admission to more advanced education.) Whether changes in 'high-content' (or 'creative') workers' jobs have increased apace we cannot judge, although the continuing expressions of concern cited above suggest that the problem has not eased.

What is of particular interest about Soviet studies of work attitudes and the possible impact of 'surplus education' is not so much what they reveal about the extent of work discontent, as the way in which they have been used as vehicles for an argument. The argument concerns the need for developing more 'participatory' forms of work organization or, as it is sometimes put, the need to extend opportunities for 'worker participation in management'. It is not always easy to distinguish between the ritualistic celebrations of 'worker participation' commonly found in the Soviet literature and serious efforts to call attention to the need for developing genuine opportunities for worker initiatives in plant-level decision-making. The usual objects of celebration are largely fictitious forms of participation like socialist emulation campaigns, attendance at production conferences, or workers' achievements in uncovering 'production reserves'. But the participatory theme invoked in some of the studies of work attitudes, particularly among younger and more educated workers, seems to reflect a more serious intent. Proposals for worker participation (and even 'self-management') in this context have been presented as partial solutions to the apparently very real problem of job dissatisfaction. A very rough indicator of the seriousness of this problem is suggested by the comparatively large proportion of surveyed workers (about 40 per cent is not uncommon in some of the better studies) whose work attitudes investigators characterize as falling into one of the three categories of 'dissatisfied', 'dissatisfied to the maximum extent', or 'indifferent'.[38]

For V. A. Iadow, a coauthor of the first Soviet study to call attention to this problem, one of the principal means of 'compensating' young workers for the gap between their schooling and their 'uncreative' jobs was the

> development of all types of participation of workers in the management of production. The highly educated worker now coming to the factory is prepared to assume greater responsibility for the affairs of production and the organization of labour.[39]

The same point was made in somewhat different form in a number of other studies of work attitudes. Thus a study of job satisfaction in a sector of the Soviet fishing fleet concluded: 'An essential socio-economic factor determining the satisfaction of the worker . . . is his participation in the management of the production process in which the work collective is employed.' The author of a study of job attitudes among oil workers urged increased 'on-the-job-independence' for workers, which in turn depended on the extent to which 'control, recordkeeping and managerial functions were present in a worker's job'. For the sociologist, V. N. Shubkin, the adaptation of youth (with their under-utilized 'educational potential') to workers' jobs would be facilitated by 'activating their participation in solving problems of management', all the more so given their relatively high educational levels.[40]

The rather general form of these statements, their failure to spell out the specific mechanisms that 'worker participation' might take, should not obscure their significance. They are simultaneously an implicit acknowledgement of the ineffectiveness of official forms of 'worker participation' and a way of encouraging the search for genuine participatory mechanisms as a means of mobilizing work effort. But there is no evidence that Soviet authorities are responding to the lessons drawn from worker-attitude studies. None of the proposals reviewed here has been translated into institutional changes that would create a sense of worker involvement in plant-level decisions. A highly authoritarian system of enterprise management ('one-man management') and the whole structure of centralized economic administration leave little scope for any real 'worker participation'. Thus the problem of adapting increasingly educated workers to the many routine and 'unrewarding' jobs that must be filled in the Soviet economy is not likely to diminish in the near future. Perhaps the best that can be said is that, like the issue of social inequality in access to higher education, it has reached the arena of permissible public discussion. To go beyond the discussion of 'worker participation' to its actual implementation would meet the resistance of both political and economic elites whose privileges rest on an authoritarian system of managing the work process.

NOTES

1. *Narodnoe obrazovanie*, No. 6 (1979) 13.
2. *Narodnoe obrazovanie*, No. 5 (1979) 3.
3. *Narodnoe obrazovanie*, No. 7 (1976) 8. The 1980 plan called for 'more than 67%' of eighth-grade graduates to continue their schooling in general-education schools, and 8 per cent in secondary specialized schools.
4. Akademiia nauk SSSR, Institut filosofii, *Kolichestvennye metody v sotsiologii*, (Moscow, 1966) pp. 308–13; N. A. Aitov, 'The Influence of the General Educational Level of Workers on Their Productive Activity', *Voprosy filosofii*, No. 11, (1966) 23–31.
5. Akademiia nauk SSSR, Institut mezhdunarodnogo rabochego dvizheniia, *Sotsial'noe razvitie rabochego klassa SSSR* (Moscow, 1977) p. 256; Murray Yanowitch, *Social and Economic Inequality in the Soviet Union* (White Plains: M. E. Sharpe, Inc., 1977) p. 80.
6. The 1970 census apparently showed that about one-third of the 'young generation' had completed daytime secondary school. The Soviet source cited in the preceeding note shows a figure of 49 per cent for the first half of the 1970s.
7. F. R. Filippov, *Vseobshchee srednee obrazovanie v SSSR* (Moscow, 1976) p. 63 (referred to henceforth as Filippov, 1). This source reports that the number of graduates of the number beginning first grade 10-11 years earlier was as follows (in %): 1965, 45; 1970, 69; 1972, 73; 1974, 80–1; 1975, 88.
8. A listing of these studies and their main findings appears in M. Kh. Titma, *Vybor professii kak sotsial'naia problema* (Moscow, 1975) pp. 112–13.
9. M. N. Rutkevich (ed.), *Zhiznennye plany molodezhi* (Sverdlovsk, 1966) p. 35.
10. F. R. Filippov, 'The Role of the Higher School in Changing the Social Structure of Soviet Society', *Sotsiologicheskie issledovaniia*, No. 2 (1977) 48 (cited henceforth as Filippov, 2).
11. G. A. Slesarev, *Demograficheskie protsessy i sotsial'naia struktura sotsialisticheskogo obshchestva* (Moscow, 1978) pp. 148–9.
12. Institut sotsiologicheskikh issledovanii, Akademii nauk SSSR, *Sotsial'naia i professional'naia orientatsiia molodezhi v usloviiakh razvitogo sotsialisticheskogo obshchestva v SSSR* (Tallin, 1977) p. 86 (cited henceforth as Institut). The figures on *VUZ* applications are from *Sotsiologicheskie issledovaniia*, No. 2 (1979) 102.
13. Filippov, 2, p. 49.
14. These controversies are reviewed in some detail in M. Yanowitch, op. cit., ch. 3.
15. V. Shubkin, 'The First Steps (Thoughts on Problems of Choice of Occupation)', *Novyi mir*, No. 2 (1976) 194–5.
16. Filippov, 2, p. 46.
17. Sometimes, especially in rural communities, it may reflect the absence of alternative schooling opportunities in the immediate area.
18. Filippov, 1, pp. 39, 107, 120.
19. Filippov, 2, p. 44. This source cites a figure of 49.5 per cent as the share of workers' children in tenth-grade classes based on a survey of some six regions in 1973–5.

20. Filippov, 1, pp. 4, 6.
21. Our discussion in this section is drawn mainly from the following: M. Yanowitch, pp. 77–9; Institut, pp. 137–9; *Sotsiologicheskie issledovaniia*, No. 2 (1974) 20; Filippov, 1, pp. 43–4, 59–60.
22. *Sotsiologicheskie issledovaniia*, No. 2 (1974) 20.
23. V. D. Kobetskii (ed.), *obshchestvo i molodezh*, 2nd ed. (Moscow, 1973) p. 15.
24. V. N. Turchenko, *Nauchno-tekhnicheskaia revoliutsiia i revoliutsiia v obrazovanii* (Moscow, 1973) p. 109.
25. Filippov, 1, p. 43.
26. For documentation of this point, see M. Yanowitch, pp. 84–5.
27. *Sotsiologicheskie issledovaniia*, No.1 (1975) 72.
28. Filippov, 2, p. 49.
29. This section draws mainly on the following: *Sotsiologicheskie issledovaniia*, No. 3 (1976) 75; N. M. Katuntseva, *Opyt SSSR po podgotovke intelligentsii iz rabochikh i krest'ian* (Moscow, 1977) ch. IV; M. Yanowitch, pp. 91–6; *Vestnik vysshei shkoly*, No. 9 (1979) 3.
30. N. M. Katuntseva, p. 175.
31. Akademiia nauk SSSR, Institut sotsiologicheskikh issledovanii, *Sotsiologiia i problemy sotsial'nogo razvitia* (Moscow, 1978) p. 135.
32. Institut, p. 14.
33. Institut, p. 89.
34. This section draws on the following: A. G. Zdravomyslov, V. P. Rozhin and V. A. Iadov, *Chelovek i ego rabota* (Moscow, 1967) pp. 304–5; V. A. Iadov, 'Orientation: Creative Work', in G. M. Gusev *et al.* (eds), *Obshchestvo i molodezh'* (Moscow, 1968) p. 134. Some of this material has appeared in translation in M. Yanowitch (ed.), *Soviet Work Attitudes*, (White Plains, NY; M. E. Sharpe, Inc., 1979).
35. N. A. Aitov, *Tekhnicheskii progress i dvizhenie rabochikh kadrov* (Moscow, 1972) pp. 66–7.
36. V. N. Shubkin and G. A. Cherednichenko, 'Social Problems of Choice of Occupations', *Rabochii klass i sovremennyi mir*, No. 2 (1978) 123–4; Institut, p. 11.
37. G. Bliakhman, 'A Social Portrait of the Modern Young Worker', *Sotsialisticheskii trud*, No. 10 (1979) 64.
38. *Sotsiologicheskie issledovaniia*, No. 2 (1975) 143.
39. V. A. Iadov, in *Obshchestvo i molodezh'*, p. 142.
40. The material in this paragraph is drawn from the following: O. I. Shkaratan, *Promyshlennoe predpriiatie* (Moscow, 1978) p. 254; M. Yanowitch, (ed.), *Soviet Work Attitudes*, p. 108; V. N. Shubkin and G. A. Cherednichenko, p. 124.

7 Society Without a Present

Fyodor Turovsky

Recently, the Soviet Union saw the publication of a work by one Yury Zhukov, a well-known journalist, party member and student of the international scene, about the life of the working class in the West. The author, who had never lived in the West, called his book Society Without a Future *and based it entirely on quotations from newspaper articles. This chapter on the working class in the Soviet Union is based on conclusions reached from the study of experienced facts, which bear irrefutable witness to the claim that Soviet society, in the form in which it has been existing for more than sixty-three years, is a society without a present.*

INTRODUCTION

My first taste of working-class life in the West came in the Montreal flat of Boris Sklyarsky, a sewing-machine mechanic who had emigrated from Leningrad. He invited me to visit him because I had only just arrived from Moscow, to talk about the old days in Russia and explain a few things about this world so new and unfamiliar for a Soviet emigre.

'Well, how are you finding things in your new country?' I asked, expecting a torrent of enthusiastic praise in reply.

'Oh, nothing special', he replied flatly, and added: 'In any case, we're no better off here than we were in the Soviet Union.'

'But you have to admit that you earn a lot more here', I persisted.

'Not at all; I earn less here in Canada.' My astonishment was so obvious that Boris did not wait for more questions, but hastened to make himself clear. 'Forgive me, but your question was about earnings, not about actual wages, and the two are very different things, you know. Here in Montreal I work in a clothes factory. I get 300 dollars a week. Then I mend people's machines at home, that gives me another 100 dollars a week. My wife works in a library and gets 200 dollars a week. Together, that makes between 2400 and 2500 dollars a month.'

'But there you are, then! As a mechanic, you wouldn't have earned more than 150 rubles a month in the Soviet Union!'

'Even less, actually 120–30 rubles, but I had another breadwinner: my Volga, which brought in 100 rubles and more in one evening, working on the side. That meant not less than 3000 a month! I had my permanent clientele – black marketeers who had to move their merchandise. They would be afraid to call a taxi in case the driver turned out to be a KGB man, and that would mean playing straight into the authorities' hands. They'd pay two or three hundred for just one trip, depending on what the load was. Textiles and footwear paid more, fruit less, because the risks involved were less. I made 4 or 5 rubles a month, on average.'

'What do you mean, four or five rubles?'

'Four or five thousand, of course.'

'What happens if you get caught?'

'If I'm had up just for working as an unofficial taxi-driver, for making money in a way that's illegal, I'll get up to three years and they'll confiscate the car as the means used in a criminal activity. That's not too bad at all: there might be a general amnesty, and anyway you can always find a way to get round a judge . . . But if I'm had up for theft of State property, I could get fifteen years, I could even be shot. If they catch Ivan Ivanovich, my black-marketeer, red-handed, there's no way he can wriggle out of it; then the investigating magistrate will start persuading him to reveal his accomplices, especially the Jews, and I'm a Jew, so he'll shop me for everything he's got, true or untrue. If Ivan says that I promised to sell his black-market goods for him, then that's it, I'm in it up to my neck, just like him, although it was his little affair and he started it. If he says that I had no idea what it was I was carrying, but that I should have guessed, since they paid me at least ten times what they would have paid in an ordinary taxi, then that makes me not an accomplice, but a secondary accessory. And so you sit there every time, wondering if your client has copped it at least, and if he has, then what sort of picture he's going to paint for the magistrate. Of course I made a lot, so the earnings were high, but then so were the expenses.'

'I suppose petrol was expensive?' I enquired.

'Petrol was dirt cheap back at home. No energy crisis over there, you know! Any lorry-driver will be only too happy to siphon a hundred litres into your tank for the price of a bottle of vodka. After all, every day of the week he must find himself a quiet street and run some of his petrol off into the gutter. He has to. Of course, it's a pity to waste it, but it would be even more of a pity, as far as he's concerned, if he didn't. You see, he writes in his day-sheet that he's made ten journeys, so as to earn his 15 rubles for the day, whereas in fact he's made a maximum of two because something always goes wrong. So he hasn't used up the corresponding amount of petrol, and that's why he has to find a dark street with sewer gratings to pour out the excess. Not the lot, of course – he leaves a little for the sake of economy. A driver like that gets rewarded for being so economical and responsible, he even gets a bonus for it; chicken-feed, of course, but a bonus all the same, and everyone's happy. The plan has been over-fulfilled in terms of goods carried and kilometres covered, petrol has been saved, and it all goes to show how devoted the carriers are to their government and to the Communist Party.'

'What were your other expenses, then?' I asked.

'Have you read your Mayakovsky?' he asked in return. 'Remember his famous slogan, "It's my police-force, and it's me they're protecting"? That's where half your profits go. I don't know how many bodyguards Brezhnev has, but I had at least twenty, sometimes more. As you pass one of them at his post, you put on the brakes, stick your head out of the window, and murmur with an apologetic smile: "Er . . . sorry, comrade sergeant, I think I just broke the rules of the Highway Code back there, won't do it again . . . " and he smiles back at you, not turning a hair, and says: "All right, all right, er . . . receiving you loud and clear . . . " You slip him a five ruble note and then you're on your way, and he's yours for the whole evening. Then you can carry as much black-market as you like, he'll wave you through every time with that baton of his, as though to say "You're one of us, now." '

'But when all's said and done, are you happy to be rid of all that?'

'Well . . . ' said Boris, considering the matter. 'Sure I'm happy that I can earn enough at my job to live well, very well. But of course there are other problems. We don't speak the language properly, and probably never will. We've left behind our friends and families, here we'll have to find new ones, and that's not so simple. We had lots of little pleasures over there which we'll never see the like of again. If you managed through some acquaintance to get hold of some beer, or a bottle of "Stolichnaya", that was a great occasion. If it was meat or fish, then you were over the moon. Everyone here talks English or French so fast there's no hope of understanding them. That's when you start feeling homesick, and homesickness is a terrible disease, not something that can be cured by bananas and tomatoes. Of course it's sad for a Russian to leave Russia; but it's not Russia he's leaving, not Russia as it could have been and as it should have been – it's a prison he's leaving, and even if they fed him well in prison, it was still a prison. I left behind my flat, my "Volga", my safe job and salary, and emigrated. Because that's no way to live.'

LABOUR AND WAGES

The Soviet Constitution declares that factories, mines and all the country's riches belong to the people, and that the land is ruled by the principle of 'Man is friend to Man'. The right to work and a guaranteed wage have been elevated into a constitutional principle, provided and protected by the State. Giving their labour is one of the ways in which Soviet citizens take part in the process of building communism, an expression of their will regulated by a body of legislation and by the agreement, freely reached, between worker and employer, protected by collective agreements worked out between trade unions (defending the interests of the workers), and state-owned firms and organisations. Wages, and therefore the standard of living enjoyed by the workers, depend upon the amount and the quality of the work they do. Safety provisions and the campaign against accidents – especially fatal accidents – at work are among the primary concerns of party and government, whose most important duty is caring for the workers' well-being.

These are the slogans: what, in fact, is the true situation?

What about the Soviet citizens' right to work?

Soviet industry suffers from an acute shortage of man-power: every factory and organisation displays large boards at the gate listing all its vacancies. Because of this there is practically no unemployment, and everyone can find work. But what gave rise to such an acute shortage of man-power?

Soviet ideology claims that the right to work is the state's guarantee to provide work for its citizens and pay them with wages according to the quantity and quality of what they produce. International conventions declare that every man has the right to work and be paid enough to live a life of human dignity.

There is no such right in the Soviet Union.

Those who are obliged to work have no vested interest in their work. Their pay is not enough to feed them and their families, and this explains the absenteeism, drunkenness and laziness of those who regard their work not a matter of 'honour, glory and heroism', as Stalin taught, but something which they are intimidated into undertaking. That is why

Soviet industry produces so many rejects, the quality of production is so low and the losses through lack of productivity so great, with equipment and lorries standing idle for days. Moreover, the worker in the Soviet Union preys upon the means of production, upon raw materials and the finished product, breaks things by accident and on purpose, and causes wastage all the time; things have come to such a pass that theft at work, not only small, but large-scale theft, has become the norm throughout the country.

But can it really be that workers steal because they do not earn enough to live on? The average wage for building-site workers – one of the highest-paid groups in the country – was 191 rubles a month in 1978, and the average wage for the country as a whole, as planned in the Five-Year Plan for 1976–80, was 150 rubles a month.

The following is a table of spending on food for a family of three (that is, the most typical size of family in the USSR) where, because of financial constraints and the housing shortage, most people cannot afford to have more than one child:

1.	Bread (900 grams)	18	kopeks
2.	Milk (1 litre)	30	kopeks
3.	Cottage cheese (300 grams)	25	kopeks
4.	Eggs (3)	40	kopeks
5.	Meat (600 grams)	1	ruble 20 kopeks
6.	Cooking oil (50 grams)	10	kopeks
7.	Margarine (100 grams)	30	kopeks
8.	Vegetables, potatoes, onions etc.	1.00 ruble	
9.	Oatmeal, flour, sugar etc.	1.00 ruble	
10.	Fruit (200 gr. each)	1.00 ruble	
11.	Sausage, fish	1.00 ruble	
12.	Biscuits,honey, jam	0.77 kopeks	

7.30 rubles per day

Based on these figures, we see that food for three people would cost 225 rubles a month (at 1976 prices; since then, many food-prices have gone up). To this sum we must add at least another 25 rubles a month for soap, toothpaste, washing-powder, a few cosmetics for the wife and an occasional ice-cream for the child.

If we take into account the fact that many fruits and vegetables are unavailable in the shops, either not to be found or else sold when they are already rotting, and therefore have to be bought at the market where the prices are many times higher, then we should add at least another 50 rubles.

So: the minimum income for this family would have to be 300 rubles a month, or 10 rubles a day, or over 3 rubles per person per day.

As far as I can see, living in Montreal, this is about the same as a Canadian family spends on food. The average worker in Montreal, however, earns an average (again, I have taken a building-site worker as my example) 1500 dollars a month. This means that in two-and-a-half days he earns as much as his colleague in the Soviet Union can earn in a month.

But man does not live by bread alone. He has to buy clothes, pay for a flat that may be cheap, but is not completely free, for a telephone, if he is one of the many thousands of Soviet citizens with his own telephone, pay for cinema, theatre, circus and concert tickets, mend his shoes, pay for public transport and so on.

Even at the most modest assessment, all these expenses would come to not less than 50 rubles per person (that is, 150 rubles a month), which would bring the outgoings in the budget of a Soviet family to 450 rubles a month.

Their incomings are a maximum of 300 rubles a month, if we take both those members of the family who work as having the average wage of 150 rubles a month.

However, these 'average' families are not in the majority. There are families where out of three people only one is working, and working not as a carpenter on a building-site but in a textile mill, a woman with two small children. Of course, there are also families where both husband and wife are professors, and together they earn more than a thousand rubles a month.

But in a country with a population of 260 million, in order to gain an accurate assessment of the general state of health it is not enough merely to determine the citizens' average temperature!

For this reason, if we take as our basic unit the family of three with two members who are working, one of them earning the average wage of 150 rubles and the other earning only a little less – say, 100 rubles – then the actual average wage of a typical Soviet family comes to no more than 250 rubles a month, and the deficit in their budget will be 200 rubles a month.

It would be impossible to cut down their needs to that level: and so people seek and find other sources of income.

What are these sources? They are many, and all of them illegal.

(1) People steal their working hours so as to make use of them in a second job. Some do not appear at all, others leave their factory during the working day, or sit idle at work so as to save their strength for

working somewhere else in the evenings. Working officially in two places at once means extending the working day by at least four hours, so that the declaration in the Constitution that the working day in the USSR is the shortest in the world can be viewed as something of an exaggeration.

This seemingly innocuous way out of the situation leads to the gravest criminal offences. Many workers officially take on a second job, but in fact they are not working: they are merely there on the list when it comes to pay day. When a man is paid these illegal wages, he shares them with those who 'employ' him and pay him. So common and well-known did this phenomenon become that 'workers' of this type came to be known as 'dead souls', after the book by Gogol. A huge inspectorate is constantly trying to seek out these disguised 'dead souls', and sometimes succeeds in 'resurrecting' them.

It was the government itself that gave the lead in this matter of getting money without earning it. This is how it happened. The whole army of 'amateur sportsmen'–footballers, speed-skaters, athletes and so on–do not, as a rule, work anywhere, but they are registered at factories where they do invented jobs and are paid their 'salaries' by post.

The entire football team of the Moscow region was registered as 'working' at the pulp plant in the town of Liubertsy. None of the team had ever even so much as seen the plant in which they 'worked' as plumbers and joiners, yet every month they received not only their wages, but also their bonuses for excellent work.

If the plant's director had been forced to take on so many 'dead souls', then why not use the same simple means to take money from the plant's liquid resources to spend where it was needed?

And if the director forced his shop foreman to take on 'dead souls' like these, then why should the latter not exploit the situation to earn a little more than the wage which the state has set for him and which is not enough to feed him and his family?

And so we find that a chain reaction of deviousness has developed at every possible level of the socialist economy.

I once had the task of defending a certain Prilutsky of the National Electro-Technical Construction Institute in a big trial, where he was accused of employing in his department several chief engineers, draughtsmen and planners, working there as a second job, and paying them for the power stations they were supposed to have designed, while in fact none of them had ever so much as set eyes either on their 'designs' or on the institute where they were supposed to have produced them.

Prilutsky rented a basement room, installed one of the institute's copying machines and employed the local yard-sweeper to make copies of plans for power stations that had already been built twenty years ago. These copies were attached to the lists from which pay slips were issued as proof of work carried out.

Among the 'dead soul' planners were well-known specialists, engineers with years of experience, who earned very small salaries in their basic job and needed money badly.

All the accused were sentenced to long stretches in prison–from fifteen to twenty-five years. Many of them never returned to the outside world, but perished in the camps.

The government tried to limit working in more than one job, and a law was made allowing a second job to be held only if it was in the same place as the first one–but this law is broken all the time.

(2) 'Fixing the books' and adding-in.

The constitutional principle of basing wages on the quantity and quality of the work carried out is something that in the overwhelming majority of cases exists only on paper. The Soviet system of labour organisation has replaced this principle by developing a reliable system for calculating wages that has come to be called 'fixing the books'.

The essence of this system is that, at the end of the month, whoever is in charge summons the 'norm-calculator', whose task is to reflect in the pay slips the constitutional principle of pay 'according to the quantity and quality of the work'.

The engineer-in-chief dictates to the norm-calculator for which workers he is to write out a pay slip, and what sum is to be their month's wages.

Why?

Sometimes machinery stands idle because some essential spare part is missing, so the men could do no work; sometimes there is no cement on the site, so the workers stand idle; if the building materials they need are not there, the workers stand idle; if the crane driver does not turn up for work, the men stand idle. . . .

If the site followed the letter of the law, hours spent idly through the fault of the employer would be paid at only 50 per cent of the normal rate, that is to say next-to-nothing.

The State Bank furnishes the engineer-in-chief with enough money only for work that has been completed. This sum does not include payment for days spent standing idle.

If the workers were paid what they had really earned, their pay slips would be so small that they would leave at once for another site with an engineer-in-chief willing to pay them a more satisfactory wage. That is why the chief tells his norm-calculator to fabricate hundreds of false orders 'fulfilled', so as to cover up for the idle days, and to include in the reports of work completed and in the figures for the pay slips, non-existent tasks which the workers have not in fact carried out.

The trade union newspaper *Trud* once published an investigation into the average wages of building-site workers in the USSR. Its author stated that the workers were earning 50 rubles a month more than what the government had planned, with 191 rubles instead of the planned 141. Then he explained that these high earnings were attained not by a rise in productivity, but by the way in which the books were fiddled. The investigators had discovered hundreds of thousands of fictitious work orders.

However, as we have already stated, the State Bank supplies the engineer-in-chief with only as much money for wages as has been authorised for a building project of this type, and all the outgoings have been calculated down to the last nail.

The professional beans were spilt by the newspaper *Literaturnaya gazeta*, which published the confessions of an engineer who had played a very important part in Moscow's apartment building programme.

'What saves our skins,' he wrote, 'are the one-off buildings, the ones that are not built according to a stereotype plan.

'Organisations which need a non-stereotype building to be built on time will comb the whole of Moscow until they find a contractor willing to take on their building over and above the buildings which he is obliged to construct in order to fulfil his plan, and which he will have to answer for with his head. And this is the saving of us: we accept the job on condition that we will have the right to readjust the estimated costs. The client looks the other way and nods in silence, since he is well aware of the true reason for our insisting on this condition: for we will include bills for work which will never be carried out, and is not even needed, except for the fact that by "doing" this work we will receive money that we need to pay the workers standing idle on the buildings being put up to ordinary stereotype plans.'

And so we see the lie-business in action. The quantity surveyors calculate how much it would cost to build contractors' roads, which no-one has any intention of building, how much to drain a non-existent marsh in a place where the bedrock lies just beneath the topsoil, and how much it will cost to divert a lake in a place as dry as a desert. When we have pumped the figure up to a couple of hundred thousand rubles for non-existent work, we offer the client the new estimate, he gulps and signs it at once, thanking us for our generous help, and we drop our work on the buildings we are supposed to be building for the plan – after all, those Muscovites who have waited so patiently for a new flat can very well wait a little longer – and set to work on our client's building.

Here we have another chain-reaction.

In the Soviet economy, everyone adds-in work which is never in fact carried out. From the norm-calculator on a building site to no less a man than Victor Vassilievich Grishin, First Secretary of the Moscow Party Committee, member of the Politbureau and of the Praesidium of the Supreme Soviet.

Thus Grishin is personally responsible to Brezhnev for fulfilling the plan as regards building in Moscow which, Brezhnev has decided, must be transformed into a model socialist city.

Two organisations are involved in building in Moscow. The Main Directorate for the Production of Building Materials and Construction, which runs a hundred factories making building materials and pre-fabricated units for use on building sites, and 'Glavmosstroi', which runs hundreds of building organisations to build the pre-fabricated units into housing, shops, schools and kindergartens, cinemas, hospitals and all kinds of other buildings.

Six hundred thousand building workers of different types are employed on the building sites of Moscow.

By the end of the month it is quite normal, so we learn, for the plan not to be fulfilled in the production of pre-fabricated units, just as it remains unfulfilled for the construction and completion of housing.

But no-one would dream of informing the Statistical Department or the Council of Ministers; that would be more than his job is worth, so Grishin gives the order to readjust the plan for those organisations which have not fulfilled it, in the hope that the deficit will be made up during the following month. But this alone is not enough to save the situation. The law demands that whatever is produced be 'realised', that is, paid for by the building firms and shipped out of the factory.

However, the building firms are not warehouses for products that they do not need. As it is, they have a surfeit of all sorts of building materials and, since there are not enough workers on the site, these materials are left lying around the hole dug for the foundations, being ruined by rain and incorrect storage.

However, the Bolsheviks of Moscow must not lose face: whatever happens, they must overcome their difficulties, and overcome them they do.

The city fathers – Grishin and Promyslov, the Chairman of the Moscow City Soviet – gave the orders for the setting up of a store for these pre-fabricated parts; although it is, of course, completely unnecessary, it allows hundreds of thousands of rubles' worth of pre-fabricated panels to leave the factory, thereby giving the impression that the plan has been fulfilled.

And so dozens of factories load their pre-fabs on to special lorries, ship them off to a piece of land owned by a poultry farm near Moscow, and there dump them in an open field, without any provision at all for storage.

It is very unlikely that anyone will ever come out here to pick them up. They will simply rot away.

This 'adding-in' of fictitious work has become a nation-wide scandal. New factories and plants are 'added-in', which do not even exist. *Literaturnaya gazeta*, again, printed an article by a special correspondent, A. Radlov, on the town of Nevyomysk, where they had speeches and papers to celebrate the completion of a large textile factory. One of those sitting at the high table during the celebrations, wrote Radlov, was a woman, the deputy director of the organisation of which the new factory was to become a part, who sat shedding tears throughout. She was crying for shame. She had been forced to sign a fictitious document declaring that the factory was completed, whereas in fact it had not even been started.

(3) Small-scale thieving.

For many years now the Soviet Union has been witness to a silent, but serious and bloody, war between two great armies.

The first army is the millions of workers condemned to poverty, who receive a minimal wage and work in the food industry, in textiles or in retail. These people can alleviate their constant poverty through small-scale thieving at work or, in the case of retail workers, by giving short-measure and short-change to the consumer, or by selling rare and sought-after merchandise at black-market prices.

The second army consists of the numberless agents of the so-called Department for the Struggle with Stealing of Socialist Property, an army of public inspectors, door-keepers, secret agents, and so on.

This army tails the workers who carry out a pair of stockings concealed in their clothing, if they work in a stocking-factory, or a pair of tights, if they work in a knitwear factory, or a couple of kilograms of meat, if they work in a meat-packers', or a watch or two from a watch factory. Of course, the ways and means of stealing are infinite, and infinitely more subtle than this. There was a trial in Moscow over the theft of a large number of watches from Watch Factory No. 2 by carrier-pigeons trained by the thieves in question. They would fly on to the window-sill of the experimental shop, where there were only a few workers; these tied the watches to the birds, which flew back off to where the accomplices of this unusual crime were awaiting them.

One of the cases I defended was that of Kolya Ivanov, a worker in a packing-materials factory, who tried to leave the factory with a kilogram or so of rusty nails to mend the old shed where his family stored its fire wood; the door keepers stopped him, wrote an official report of the theft, and this 16-year old boy was sentenced to *fifteen years of prison*. The court did not take into account the fact that Kolya's father had recently hung himself in that same shed, in despair that he would never get his family a decent place to live. The whole family lived in one rented room in a private house, no more than three metres square, with rotting floor boards and no central heating or insulation. Kolya's father was a veteran and invalid of the Second World War; he had been badly wounded in the lungs and now suffered from tuberculosis. All his attempts to get somewhere for his family to live had ended in failure. They had been on the waiting list for a flat for more than ten years, but they lived not in Moscow, with its shining new housing estates that so impress tourists from the West, but in Volokolamsk, fifty kilometres from the capital. Volokolamsk could not, of course, boast any kind of a housing estate at all, and the authorities were forced to refuse requests for housing even from families like the Ivanovs.

But why fifteen years of prison, the reader will ask. Kolya was unlucky. Not long before this sad affair, the Praesidium of the Supreme Soviet had published a decree raising the penalties for the theft of state property. The irony of the new law was that the theft of property owned by some co-operative carried a lighter punishment than that of state property: as though the state was declaring to its citizens that if they could not help stealing, then they were at least to steal not what the state owned, but what groups of individuals owned collectively. It was this which sealed Kolya's fate: he came under the terms of reference of the new decree.

I heard the summing-up for the defence by the Moscow lawyer Goldberg in the trial of a textile worker from a factory near Moscow. She was accused of trying to smuggle a five-metre piece of cotton, from which she was going to sew a dress for her little girl, out of the factory in her clothes.

Her name was Ananieva and her husband had been killed at the front, leaving her with two children. She earned 120 rubles a month, which was simply not enough for the family to live on.

Goldberg remembered an occasion from pre-revolutionary legal history, when the famous Russian lawyer Plevako was defending an old woman on trial for attempting to steal a state-owned teapot. The Public Prosecutor was demanding that she be given a prison sentence, since Russian state property was holy and inviolable, and anyone who breached this inviolability should be made to pay for his actions with the full weight of the law. Plevako agreed with his opponent's evaluation of the importance of state property, but noted that when the Teutonic knights had attacked great Russia, she survived unscathed: then when she was attacked by the Mongols, she remained unscathed . . . and so Plevako finished his speech with the words: 'And now, when my client has attacked Russia in her turn, I hope in the Lord Almighty and have every confidence that Russia will survive unscathed once more.' Goldberg found Plevako's approach very tempting.

But even if a Tsarist court acquitted the old woman, how much more fitting was it that a Soviet court should acquit a woman with two children on her hands and whose husband had died a hero's death defending his country, all of which Goldberg mentioned in his concluding address.

The court sentenced Ananieva to prison, whence she was taken straight from the courtroom, to the heartbreaking sobs of her children, while Goldberg was expelled from the College of Advocates for making a politically dangerous speech in court and shutting his eyes to the enormous damage done to society by all the petty thieving that went on from people's places of work.

Unable to stand the strain of not being allowed to practice the profession in which he had served more than fifty years, Mikhail Moiseyevich Goldberg died of a heart attack.

(4) Large-scale thieving and mis-use of power.

The whole country used to follow breathlessly the trials of those accused of large-scale thefts of so-called 'socialist property'. The methods used were simple and always so similar as to give the impression that all the defendants were following a rule-book passed on to them by their superiors.

Experienced workers manage to make things, behind the back of the Accounts Department, out of raw materials that have been acquired illegally, either by economising on materials for the 'official' production or by not using quite enough. Then the retail outlet passes on this stuff produced, as they say, 'on the side', to those who work in the state shops (there are no private shops in the USSR). Finally, the money which these goods bring in is shared between all those who took part in the theft. A part is played in this operation by the workers who actually make the goods that do not find their way into the books of the Accounts

Department; and so for the work they put in on these 'side' goods they are paid directly by those who organise the theft, and at rates much higher than those the state pays.

However, in spite of an army of investigators, these 'economic' crimes, as academic lawyers call them, continue unabated. It is the system itself which forces the workers into crime: the whole of industry and management is contaminated with a massive illegality, starting with the illegality of the system itself.

Besides this, the army of investigators is itself infested at every level with bribery and corruption. For this reason, those who break the law can act, up to a certain point, with complete impunity: more than that, those who occupy the relevant posts protect them effectively from all mishaps once they have been 'bought'.

The former director of the central distributing agency for textiles in Kiev, a certain Khaikin, used to 'lose' several thousands of rubles almost every evening to the secretary of the Kiev District Committee of the Communist Party.

Later, Khaikin was arrested and accused of selling, over a long period of years, to black-marketeers the imported textiles that were intended for sale in the state shops. The black-marketeers paid a black-market price for the goods and re-sold them privately at a large profit. Khaikin was known in Kiev as a big spender who haunted the most expensive restaurants. When the Kiev football team were playing in Moscow, he would fly up in a special plane, for which privilege he paid a fortune to the employees of Aeroflot. But he never lost a moment's sleep: the man who ran the city was 'in his pocket', and he was all-powerful.

Khaikin made a clean breast of it and was given the longest sentence appropriate for misuse of power or position: since he had not actually stolen, but simply misused his power in selling not to shops but to private individuals, thereby making a profit for himself, he was given ten years.

But Stalin heard about the case and, in his anger, ordered Khaikin to be shot, although judicially there was no justification for such an extreme measure. And Khaikin was shot.

The beginning of the 1960s saw a wave of trials in which dozens of people from the prosecuting apparatus, at all levels from local prosecutors' offices to that of the prosecutor for the Russian Federation, from the magistrates of local People's Courts to those in the Supreme Court of the Russian Federation, were sentenced for taking bribes from workers in industry and the retail trade in return for suppressing investigations and trials. And a few years before that we heard of the suicide of a certain Solodilov, former deputy chairman of the Supreme Court of the USSR, who committed suicide when they came to arrest him for taking large bribes over a number of years in connection with the business of the court.

How harsh and unbending had that same Solodilov shown himself to be when faced with a defendant whose only crime lay in the fact of having to support a family on a miserable wage, and stealing a box of sweets from the factory for the children or a headscarf for the wife. He used angrily to brush aside all their lawyers' remonstrations that these first-offenders had been forced into their crimes, and flung out of his office any lawyer who came to see him privately on this score.

LEGAL RIGHTS

I would now like to acquaint my Western readers with the fact that Soviet workers enjoy no rights at all *vis-à-vis* the authorities and the courts. One of the results of this fact is the extent to which their lives are entirely dependent upon the sway of chance.

Soviet ideologists claim that the Soviet state is founded upon respect for the rights of the citizen and for the law, which in its turn is seen as an expression of the will of the Soviet people. However, as we have seen, Stalin had no difficulty whatsoever in overriding the law and ordering Khaikin's execution for a crime whose legal punishment went only as far as a term of imprisonment.

When his lawyers told Stalin that the order to shoot the defendant could not be carried out because the law did not allow for execution in the case of this crime, Stalin rounded angrily upon them and asked:

'So you say that the law does not allow for execution here? But who makes the laws in the Soviet Union?' Then he gave the order for Khaikin to be shot.

Khrushchev, the great exposer of Stalin's 'violations of socialist legality', himself had Rokotov and Faibishevich shot after the famous Moscow trial over their foreign-currency dealings, although the law which they had broken allowed for nothing beyond a term of imprisonment as a punishment. It was, in fact, after the defendants had been found guilty that he published a decree making death the maximum punishment for currency offences. But all civilised societies agree that a law which increases the relevant punishment should never be retroactive, and enshrine this principle in their legal systems.

When the lawyers told Khrushchev that his orders to shoot Rokotov and Faibishevich could not be carried out because a new decree could not be made retroactive, Khrushchev lost his temper and demanded: 'Who makes the laws in the Soviet Union?', and gave orders that the decree be published with a special clause about retroactivity to cover Rokotov and Faibishevich, duly signed by the then chairman of the Praesidium of the Supreme Soviet, Leonid Brezhnev. Rokotov and Faibishevich were shot.

Anastasia Vinogradova, who lost four sons fighting at the front during the Second World War, appealed at all levels of the Soviet judicial system for mercy on her fifth son. He had knocked down a pedestrian who later died in hospital.

Vinogradova's son was sentenced to ten years' imprisonment and had already served more than half his sentence. His mother was over 78 years old, all alone in the world and a very sick woman when she asked to have her fifth returned to her so that she could see him again before she died.

But all her efforts were in vain. No-one took pity on the old woman, and she died alone.

Compare this with the case of the elder son of a former minister who was so drunk that he tried to walk along the eighth-storey ledge outside the window, fell and was killed. The minister's second son was at the time doing a stretch in a camp for rape. Of course, we can understand how deeply affected were the minister and his wife. He asked the present chairman of the Soviet Supreme Court, Smirnov (the same Smirnov who personally presided over the trial of the writers Daniel and Sinyavsky), to take account of their situation, left as they were without either of their children, pardon their son and set him free. Smirnov pardoned the rapist and let him go.

As for the field of labour and labour relations, it is again the sway of chance, rather than concern for the rights of the Soviet citizens, that reigns supreme.

The head of the bakery in Shargorod illegally dismissed his boiler-man without the permission of the trade union that is demanded by the labour laws. The trade union did not object either on behalf of its member, nor in its own right. The worker, Radetsky, spent two months re-establishing his rights over which the director had ridden rough-shod, and only by going to court did he succeed in being re-installed in his job.

This fact was reported with pride in an article published in *Trud* on 24 July 1979 by G. Tarnavsky, Chief Prosecutor of the Vinnitsa region, entitled 'Where the Strength of the Law Lies'. The Prosecutor took pride in the triumph of legality, but seemed unaware that in order to put right a violation of the labour laws it was hardly necessary for a boiler-man, who earned 70 rubles a month, to chase from court to court in order to teach his party-member boss what it meant to break the law.

This is how the same author describes the position *vis-à-vis* the question of defending the workers' interests adopted by the trade unions when the employer has violated their rights:

> Often we find the following situation: the chairman of the trade union committee does not succeed in convincing the management that the latter is acting wrongly in some matter, and he lets it slide. Often he lacks the courage to take the next step, that of referring the matter to court – even though he would always be supported by the higher ranks of the trade union organisations and by us at the Prosecutor's office. In this way much illegal action on the part of management could be prevented.

But why are trade union officials so timid? Because, as everyone in the USSR is aware, it is the management, the head of any factory, that 'elects' or rather appoints that factory's trade union leader, and it is the same man who decides whether the leader be chosen for a second term or not. The actual 'election', when the workforce votes, is merely a piece of second-rate play-acting, where everyone in the audience is only too well aware of who is writing the play and how it will end.

Ninety per cent of union officials are workers who receive their orders from the management, are dependent on the latter for their wages, and look to the management for all their 'perks' like bonuses, new flats and subsidised holidays. Is such a union leader likely to defend the workers' interests, or would he not prefer to remain good friends with the management?

From time to time in legal journals and even in the newspapers we read that the vast majority of cases for reinstatement, where someone has been unfairly dismissed, are resolved either at the first court hearing or else after several appeals. Sometimes the process takes years and the worker's quarrel with an overweening manager goes as far as the Supreme Court of the USSR or the Public Prosecutor's office. Legions of lawyers support the high-handed director and then, when the matter comes to the final court of appeal, often purely by chance – a telephone call from the Party Central Committee to the Supreme Court or the Prosecutor's office – the whole affair takes a sharp turn-about and truth finally prevails. The worker is reinstated and his place of work made to pay him up to two months' wages for the time he has been idle.

The situation becomes even more dramatic when the workers

concerned come from the so-called 'No. 1 list' – master craftsmen, shop-foremen, chief mechanics and so on.

According to the law as it stands, if any of these are dismissed illegally, they have no right to seek the protection of the law. They can be reinstated only by their management to which their director himself is answerable. But what redress can the illegally dismissed 'No. 1' man have if the director, before issuing the illegal orders for his sacking, has anyway consulted his own superiors beforehand? The dismissed shop-foreman comes to them to make a complaint about the director of his factory. He is heard out with all apparent gravity, he is promised an investigation, and addressed only in the most respectful terms, as constantly laid down in resolutions passed by the Party Central Committee on the way to treat complaints; but as soon as he leaves, buoyant with new hope, the official will write on his complaint that his request to have his dismissal reviewed has been refused. The same comedy is played through a million times a day at every level of the mechanism for complaints to which Soviet citizens have recourse when their rights have been violated.

There is another field governed by a complex system of regulations, the violation of which leads to the deaths of thousands and thousands of workmen on the job and tens of thousands of industrial accidents.

In 1976, a boiler exploded at Moscow's No. 3 woodmill. It had supplied steam for making chipboard building-panels, and the accident resulted in the deaths of the twenty-two men who had been in the shop at the time.

The boiler exploded, shot up through the roof, flew over the wall of the shop and came to earth only a metre away from a large block of flats. If it had fallen a metre further, there would have been many more victims.

The boiler had been installed forty years before and was long since obsolete. Its walls were full of cracks, a sure sign of metal fatigue, but it was still kept in use and the cracks merely soldered over. The mill had begged Grishin at the City Party Committee and Promyslov at the City Soviet to authorise them to spend the necessary foreign currency on a replacement. The city fathers, however, refused. Just at that time, Moscow was building the Hotel Russia; it was a question of the city's prestige, and panels were needed for this building that was under direct government supervision. The result was this explosion with a large number of fatalities. And who was held responsible? The shop-foreman, a hero of the Second World War, who had shot down two enemy planes and suffered severe burns in his fighter. He was given five years in prison, the maximum stretch.

Grishin, meanwhile, was receiving the highest peacetime honour: he was made a Hero of Socialist Labour on his sixtieth birthday.

The wife of a driver who was killed in the explosion applied for a grant to help her to send her handicapped six-year-old son for a rest-cure. The child was given an allowance because of the loss of the family breadwinner of 56 rubles a month. His mother earned 90 rubles a month and had an older girl as well.

Lev Alexandrovich Lebedev, deputy chief of the head office, consulted me on the legal aspects of the matter.

'You must help her,' I replied somewhat evasively.

'I know that already, but what does the law have to say?'

'The law,' I said, 'has nothing to say. But you still have to help.'

'The organisation isn't a synagogue, you know, we don't run a charitable institution. If she's legally entitled to money, I'll give it to her, but if she isn't – then I won't. That's all there is to it.'

'Yes, there is a law,' I said. 'The organisation has a special fund to help workers temporarily in difficulties.' (That is how they formulate the laws in the USSR. They are willing to admit of the possibility of temporary difficulties, but never of permanent ones.)

'You're no good as a lawyer,' said Lebedev. 'Shirayeva [that was the woman's name] doesn't work here; where she works they must also have a fund, let her ask them for money.'

'But we killed her husband, not the place where she works herself,' I objected. 'The moral onus is on us.'

'That's just propaganda,' cut in Lebedev, and wrote on the bottom of the sheet: 'Refused.'

Every winter for decades, usually at night, the foremen from reinforced concrete factories send the women who work under them out to the loading-bays where they have to unload frozen sand or gravel from railway wagons. If a large consignment arrives, the foreman stops all work in the shop and sends the whole workforce out to unload. Women in padded jackets and canvas mittens, which have no effect against the fierce frost and a wind strong enough to blow them off their feet, clamber up on to the open wagons and, armed only with crowbars and hammers, chip away at the frozen sand and gravel.

There is a law against making women do this hard and damaging work. This is a task for bore-loaders, which would work much faster and more economically. The wagons stand for days here in these unloading bays, so that the factory has to pay large sums in compensation to the railway. But driving out the women like slaves still works out cheaper.

As the women work they weep and rub their frozen hands and feet, they get frost-bite but dare not refuse to do the work: they are on the waiting-list for a flat.

If they refuse to do the work, then there will be no flat.

What does the trade union committee have to say?

'An industrial necessity . . .' and it pretends not to notice the mockery that is being made of the law and of these women.

The state's irresponsible attitude to the lives of its workers means that the officials who work in industrial management have complete disregard for their workers, who in their turn are quite resigned to their total lack of rights.

Sometimes, however, things come to such a pass that the workers strike in protest.

The workers in the best shop at Reinforced Concrete Factory No. 5 in Moscow announced that they would strike if the newly-introduced production norms were not lowered to their previous level. These new norms had not been discussed with the workers, the workers had not even been told, nor had the trade union committee discussed them in the presence of the workers. When the workers came to receive their pay-packets, they found that they had only earned 20 rubles in two weeks. They also learned that the chairman of the factory's union committee had taken his decision to raise the norms by himself, considering it a mere formality to discuss the question with the workers or even with the rest of his committee.

This low-key strike lasted for two days. The workers sat about in the shop, doing nothing. The conveyor-belts moved emptily along. The shop-foreman begged his men to get to work, threatening them with legal action, but they demanded to see the factory director. The director, terrified by the strike, was afraid to enter the shop. At that point, one of the strikers telephoned the local party committee and announced the strike.

The local party secretary came straight to the factory with a promise to lower the norms, and the conflict was over.

A few days later a group of the workers came to me and asked me to find out if they had the right to be paid for the days when they were on strike.

What could I say? There is no legislation about strikes in the Soviet Union except for the fact that if strikers are being taken to court, they can be accused under any of the articles in the criminal code dealing with crimes against the state. However, I wanted to help them, so I had thought up the following argument: if the factory management had acted legally, they would have lowered the norms as soon as the workers demanded it, and there would have been no idle days. But since the management had illegally introduced new norms and illegally maintained them, then the workers' idleness had been the fault of the administration. And idleness of this type had to be paid at 50 per cent rates.

The workers were somewhat disappointed to hear this and one of them, evidently the bravest, said, 'To hell with him, why do we bother?'

And at that they set off to see the boss.

Soon, however, none of those who had taken part in the strike was left. The management had found various excuses to make sure that each and every one of them 'left his job' sooner or later . . .

Twenty drivers from one road-transport organisation in Tadjikistan wrote a collective letter to the union committee in their organisation asking it to force the management to pay them for idle days incurred through the management's fault and to make sure they were kept in work.

The reason was that because the garage had not stocked up sufficient numbers of spare-parts, many of the lorries were out of use. The law states that in such cases the workers must be paid at least 50 per cent of the usual rate. However, these workers were not getting a penny and, moreover, the drivers were not being issued with petrol, but were having to buy it with their own money instead.

The day after he received their letter, the director of the garage replied to their complaint by transferring all the drivers who did not have work to the repair of farm equipment. For this month of work in which they were not qualified, these workers were paid 30 rubles each, while by law they should have been paid from 63 to 103 rubles, depending on their qualifications. After their complaint was received by the union committee, these violations of the labour laws not only did not cease but, on the contrary, they became even more marked. Drivers were not paid for idle days and, so as not to be idle every day, they had to buy their own petrol. It was then that they wrote to the newspaper *Trud* which, on 20 June 1979, published an article by a correspondent called Y. Krasnopolsky entitled 'At the Source of the Conflict'.

The reader would be justified in concluding that the director begrudged spending the state's money on petrol. But, of course, he did not begrudge the state's money; his concern was less for the state than for himself, his job and the privileges that went with it. As we have said before in another context, the state supplies the director with money to pay only for working days, and not for days spent idle.

For this reason, if the director pays out for idle days as well, he will forfeit his bonus and never be considered 'progressive', which in its turn may lead to the loss of his post and in any case would never lead to promotion. In order to consolidate his position in this respect, this director risked not paying his workers for months. Sometimes, however, the director's interests are best served by the opposite tactics. The director of the bus garage in the city of Kaunas told me the following tale:

> At the beginning of every year the government sends out a general instruction telling everyone to cut down their workforce by 10–15 per cent. The fact of cut-backs does not in itself provoke any objections, since often we have too large a workforce anyway, but they ought to trust the management to cut down on the administrative apparatus as and when it can. However, there is no such trust, and each year a campaign is organised to get the cut-backs going. Now it is only May. I know that I have three or four people in the office for whom there is not enough work: we have simplified our accounting procedure, mechanised it to a certain extent, and now there is nothing for them to do. I have not made them redundant however; I am merely fattening them up for the slaughter, as it were, waiting for next January.
>
> When the instructions come to make the cut-backs, I will sack them at once, but until January let them live here off the fat of the land, getting their salaries and doing nothing. I am wasting a lot of money that I could have saved by sacking them now, but that would not impress my superiors come January. And so I bide my time till then, knowing that during the first week of January there will be a long article about me in the paper, saying how progressive I am, an example to all those irresponsible people in management who avoid cutting back on their workforce.

But why, to return to the Tadjik garage, is a Soviet director not ashamed to refuse his workers even the miserable wages that are their due? Because there is an unvoiced agreement that the director will not take issue with the workers over the fact that they spend the greater part of their working day working 'on the side' so as to earn more money. There are not enough lorries for hire to the public in the country, and if you need a lorry to transport furniture, or make the move in spring out to your little house in the country, then this is almost the only way to do it. The drivers of state lorries turn this fact to their advantage and charge high rates (100–200 rubles) for their services in such things. And so they are 'forced' to buy petrol with their own money, so as to carry on their business. The director, on the other hand, needs to show that he has saved on petrol; this is considered very important and something for which the director will receive a bonus in rubles. And so each side can both have its cake and eat it. The author of this article points out that over the year it was estimated that the garage had saved 10.3 per cent in petrol and adds sarcastically: 'It's a pity that we do not know exactly who is profiting.'

The same article also revealed that drivers buy the majority of their spare-parts themselves, which proves that they are using the state's vehicles for their own ends if they are prepared to share in the running costs.

For a long time there were eight taxi-garages in Moscow, but the largest and most dependable was the so-called 'Garage No. 9', that is to say the row of cars parked on Pushkin Square whose 'owners' (ministers, the heads of national organisations and others whose responsible posts carried with them a personal car and chauffeur provided by the state) allowed their chauffeurs to make money on the side, and in return for this favour the chauffeurs were ready to serve their masters and the latters' families outside their official working hours, and never to run out of petrol although this was rationed out by the state in accordance with the rank of the 'owner'. A high-ranking official from a national organisation has the right to a twenty-four hour service, that is to say his chauffeur is on duty all round the clock outside his house; an official in one of the Soviet republics has the right to 'two-shift service', that is, sixteen hours a day; and a local official has his car for eight hours. All of them are well aware that their chauffeur receives a minimal wage, that if the car breaks down and is repaired through the official channels the garage will take a long time to mend it, doing it badly, so that it is better if the chauffeur sees to his own repairs. And so they come to some agreement.

Women often have problems finding a job. There are employers who regard it as a grave disadvantage if a woman is married, since there is always the threat that she will leave her work for a few months (since we are all human) to have a baby, putting her own interests before those of her place of work. This independent behaviour on her part robs the organisation of one of its slaves for four months, two of which have to be paid before she has the baby and then another two afterwards, following which she has the right to a whole year of unpaid leave. If she returns to work when she is still breast-feeding, she is entitled to extra time-off every day to go and feed the baby; and if it is ill, she can stay off work until it is recovered. When the child is a bit older, she comes up against the problem of waiting lists for creches and kindergartens, which leads to absenteeism amongst women; and when at last her turn comes and her child enters one of these pre-school organisations, it will be ill even more often, since colds and stomach upsets spread quickly among the children, and as often as not the mothers are at home with them. True, a woman who has to stay off work in order to look after a sick child is paid for only three days, and if her child is irresponsible enough to be sick for longer, all the mother receives is a doctor's certificate saying that she had to look after a child and has no grandparents at home to do it for her. This certificate gives her the right to miss work, but does not give her anything to live on.

Not only are the problems that face women in the USSR not exaggerated here, but the truth of these claims and the widespread violation of women's right to work are further proved by the fact that a law exists making it a criminal offence for the management of any organisation to refuse work to a woman.

On paper, women are allowed to work a shortened working-day and be paid only for the hours which they have worked. In practice, this is very rare and happens only in offices (never in factories), mostly those where the wives of the elite work.

I was consulted by a woman with three small children, all handicapped from birth with partial paralysis of the limbs. Their father was an engineer and earned 200 rubles a month; their mother was also an engineer, working in the Planning and Technology Department of our organisation, and earned another 200 rubles a month. They could live on that money, but they could not afford someone to help in the home, besides which it would be almost impossible to find someone willing to take on so much work at once. Anna Izrailovna was therefore requesting permission to work a four-hour day and earn 100 rubles a month.

The director did not, however, give his permission. He expressed his sympathy for the poor woman, but asked her to understand his point of view as well. For there were 800 engineers working in the department, and at least half of them were women. 'And so,' answered the director, 'you must understand that if I allow you to shorten your working-day, hundreds of other women will want to follow suit, and then we will have to close the department.' In his way, he was right: although, of course, other women could not possibly be in such a hopeless position as Anna Izrailovna, each of them could produce enough good reasons to earn them the right to a shortened working-day.

The extraordinary thing was, however, that there actually was one woman who worked a shortened working-day in that department, then went home at 12 o'clock. She was brought to work in the personal car of the head of the whole organisation and, at lunch-time, it returned to take her home. She was the wife of the head of the whole organisation.

The director was not afraid to allow her to work a shortened working-day, for he knew that none of her colleagues would ever ask why she, the wife of the boss, should be allowed a privilege denied to the rest. All 400 women in the department were well-acquainted with the fact that one law applied to the elite, another to the rest. And so they worked like cattle, these emancipated women, one shift at work and another at home afterwards.

I advised Anna Izrailovna to write a personal letter to the head of the organisation in the hope that in view of all this his conscience would not allow him to refuse this poor woman her perfectly legal request – but it was rejected.

I would like to draw my readers' attention to another aspect of the life of working women in the USSR.

If you look down the lists of deputies elected to the local Soviets, those of the various republics and the Supreme Soviet of the USSR, you will see that there is full equality for women in Soviet politics. At least in all the state and political and social organisations where representatives of the working people are required to raise their hands together in unanimous votes, women are the equals of men.

But in the posts where a man can show his true mettle and demonstrate his ability to find the solution to problems, unite his fellows in creative work, that is be in charge of others, there is no room for women. Here are my proofs.

The building industry runs more than 100 factories, institutes, trusts and so on. Among those in charge of all of these there was not a single woman director of a factory, or woman chief engineer, except in a couple of unimportant little organisations. And that was not all. A woman, Anna Vassilievna Stroganova, had worked for many years as deputy head of the trust which supplied sand and gravel, serving it faithfully. A new head was appointed to her trust, a certain Nikolai Alexeyevich Korzhevsky, who had been relieved of the post of assistant head in another trust because of constant drunkenness at work. He continued the same tradition in the new post.

However, since the modest and conscientious Stroganova did not wish to keep him company, he fabricated a false accusation against her that she was misusing her position, claiming that she was selling sand and gravel to collective farms for the building of cowsheds (this is against the law in the Soviet Union, since both sand and gravel are in short supply for the building-materials organisation's own factories); and so the only female administrator in this enormous organisation was dismissed.

As chief legal consultant, not only did I refuse to sign the order to dismiss Stroganova, but I wrote a detailed objection to the obviously false references in the order and to the accusations of guilt. The Director, however, not only signed the illegal order, but attacked me for obstructing his attempts to reform the senior management. For eight months, Stroganova haunted the offices of his superiors until at last she was admitted to see the head of the Party Control Committee of the USSR, the highest controlling organisation in the land. Stroganova was lucky, her dismissal was recognised as illegal and her former employers ordered to change the formula by which she had been dismissed and pay her two months' salary (in fact, she had not worked for eight months). But that was all. No, there is a little more to tell. In another few months, Korzhevsky had drunk himself to such a state that his drinking companions in the organisation could no longer see any way of allowing their friend to retain his post and they felt obliged to demote him to deputy director of a large reinforced-concrete factory.

Stroganova had been without work for eight months. Nobody would take her on with a dishonourable discharge to her credit and, of course, there was no unemployment pay for her and her children. She went hungry and sold everything she had while having to listen every day to propaganda from the ideologists about full employment in the USSR.

Theoretically, the 'law' is a help to people in sorting out life's problems. Soviet law claims to be particularly concerned about the working man. But how does this work out in fact?

Igor Svetlov was a young man of twenty-six with tuberculosis, married, supporting two small children who also coughed (they must have inherited it), and aged parents. I first met him in the part of the Butyrskaya Prison set aside for those whose cases are under investigation. I did not know what I was going to do with poor Igor, who was threatened with fifteen years of prison or more, but who asserted his innocence and offered a seemingly ridiculous version of the facts to counter the investigating magistrates.

On his way home on his last night of freedom, Igor was seized in a dark doorway (the authorities were evidently saving on electricity) and dragged home, or rather to his little shed in the courtyard of the house.

There, by the light of police torches, Igor was shown the warrant for a search and his arrest.

They searched the shed, and then the little room, three metres by three metres, where five people, grown-ups and children, lived together with a sufferer from tuberculosis, and discovered fifty sets of parts for sewing machines from the factory in Podolsk, the largest sewing-machine factory in the Soviet Union and maybe in the whole world.

The parts were carefully recorded in the transcription of the questioning, which went on until the morning. Towards morning, the police took Igor off to prison without even letting him go over to the children's beds to take a last look at them, and when the heartbroken parents tried to kiss their son goodbye they were rudely shoved aside and Igor pushed out into the corridor. And after this, professors of law will still continue to declare in their lecture-halls and at their international congresses that only in the socialist countries is a man really innocent until he is proved to be guilty.

This is, of course, a mirage. Sentence had been passed right at the moment when some half-illiterate policeman wrote out the warrant for his arrest and the search. The car carrying Igor was waved through all the red lights, since it carried an important criminal who might be the subject of a rescue attempt by his accomplices . . .

In the morning, the investigating magistrate inquired after Igor's health and then showed him the account of the search and a list of 200 peasants from various villages in Azerbaijan who had testified that at various times over the past three years they had visited Igor in Moscow, having been given his name by other people from the same village, and had bought sewing machines from him at the market price.

'There's no point in denying it,' said the investigating magistrate. 'You have been caught red-handed; tell us everything, name all your accomplices, and especially those members of the factory management who incited you to commit this crime, and you will be free to leave the prison at once. Because of your illness you will receive a suspended, sentence, but we need you because through you we can get the bigger fish.'

Igor shrugged and said that he did not understand why he was being accused of stealing sewing-machine parts that he had not stolen, but had picked up on the factory rubbish dump outside Podolsk. Every day the factory's lorries dumped the rubbish from the various shops in that spot, and many workers collected the parts that had been thrown out as rejects, put them right on primitive home-made lathes, then built them into machines and sold them to farm-workers.

The magistrate opened the criminal code and showed Igor the article stating that for making a confession and helping in the investigation a prisoner could earn himself the right to a reduced sentence.

'You must understand, Igor, that it's not you we're interested in. Help us to catch the director of the factory, his deputy for commerce, or the chief engineer. Just think of your parents and your children. Remember that you're a sick man – you'll be rotting in prison while they spend their weekends in the country cottages they've built by cheating the state. Give us evidence on how the thefts were accomplished, who drew you into this crime, and then you can go home. If you don't believe me, here's the order for your release signed by the Public Prosecutor. If you'll give evidence, you'll go home; if you don't, I'll tear it up before your eyes.'

Igor sat silent, then rose and said: 'Tear up your dirty little paper.'

Igor's fate could have been decided by an experimental investigation, if an investigating magistrate went out to the rubbish dump with him for him to demonstrate his innocence *in situ*; the testimony of an expert witness, saying that the parts from which Igor made machines were rejects which had to be finished by home-made methods, would have supported his version of the facts. But both the magistrate and the court rejected these moves by the defence as merely playing for time.

I decided upon a desperate measure. I asked Igor's friends, also sewing-machine mechanics, to go out to the rubbish dump, find the parts to build as many sewing machines as possible, write an official report on what they had done, sign it, and bring the machines to the court room with the report· and a written request that the court call them as witnesses. This action on my part was quite illegal from the point of view of the brief of a Soviet lawyer. Not that I was acting criminally, but I could have been banned from my profession, since a lawyer does not have the right to carry out any investigations of his own. He is the man who stands before the court in supplication, whose only right is the right to beg. But I was convinced of Igor's innocence, since long before the trial I had visited the dump myself and seen with my own eyes how many parts lay rusting under the open sky. I was only sorry that Igor was not by my side to put a machine together on the spot for my wife, who longed for one even more than I longed for a car.

During the recess, I told the judge and the prosecutor of the expedition I had organised, said that it had been a success and that there were now witnesses asking to be questioned and to show the court the machines they had built. I had no desire to make such an unusual request, which must shock the judge and the prosecutor, without first warning them. They asked me politely to leave the judge's room, where the prosecutor remained behind with the judge. When the court reconvened, the judge announced that the court, with the lawyers and the accused, would go out to the scene of the crime, that is to the dump, to view it for themselves. The expert witnesses and the witnesses who had just arrived with their sewing machines were also invited, and the next day this solemn procession duly made its way out to the dump.

That was many, many years ago. That dump has probably been replaced with the high-rise dwellings of Greater Podolsk, but that morning – it was one of the few happy days of my career as a lawyer – all of us who took part in this extraordinary court-sitting were faced with an astonishing spectacle. Over an enormous area lay little hills of rubbish, yellow metal-shavings, oily rags, all sorts of rubbish like bits of the boxes in which the bolts were delivered, nuts, odd pieces of machine and, here and there in the sunlight, glittered thousands of sewing-machine parts of all shapes and sizes. In places they were in little heaps, as though they had been thrown down like that on purpose to impress us.

The judge and prosecutor had also thought of that, and a policeman was sent by car to the factory to check that the parts had not been brought out specially to coincide with the arrival of the court; but no, the factory gave us an officially-signed document stating that this was not so and that for more than a month there had been a ban on dumping rejects from the shops out here. A special place had been prepared inside the factory gates, where the rubbish was sorted and parts returned to the factory stores to be melted down again as scrap metal. This was an unexpected victory, since it meant extra confirmation from the factory that parts used to be dumped and that this was not merely something Igor had invented.

Igor's parents, who were present, were weeping with happiness and already imagining the welcome they would give when their poor son returned.

The court's investigation was soon over. For some reason, in his summing up the prosecutor spoke at length of the fact that socialist property is holy and inviolate, and that anyone who attempts to steal it is an enemy of the Soviet people; I could not understand why he spoke thus, when by now it was quite clear that the defendant was no thief, but a hard-working man who, unable to earn enough to feed his family, was forced to pick over a rubbish dump, all the year round, to supplement his income. And all this while I could not put out of my mind the fact that the prosecutor who was speaking had seen for himself, along with the rest of us, the story that the dump had to tell . . .

'And so,' he finished, 'in the name of the Soviet state and the Soviet people, I ask that you should condemn Igor Svetlov to fifteen years of hard labour in a camp. It is no secret,' he went on, 'that if the defendant had wished to reform, told us who were his accomplices and admitted his guilt, we could have considered requesting a less extreme penalty, but as the great writer Maxim Gorky tells us, "If the enemy does not surrender, he must be destroyed".'

There is no need to repeat the line taken by the defence, since the court ignored it. It was clear to all those present at the trial (and there were more than a thousand of them, since this was a show-trial held in the hall of the factory's social club 'as a warning to the rest') that the defendant was an arbitrary victim of the investigative procedure who had been deprived of the right to a defence during the investigation, since the investigating magistrate had collected only negative evidence and was not interested in getting to the truth. The summing-up for the defence was greeted with wild applause, and that of the prosecutor with cries of 'Shame!' and 'Building a career, are you?' The judge was distraught, shouting at the public that they were not in a theatre and threatening to have them all ejected from the court room and arrested as hooligans.

The sentence passed was fifteen years in a hard-labour camp and the confiscation of all Svetlov's property.

A few moments previously the hall had been full of noisy reaction to the events taking place, cries of protest and even personal insults for the prosecutor, a storm of applause after the summing-up by the defence and the last words of the defendant, who thanked the court for the care with which it had heard his case and for making the journey out to the rubbish dump dispelling all doubt; now there was dead silence when the judge pronounced his sentence of fifteen years' imprisonment, that is to say, fifteen years of dying, slowly but surely, for a man who could hardly last fifteen years even in freedom with the state of his lungs. The silence was total: not a word of protest, not even a glance of contempt towards those who had trampled upon the life of a young man and upon justice itself.

The sentence stated that the defendant Igor Svetlov, together with unidentified accomplices, had stolen parts for sewing machines from the state sewing-machine factory in Podolsk, with the intention of undermining the economic might of the Soviet state.

During the appeal, the defending advocate will say that the law requires a sentence to state what crime the defendant was supposed to have committed and then furnish proof that the crime had been committed and an account of the way in which it was committed, and give a list of those who had taken part. To state only that the defendant had committed theft 'with unidentified accomplices' was admission that the sentence was based not upon proofs, but upon suppositions, that is, that this sentence was illegal.

The court of appeal and all the other organisations and government departments to which lawyer, defendant and his relatives will apply for this miscarriage of justice to be rectified will furnish a stereotyped reply that the sentence was correct and tallied with the evidence presented, so that the complaint is unjustified and will not be taken up.

The collective agreements which are signed by the union organisations on behalf of the workers and the management of the factory have long since become mere bundles of paper, forgotten by both sides, neither of whom checks to see that they are being observed unless they receive the command from above to do so. In fact, they are not even agreements, since the idea of an agreement is that it is an expression of the free will of either side. Here there is only one 'side', the Five-Year Plan all-foreseeing and all-regulating, which gives neither side the right to depart from its rigid rulings.

The so-called 'collective agreement' lists the requirements of the Plan: the amount to be produced, usually an inflated and unrealistic figure, the growth in productivity, also inflated and unrelated to any organisational or technological streamlining, capital investment in improvements to the standard of living and the cultural life of the workers. This includes canteens, social clubs, pre-school organisations like creches and kindergartens, public baths, laundries specialising in overalls, and so on.

Even here, however, official disregard for the needs of the workers makes itself felt. Building in this last category is considered to be of only secondary importance and usually takes much longer than planned; and when finished, all the services they offer, so important in the every-day lives of the workers, are usually highly unsatisfactory.

Considering the constant shortages of foodstuffs throughout the country and especially in the provinces, factory canteens are especially important. Often it is quite impossible for the worker to bring his food from home, though he will be away for a minimum of ten hours – that is, if he is not forced to work overtime. This is why it is very important that the workers should be able to eat in a canteen during their lunch break, both for the workers themselves, and for the employer, for a hungry worker is never very productive.

Let us hear what one of the most important union leaders in the country, Viktorov, Secretary of the All-Union Central Council of Trade Unions, has to say on this count. The following quotations are taken from his article 'The Workers' Canteen', published in *Trud* on 5 June 1979:

'The past three years in the tenth Five-Year Plan (1976–8) have seen the building of workers' canteens with seating for 816,000 people.' A very impressive figure. But if we divide this figure into the 130 million industrial workers, we end up with only one place per 130 workers, or 8 places per 1300 workers. What now impresses us is the *paucity* of provision. And these few canteens have taken three years to build . . .

'The number of industrial and office workers who use the canteens,' boasts Viktorov, 'grew from 49 million in 1975 to 60 million in 1978.' What this figure proves, first and foremost, is that even now not all the workers use the canteens, not because they prefer to patronise the elegant restaurants in hotels, but because they do not have a canteen or, if they do have one, it is open for only a few hours a day and closed at night, although some of the workers work a night-shift. From these figures we can see that up until 1975 it was only every third worker who ate in a canteen, and that now the figure has risen to one out of two.

'By the end of this Five-Year Plan, that is by 1980,' writes Viktorov, 'another 500,000 places will have been built.' That means another half-place for every 130 workers. Not too good! In practice, not more but fewer canteens are being built with every passing year.

The disregard for the workers' needs which we noted earlier is confirmed in this same article.

'This year the various ministries built 57,000 fewer canteen-places than was planned; some of them, Ministries responsible for the paper industry, for ship-building, for heavy industry and for oil built only between 30 and 60 per cent of the canteens that had been planned.'

Let the reader note which important Ministries could not complete the insignificant amount of building that goes into a few canteens. Building a canteen is far easier than building a car factory. But even so, tens of thousands of metal-workers, oil-riggers, ship-builders and pulp-workers will not be able to have a meal during their working-day. Many of these are doing a dangerous job in an unpleasant climate.

Viktorov also admits that there are queues in the workers' canteens. 'How unpleasant for them,' he complains, 'to spend so much time in the canteen queue, being put in a bad humour for the rest of the day, wasting the lunch break and sometimes their working time as well. In order to serve meals more quickly we need more serving hatches, but the Food Ministry planned only 10,000 hatches for this Five-Year Plan, while we need at least 30,000.' From this we can work out that in about another fifteen years, workers can hope to be served their lunch without a queue.

Viktorov is likewise unsatisfied with the quality of the food.

'A survey by the Council of Ministers' Central Bureau of Statistics established that 52 per cent of the workers questioned and criticised the quality of the food, and called it monotonous.' Viktorov's findings are not out-of-date, for they still continue to be quoted. 'We find incorrect preparation and serving of the food . . .' Viktorov is too polite to say what he means. It would have been more correct to state that those who work in the canteen steal from the workers by not using the ingredients in full measure and giving out portions that are far too small.

But a report by some ordinary workers, who carried out a lightning inspection of the canteens at the Kemerovo mines, showed Viktorov how he should have put it. The results of their inspection are also quoted in the *Trud* article.

Three union committees from the chemical and oil industries in the Kemerovo region, together with workers from the State Retail Organisation, passed a resolution last year to liquidate the faults in their workers' canteens. The first lightning inspection was carried out at the 'Carbolit' factory and demonstrated that 'over nine portions of beetroot salad with sour cream, the average loss was 155 grammes per kilogram. Portions of cottage cheese with sour cream and sugar and other dishes were also underweight. The dishes purchased and the amount on the bill did not tally' (that is, they had simply been overcharged). A second inspection was carried out by the same team and showed that seven portions of cottage cheese were 105 grammes underweight. The complaints-and-suggestions book contained a collectively-written complaint: 'We have asked the management several times to look into the way the workers are being fed, with meat soups containing no meat and vegetables that have started to go off, or slices of sausage and cold macaroni for the main course. And no choice: no salads, no sour cream or puddings . . . ' Their third inspection revealed cottage cheese that smelled sour and had a hard yellow crust. For several of the dishes there was no way of finding out how much they ought to weigh, since they were not included in the menu. At another factory, 'Khimprom', they established that on some nights, by no means regularly, there was a buffet on wheels, but it did not have time to do the rounds of all the shops. It served only cold main courses, since there was no equipment for keeping them warm. In size and equipment, the 'Khimprom' canteens did not satisfy the sanitary regulations. The following fact shows how seriously the administration took its duty of feeding the workers: at the end of last summer, the canteen took delivery of an essential cold-storage system, but the factory did not take the trouble to install it until the deputy director was threatened with a fine.

In the 'AZOT' organisation, there is nowhere to eat between 11 p.m. and morning. The workers have to send someone on foot with a saucepan to bring back hot food, either from the central distribution point or the canteen at the nearby Novokemerovo Power Station. 'And what does Y. Tusyuk, chairman of the organisation's union committee, make of that?' asks the article:

> He has a ready answer: between the hours of 11 p.m. and morning, he claims, the chemical workers do not need to eat and anyway they could not, since they are not allowed to stop working: as for the doctors' recommendations that the workers should be fed at night because of the harmful nature of their work with chemicals, he feels that this is pure invention (*Trud*, 3 July 1979)

The reader will note that neither in Viktorov's article nor in the inspection-teams' reports is there any mention of the employer's duties as defined in the collective agreement or of his responsibility, moral, administrative and even monetary, for not fulfilling the promises he makes to provide suitable working conditions, especially important in factories where the work can be harmful or dangerous.

We can see in other spheres, too, how useless these collective agreements always are.

Let us take the question of organising the workers' leisure.

This question seems to interest the party organisations much more than the other services provided for the convenience of the workers. Leisure is tied up with ideological questions including the fight against alcoholism, atheist propaganda, the struggle with hangovers from capitalist attitudes (this ridiculous formula has now become something of an embarrassment and has been replaced by a new one, 'hangovers from the past'), the inculcation of patriotic fervour and loyalty to the party cause.

However, all this political effort to educate the masses is carried out so uninspiredly that no-one takes it seriously, as we see from the state's attitude to the work of cultural centres, the so-called 'Palaces of Culture', factory clubs and so on.

I have before me an article from *Trud* about the state of these palaces of culture and clubs and, by inference, about leisure provisions in general in one of the USSR's largest coal-mining areas.

The authors inform us that a few thousand people live in Shakhtyorsky Novodruzhesk. The little town has the club run by the

Novodruzhesk Mine, and no other leisure provisions at all. No cinema, no concert hall and the only club is falling apart.

In winter, the temperature indoors falls below zero (and that in a mining town, producing first-class coal). The roof is leaking, the plaster has fallen off the ceiling, the mouldings are crumbling and the furniture is falling apart. There are almost no musical instruments left, and it has been in this state for over three years.

The same thing is happening to several other clubs in the region. When asked for help, Khomitsky, the head of the organisation, and Kretinin, chairman of the miners' union in the town, replied that they had more pressing problems on their hands . . . The heads of the relevant organisations have stood by and watched as Palaces of Culture and clubs all over the region, including Donetsk itself, are falling apart.

'The situation is most alarming,' conclude the authors of the article.

'The worst thing,' they add indignantly, 'is that nobody seems to care even now, after the publication of the Central Committee's resolution entitled 'On Improving Ideological and Political Education', which demanded that those in charge of the buildings and the union organisations should see that repairs are carried out on all existing clubs and palaces. 'Why are those responsible for the Pervomaisk Coalmine taking so long to start?' ask the authors dramatically. That is all the reproach they have for those who are presiding over the decay of the cultural life of this huge army of miners, robbing them of their cultural leisure activities and almost literally 'driving them to drink'. For that is the usual recourse of those who have nowhere to spend the free time of which they have so little. Outside each shop selling wine and vodka there is always a crowd of workers of all ages, including women, young boys, drunken old crones, hoarse old men who seem to live in a constant stupor, and young people only just starting to acquire the taste for spirits. Soon the crowd divides into groups of three, one of whom goes off to join the queue for the vodka, the second to seek an automatic soda-water dispenser in order to steal the glass, while the third tries to persuade the man selling vegetables from a booth on the corner to let him have a salted cucumber or an onion to go with the vodka. Then this cosy threesome is reunited under a nearby archway or in a dark doorway to start its cultural leisure-time activities. Each of the three, fired by an awareness of their collective responsibilities and a sense of fair play, marks off his third on the label and knocks it back unselfconsciously, usually straight from the bottle, since it is not always possible to steal a glass. If the expedition to the vegetable booth was successful, then each in turn can chase his share of the vodka down by biting off his third of the salted cucumber or the onion. Then, when the last drop has been drunk, the empty bottle remains with the one who had purchased the most 'shares' in this company, and the group evaporates like the morning dew, until the next meeting. That might be in a few minutes' time, or in a few hours, depending on how and where they get hold of the magic ruble that buys them the right to a drink. If there is no ruble to be had, the same effect can be produced with less capital outlay: twenty kopeks is enough. In that case, however, the group will make either for the chemist's dispensary or for the place where they sell methylated spirits.

The drinking circle will buy primus-stove fuel, or poison for the bedbugs and cockroaches that infest the communal flats, or the cheapest brand of eau-de-Cologne, as long as it is made of alcohol; and from this point onwards, the whole process is repeated, the archway or dark doorway and the quick slurp followed by the bite of onion or a sniff at the sleeve. (If there is no cucumber or onion, then the seasoned drinker, after he has spat to express his pleasure, will sniff at his sleeve instead of taking the traditional bite of something . . .) And then the fog settles in again . . .

Sometimes the price paid for this fog is fifteen years in prison, sometimes – and not all that rarely – it is the death penalty. Men who are so drunk that they have lost all control of themselves, oppressed by unfulfillable and inchoate desires and desperate for another drink, will commit crimes of theft and violence or even murder. Those who work in the courts and the prosecutor's office, in the police, the press, the radio and television never cease to affirm that the lion's share of crimes are committed by people under the influence of drink. They are constantly urging management and union leaders to improve the cultural facilities put at the disposal of the workers and build them clubs and palaces where they could spend their time in a civilised way over a cup of tea or a soft drink with something inexpensive to eat.

Now let us pass from the coal-country to the land of cotton and fruit, Tadjikistan, and lend an ear to A. Nedachinov, deputy chief of the crime-prevention section in the Criminal Investigation Department of Tadjikistan's Ministry of Internal Affairs.

In his article 'Why Give in to the Absenteeism?', published in *Trud* on 5 June 1979, he writes:

According to the statistics of the Leninabad Police Department, last year in the space of only twelve months workers from the Leninabad Tinned-Fruit Factory committed 87 crimes of various kinds. Thirty-five workers were found drunk on the streets and taken in to be sobered up. For the sake of comparison, in the previous year, 1977, there were only 17 such cases. The number of arrests for small-scale hooliganism and for theft also rose.

Taken altogether, 1978 saw a rise of over 50 per cent in crimes committed by workers from the factory. The same pattern can be observed in the other factory run by the same organisation, and last year there were more than 200 workers who committed some offence connected with their work, i.e. one in every six workers. The loss of working days for this period was almost three thousand man-days, and from this cause alone the organisation lost 130,000 rubles' worth of revenue through work left undone. Here are some of the typical absentees: Orinov, a workman who was absent for six working days in January alone; Eshmatova, absent three times; Abdulayev, four times.

Many other authors, in newspaper articles and other publications, admit that at least 20 per cent of the workforce indulges in absenteeism, which means that every day millions of Soviet workers simply do not turn up for work as though, for all practical purposes, they were on strike. It cannot be that they are absent because their monthly wage is usually too high for them. It cannot be that they are simply lazy. These absentees are people who cannot stand their work and would rather stay at home any day, either working somewhere on the side or else drinking themselves into a stupor.

Those for whom one feels sorriest are those Soviet citizens condemned to a slavery made legal by the state: the soldiers of the Red Army, who are sent by their commanding officers under military discipline and the threat of a court-martial to work in the factories. In return for their free labour, the factories supply army units with their products.

There were many soldiers working in our building-materials organisation, and in return for their labour our factories supplied reinforced concrete and bricks to the army units stationed near Moscow.

How many times have I visited a factory and seen sad-eyed young lads in dirty soldiers' overalls working in the worst and most dangerous jobs in the factory? They lived under the constant threat of criminal or military proceedings against them for any violation of military discipline in this civilian factory.

However, their slavery does not last long.

There is another, much larger group of people who are sentenced to slavery for an unlimited period, those who are hoping for a residence-permit. They are ordinary Soviet citizens who enjoy the right to work and to freedom, but not the right to live in Moscow, the dream of many. The representatives of an organisation called the 'Organised Selection of the Work-Force', that is recruiters of cheap labour, sign contracts with those who wish to work for a year in a Moscow factory, but only as unskilled labour, not for any other posts. Teachers, dispensers, librarians, accountants set off to work in Moscow, to the envy of their fellow-villagers. These fortunate few will live in Moscow, eat sausage and go to the theatre. To be completely happy, however, young people need love, a family, children and a home, but these are forbidden: this category worker has only a temporary residence-permit and has to live in a hostel.

My help was sought by a man who had been working like this for over five years in Moscow. His name was Sidorov, and he told me that he had hidden from the examiners the fact that his residence-permit was only temporary and had passed the entrance examination for the Bauman Institute. After five years of combining a full programme of study with his job, he had just graduated. 'Now,' he complained, 'I am not being allowed to work as an engineer, but am being forced to remain a porter or to leave Moscow.'

The head of the Personnel Department where he worked had flatly refused to allow him to work in a job for which he was trained.

Such is the fate of these people, and nobody can do anything to help them.

At the same time, there is an element of slavery in the life not only of the residence-permit seekers and of the soldiers who spend their military service in a factory, but also of every worker in the country.

Those who leave a job on their own volition are punished through the loss of the uninterrupted stretch of working years that is necessary in order to be eligible for sick-pay.

If, in the space of one year, you have twice left jobs on your own volition, or have been sacked for breaking the rules, then you are stripped of your right to choose your job for yourself and are forced to take the job designated by a special committee in the local executive, usually an unpleasant and difficult job that is likely to be miles from where you live. Often it is a job that has nothing to do with your qualifications.

If you have been educated at a university, institute or technical school you have to work a given number of years in a job chosen by a special committee that not only takes no account of your own wishes, but actually goes against them. Husbands and wives are separated, as are parents and children.

Here we see the essence of that inhumanity which penetrates the economic and political life of Soviet society.

8 Welfare and Social Security

Alastair McAuley

In the USSR, as in other industrial economies, families derive benefits from the state's social security system; the state also provides a range of goods and services either free of charge or at subsidised prices. Soviet economists and statisticians refer to expenditures for these purposes as social consumption; one might also refer to them as the Soviet welfare state or, from a different point of view, as the social wage. It is the purpose of this chapter to describe the main features of the Soviet welfare state, to outline its major programmes, identify their beneficiaries and assess the contribution that they make to the wider goals of Soviet policy. Section 1, therefore, deals with Soviet attitudes towards welfare and inequality, Section 2 describes the composition of Soviet social consumption and its sources of finance. Sections 3 and 4 examine individual programmes in an attempt to assess their impact. The chapter ends with a brief assessment of the achievements and shortcomings of the Soviet system.

1. SOVIET ATTITUDES TO WELFARE AND EQUALITY

For most people in the West, communism is associated with distribution according to need; it implies a concern on the part of the state for the well-being of individual members of society and an official commitment to equality. This, in turn, is thought to involve the development of an extensive welfare system based on egalitarian principles. And, in this respect, few people distinguish between communism and socialism. In Soviet official ideology, however, this distinction is of crucial importance. Communism is certainly the long-term objective of the Soviet authorities but, at present, the USSR has only reached the socialist stage of development. In consequence, rather than being guided by communist principles, both incomes policies and the Soviet welfare state embody those of socialism. To see what this entails in practical terms, one must turn to the Soviet exegesis of these Marxist categories.

Communism requires two conditions for its realisation: it requires an abundance of material goods and the development of new attitudes to work and leisure or, in Marx's own words, it presupposes that '. . . labour, from being a mere means of life, has become the prime necessity of life'. Without these preconditions, any attempt to adopt communist distribution principles is bound to fail – and that failure will lead to social and economic disruption. Socialism, on the other hand, is characterised by a relative scarcity of material goods and by social attitudes according to which people work to live rather than live to work; that is, incentives and economic coercion are still needed to elicit the necessary supply of labour. In such circumstances, income distribution and welfare policies should be formulated on socialist principles. These are usually paraphrased in the USSR as: from each according to his ability, to each according to his labour. This meritocratic conception of socialism not only determines the official Soviet approach to earnings differentials and inequality, it also affects the terms and conditions on which income-support programmes are made available to Soviet citizens and the range of non-cash services provided. Let us consider each of these issues in turn.

As far as earnings differentials are concerned, Soviet economists start from the proposition that, under socialism as under capitalism, individuals are unequal: they are unequal in their capacity for work, in their skills and abilities, in their needs, tastes and preferences, and they should be unequal in their incomes. The sole gain from the revolution (but, they would argue, it is a crucial one) is that the elimination of private ownership of the means of production, and hence of exploitation, imposes upon all an equal obligation to work, to be judged by their work. All are agreed that there should be earnings differentials, that those in positions of responsibility should receive more:

> It is possible to guarantee the participation of the majority in work only if the possibility of receiving a share of society's output is made conditional upon undertaking socially useful labour and if the size of this share depends upon the importance of the contribution made. (Maier, 1968, p. 19)

While there is some disagreement about the size of differentials that are appropriate at any given point in time, a substantial majority of both academic economists and official spokesmen agree in condemning egalitarianism:

> [Socialist] forms of payment for labour are in no case compatible with egalitarianism. All such tendencies are harmful, in conflict with the rapid development of productive forces and the creation of conditions necessary for the continuing growth of workers' welfare. Egalitarianism undermines material incentives and, in the last analysis, causes irreparable harm to the building of communism. (Kulikov, 1972, p. 58)

Two further points are frequently made. First, economists are at pains to point out that the authorities have little autonomy in deciding upon the size of differentials. Basing themselves on the Marxist doctrine of the reducibility of labour, Soviet economists have recently asserted that wage relativities are objectively determined, that they must correspond to the structure of skills found in the labour force. Consequently, attempts to reduce inequality prematurely, however well-intentioned, are misguided; they can only result in economic disruption. Second, many economists have quoted Lenin's strictures against attempts to use wages to achieve welfare ends. As two authors put it recently, '. . . all that bears the stamp of social security, that is not connected with production, should be separated from wages'. (Rabkina and Rimashevskaya, 1972, p. 26)

Thus, one may paraphrase official Soviet attitudes towards earnings differentials and equality as follows. Both equity and efficiency considerations require that in a socialist society reward should be commensurate with effort and status. Attempts to introduce an egalitarian structure of earnings or to use the wage and salary system for welfare purposes, even if successful in the short run, will result in the dislocation of the labour market, high labour turnover, bottle-necks and a collapse of labour discipline. They will adversely affect economic growth and consequently defer the attainment of communism.

In the 1940s and 1950s, it was often claimed in the Soviet Union that expenditures from the state's social consumption funds were governed by the communist distribution principle. Consequently, it was argued that, with continued economic growth, with an ever closer approach to the preconditions for communism, the sphere of free distribution would increase indefinitely. Such a view is embodied in the 1961 Party Programme. In the 1960s and 1970s, however, this argument has been extensively criticised; in its place it has been asserted that socialism and the socialist principle of distribution imply the provision of a limited range of specific programmes that have as their aim the modification of patterns of consumption in the interests of continued economic development. These recent views have been restricted to the state's provision of goods and services (as I show below, transfer payments had already been brought within the ambit of the socialist distribution principle) but, in general terms, it can be asserted that they have had the effect of replacing a commitment to equality with the more limited goal of equality of opportunity.

Starting from the proposition that under socialism individuals are unequal in their abilities and capacity for work, a number of economists have pointed out that, if distribution according to labour were the sole form of distribution in the USSR, this inequality would be perpetuated. Those with higher incomes would secure for themselves and their dependants a lion's share of available resources. As a result, their children would be better educated, better able to secure for themselves positions of dominance in their turn. At the same time, the human potential of the labour force would remain underdeveloped. The children of the unskilled would be in no position to develop their own capacities. It has been pointed out, however, that such considerations as these only imply that the state should intervene in the income distribution process. They do not determine the form that that inter-vention should take. This follows from the proposition that individual tastes and preferences are conditioned by experience and that the latter is mediated, in general, by income. As a result:

> if the whole of the social consumption fund were distributed among members of society in cash and if consumption goods and services satisfying intellectual and social needs were paid for, the money allocated from social consumption funds for, let us say, the education of children or for physical culture and so on might be partially or wholly spent by consumers on the satisfaction of needs that they regarded as more important – on goods like clothing, footwear, food etc. (Rakitskii, 1967, p. 121)

Thus, it is recognised that planners' preferences and those of individuals may not coincide. If the former are to prevail, the state should provide a range of specific goods and services either free of charge or at subsidised prices.

This analysis of the functions of social consumption expenditure in a socialist society conflicts with the rather superficial views advanced in the 1950s. It implies a definite limit on the sphere of free distribution. This should be restricted to those goods and services that contribute to economic development. The purpose of such provision should be to 'ensure that all individuals enjoy a real possibility of acquiring the highest qualifications and, as a result, can conceivably occupy any position in production or in society' (Maier and Rakitskii, 1976, p. 192). Equality of educational (and, to a lesser extent, medical) opportunity will lead to reductions in the inequality of earnings and income in the long run through its effects on the distribution of skills. Equality of opportunity is also invoked as a mechanism to counter tendencies towards elitism and social exclusiveness (or what Western sociologists would call social stratification) that are still present in socialist society. But attempts to go beyond equality of opportunity, to introduce equality prematurely, can only undermine the primary objective of a socialist state – the building of communism.

Adherence to the socialist principle of distribution has also influenced the range of income-support programmes provided by the Soviet welfare state and has affected the terms and conditions on which citizens have had access to them. Some of the earliest legislation adopted by the Soviet government after the revolution was concerned with the establishment of a social security system and, it is claimed, during the 1920s entitlement was based on need. But the resources available for these purposes were meagre and cash transfers made little contribution to the budget of the average Soviet family. Social welfare continued to enjoy a low priority after the introduction of central planning, and at this time it came to be accepted that '. . . the principle of each according to his labour should operate in the field of social security as well' (Acharkan, 1974, p. 122). In practice, this had the result of making most cash benefits dependent on prior employment, of introducing the principle of earnings-relatedness for those who were entitled and of excluding substantial occupational groups from coverage by the state's social security system altogether. A greater priority for social welfare in the post-Stalin period has led to the commitment of more resources to income-support programmes in recent years. It has also led to the partial erosion of the three characteristics of the Soviet system set out above. But socialist principles still command widespread support among specialists; there is little open advocacy of what one may call the Beveridge principle, that the state's welfare system should act as a provider of last resort, should guarantee an income below which no one should fall. And the public assistance component of the Soviet welfare state is particularly underdeveloped.

The major cash-benefit programmes in the USSR, old-age pensions, disability pensions and sick-pay, all require prior employment as a condition of entitlement. The same is true of maternity benefits, although in recent years the link between previous employment and the size of these latter has been weakened. Only student stipends, child allowances and, since 1974, a family income supplement do not depend upon prior employment. And there is evidence to suggest that this last scheme was opposed for several years on the grounds that its introduction would undermine work incentives. (For more details, see McAuley, 1979, chapter 11.) There is no unemployment pay in the Soviet Union. Soviet spokesmen justify its absence by the lack of unemployment in their country. In fact, unemployment in the USSR, though modest by Western standards, does exist, and the absence of financial support in times of unemployment imposes a certain hardship on workers and their families. One or two economists have advocated the re-introduction of unemployment pay in the USSR but this suggestion has been resisted on the grounds that, since ample job-opportunities exist, the payment of unemployment relief would only encourage the work-shy, would enable them to live at the expense of the state.

The principle that benefits should be related to prior earnings was introduced into the Soviet social security system in the early 1920s. It is argued that benefits cannot exceed earnings while in employment without undermining work incentives and that the egalitarian principle of flat-rate payments therefore implies that benefits must be low. This undermines the ability of the social security system to reinforce the differentials built into the wage and salary system. Earnings-related benefits provide added incentives for individuals both to participate in the labour force and to acquire desirable skills. Court practice in the USSR has interpreted the principle that benefits cannot exceed earnings while in employment in a particularly rigid fashion with the result that substantial numbers of pensioners have been condemned to receiving the minimum pension. (Existing pensions have only partly been adjusted to take account of inflation and rising money incomes.) In the 1970s, the link between the value of benefits and prior earnings has been weakened by the introduction of fixed ruble supplements, for example for those pensioners with dependants, but the Soviet system is still characterised by substantial differentiation.

The Soviet system of social security, as it developed under Stalin, did not apply to collective farmers. These had to wait until 1965 for the introduction of an All-Union system of pensions and other benefits. Prior to that date, *kolkhozniki* were dependent upon the charity of relatives or their collective farms in times of need. Also, statistics on the numbers of pensioners seem to imply that entitlement regulations were applied in a rigid fashion; employment outside the scheme (for example in Tsarist industry) was not counted and, as a result, few people qualified for old-age pensions in the early years of Soviet power. But the passage of time and the extension of schemes has made the system more comprehensive.

The Soviet approach to income maintenance, then, has been based on a desire to encourage high levels of labour-force participation and to reinforce the work incentives built into the wage and salary system. Only reluctantly have the authorities responded to social need, for example by introducing the family income supplement. Whatever may have been the views of Lenin and his collaborators at the time of the October Revolution, the material presented here suggests that equality of incomes and distribution according to need are not among the short-term goals of the Soviet government. In earnings, in income-maintenance, in the provision of welfare services, the authorities are guided by meritocratic principles. This philosophy is not without its critics in the USSR, both among academics and the population at large, but it is my belief that it commands a substantial measure of support among those responsible for the formulation of policy.

2. SOCIAL CONSUMPTION: STRUCTURE AND FINANCE

The Soviet government devotes considerable resources to the provision of cash transfers and welfare services, and these have grown rapidly in the post-war period. These now make a significant contribution to average living standards. Post-war growth has been accompanied by changes in composition, with income-maintenance gaining at the expense of health and education. However, the terms and conditions on which income support is available probably make the Soviet social security system regressive in its impact (in the sense that the absolute value of benefits increases with the incomes of recipient households) and this characteristic will have been reinforced by the change in composition alluded to above. Methods of finance also probably contribute to the regressivity of the system, although it is difficult to be definite on this point.

There are various ways in which the scale and structure of welfare services in the Soviet Union might be measured. But in this chapter I have decided to rely almost entirely upon Soviet statistics. Since the Soviet approach to the definition and measurement of national income differs from that commonly adopted in the West, this has the disadvantage that some components not normally considered to be part of the welfare state will be included as social consumption and others may be excluded. For example, Soviet statisticians include holiday pay as part of social consumption whereas their Western counterparts would classify it as part of wages and salaries; on the other hand, Soviet statisticians exclude food subsidies while most Western statisticians would include them. The use of Soviet concepts has the advantage, however, that statistics are available with a minimum of interpolation and estimation.

Table 8.1 gives an idea of the size and structure of the Soviet welfare state. The figures given show that, in nominal terms, expenditure on social consumption has increased almost eightfold in the last two or three decades. If allowance is made for changes in the cost of living, the increase will be less; but since in the post-war period the USSR has not suffered as badly from inflation as the market economies of the West, this increase would still be sizeable. Over the period covered by the table, *per capita* expenditure grew at an average rate of 6.4 per cent per annum, or somewhat more slowly than national income. (This grew at an annual average rate of 7.8 per cent on official definitions.) Growth in social consumption expenditures was somewhat higher in the 1960s (7.5 per cent per annum) than in either the 1950s or the 1970s (5.8 per cent and 5.5 per cent per annum respectively). The more rapid growth in the 1960s is a reflection of the introduction of major new programmes during that decade as well as rising expenditure on existing programmes brought about by demographic evolution. The declining growth in the recent past in part reflects increased stringency occasioned by falling growth-rates.

Table 8.1 also shows that there has been a change in the structure of Soviet welfare expenditures since the end of the Stalin period. In general, income transfers have become more important while expenditure on goods and services has suffered a relative decline. The main beneficiary of this change has been pensions, whose relative share increased by nine percentage points between 1950 and 1977; the main loser has been education, whose relative share fell by about the same amount. In fact,

TABLE 8.1   *Social consumption expenditures: USSR, 1950–77 (%)*

	1950	1960	1970	1977
Total Expenditure (milliard rubles)	13.0	27.3	63.9	99.5
Pensions	18.5	26.0	25.4	27.2
Allowances	9.2	9.5	9.6	10.2
Stipends	3.8	2.2	2.0	2.3
Holiday pay[a]	13.1	11.7	14.2	13.6
Total cash transfers	44.6	49.4	51.2	53.3
Education	33.8	26.7	27.1	25.5
Medical care etc.	16.9	18.3	15.5	14.6
Social security	0.8	1.1	0.8	1.0
Housing subsidies	3.8	4.4	5.5	5.6
Expenditure per capita (rubles per year)	**72.8**	**128.5**	**264.4**	**384.3**

a. This is included as a welfare benefit according to Soviet conventions; in most countries, holiday pay is included in wages and salaries.

SOURCE   McAuley, 1979, p. 262; *NK SSSR*, 1977, p. 408.

two out of the three major non-cash components of social consumption showed a relative decline in the 1950–77 period; only housing subsidies have increased in relative importance.

The expenditures reported in Table 8.1 are financed from a variety of sources, the state budget, a social insurance fund and the funds of various organisations and institutions. The contribution that each of these has made for a number of years since 1960 is shown in Table 8.2. Unfortunately, I have been unable to locate figures for earlier years. The

TABLE 8.2   *The financing of social consumption: USSR, 1960–75 (%)*

	1960	1965	1970	1975
Total expenditure	100.0	100.0	100.0	100.0
Social insurance fund	26.4	25.4	26.6	29.1
Enterprises etc.	17.0	17.9	20.8	20.0
Kolkhozy	1.4	3.0	3.5	4.0
Trade unions etc.	1.5	1.5	1.7	1.6
State budget	53.7	52.4	47.4	45.3

SOURCE   McAuley, 1979, p. 264.

social insurance fund is derived from an ear-marked payroll tax (differentiated by sector) and is used to finance pensions and some allowances. These are also financed in part from general budgetary revenues. Enterprise funds are used to finance holiday pay and certain benefits in kind (for example, pre-school child care and certain medical services). The same is true for *kolkhoz* and trade union funds. Finally, the bulk of benefits in kind are paid for out of general budgetary revenues.

It is impossible to ascertain the incidence of the various levies used to finance Soviet welfare expenditures on the basis of published statistics and the topic has not been studied by Soviet economists. But general considerations suggest that the overall impact of the system may be regressive. For instance, insofar as variations in the rates of payroll tax are less than variations in average sectoral earnings, this tax is probably regressive. (That is, a disproportionate share of tax receipts comes from sectors in which average earnings are relatively low.) Further, since income-tax receipts form a relatively small part of total budgetary revenue and the turnover tax a rather large part, this component is also probably regressive in its incidence. Since these two components account for some three-quarters of the total, their impact is probably decisive. It should be pointed out, however, that the trend towards greater reliance on deductions from profits as a source of budgetary income in the 1960s has probably led to a reduction in regressivity in recent years.

So far, discussion has centred on the composition and finance of Soviet welfare programmes as a whole. But these are not the only questions of interest. In Table 8.3, an attempt is made to assess the contribution that social consumption expenditures make to the living standards of the average Soviet family. It contains estimates of the structure of personal and total income for collective farm and industrial worker families for the three years, 1940, 1965 and 1977. It is unfortunate that estimates of income structure for 1950 and 1960 do not appear to have been published.

Before turning to the lessons that can be drawn from the figures in the table, a few words of warning are in order about the limitations of the data it contains. First, it is as well to be clear that industrial workers and *kolkhozniki* do not make up the whole of Soviet society and it is problematical how far inferences based on the table can be generalised to the urban and rural populations as a whole. To be precise, I estimate that in 1950 these two groups accounted for about half of the occupied population (or two-thirds if one includes members of the families of *kolkhozniki* wholly engaged in private agriculture). Of these, two-thirds were employed in agriculture. The industrial labour force was surely smaller in 1940 than it was in 1950. Twenty years later, in 1970, *kolkhozniki* and industrial workers together made up about a third of the occupied population. At this date, there were three industrial workers for every two collective farmers. Thus, at best, the figures in the table refer to half the population, and this proportion has declined over the period covered by the table. In the early years, moreover, the income structure of *kolkhozniki* was probably more typical than that of industrial workers. More recently, the latter's structure should have come to predominate – although there is no guarantee that the structure of incomes accruing to groups excluded from the table parallels that of those included.

Second, the figures in Table 8.3 have been derived from the Soviet family budget survey. In the 1960s, the sample-selection procedures used in this programme were criticised by Soviet economists for yielding biased samples. It is believed that some, if not all, of these shortcomings have been overcome in recent years, but doubt must remain about the representativeness of the data referring to the first two years listed. For all their limitations, these estimates are the best published by the Soviet authorities; what do they show about the contribution of the Soviet welfare system to rural and urban living standards?

Before the Second World War, cash transfers made only a small contribution to the budget of the average industrial worker family. They yielded only half as much income as private (largely agricultural) activity did and were on a par with receipts from bank interest and so forth. Since industrial workers were among the better-paid sections of the urban population and since cash transfers tend to increase with income, it is to be supposed that the contribution that this source made to the budgets of the rest of the urban population was less than that for industrial workers. By the end of the Khrushchev period, however, the relative importance of cash transfers in the industrial worker's budget had doubled. At the same time, there had been a marked decrease in the average family's reliance on sources of income other than wages. Neither private activity nor receipts from the financial system made any substantial contribution to the family budget. In spite of continued increase in the absolute value of cash transfers under Brezhnev, no further significant change in the structure of family income has occurred in the past fifteen years or so. Again, one presumes that cash transfers form a more significant part of the budget of industrial workers than that of other sections of the urban population.

In view of the recent preoccupation among Western economists with the importance of the so-called second economy to the living standards of Soviet families (prompted by the accounts of recent emigres), the figures in Table 8.3 may give rise to a certain scepticism. There seems to be no allowance made in them for substantial earnings from unofficial or illegal activity. Perhaps the respondents to the budget survey failed to report income from these sources; perhaps statisticians have classified such earnings as wages; perhaps recent emigres are mistaken about the significance of the second economy. There is not enough information to decide which of these explanations is the most plausible.

Before the Second World War, *kolkhozniki* in the Soviet Union were dependent on their private plots for half their incomes. Work for the state or collective farm provided the bulk of the remainder. Cash transfers yielded less than 2 per cent of the total. Since at this time the overwhelming majority of those who worked in agriculture were *kolkhozniki* and agricultural employment covered the bulk of the adult rural population, one can conclude that the Soviet social security system made at best a derisory contribution to rural living standards. By the end of the Khrushchev period there had been some small improvement. The relative share of cash transfers in total *kolkhoznik* income in 1965 was of the same order of magnitude as that in the incomes of industrial workers twenty-five years previously. But *kolkhoznik* families still derived more than a third of their total income from their private plots. On the other hand, the growth in the number of *sovkhozy* and the expansion of rural non-agricultural employment in the post-war period means that the rural population as a whole derived more benefit from the Soviet social security system that did *kolkhozniki* themselves. Both earnings from *kolkhozy* and cash transfers from the state have assumed a greater importance in the collective-farm family's budget under Brezhnev. And reliance on earnings from the private plot has continued to decline. By 1977, the role of cash transfers in the *kolkhoznik*'s family budget was almost as large as in that of the industrial worker. Thus, by the 1970s, the Soviet authorities had more or less succeeded in eliminating this source of difference between town and country.

Table 8.3 also casts light on the contribution that state expenditures on education, health and housing, the social wage, as it has been called, make to the living standards of workers and peasants. In 1940, the value of educational and medical services and so on available to the average industrial worker and his family added almost 10 per cent to their personal income. This contribution was almost twice as large as that provided by various income-support programmes. In the post-Stalin

TABLE 8.3 *The structure of household income: industrial workers and* kolkhozniki, *1940–77* (%)

	Industrial worker family			Kolkhoznik family		
	1940	1965	1977	1940	1965	1977
Wages from state employment	71.3	73.1	74.3	5.8	7.4	8.3
Earnings from kolkhoz				39.7	40.0	45.3
Cash transfers	5.5	9.0	9.2	1.5	4.2	8.4
Receipts from private plot	9.2	1.7	0.8	48.3	36.5	24.9
Other receipts	5.0	2.4	2.3	1.3	1.9	1.2
Personal income	91.0	86.2	86.6	96.6	90.0	88.1
Social wage[a]	9.0	13.8	13.4	3.4	10.0	11.9
Total income	**100.0**	**100.0**	**100.0**	**100.0**	**100.0**	**100.0**

a. State expenditures on education, medical care and so on.

SOURCE Derived from *NK SSSR*, 1977, pp. 409–10.

period, the social wage has assumed an even greater importance: it now amounts to somewhat more than an eighth of the income of the average industrial worker's family. This change in structure was largely complete by the end of the Khrushchev period. Since 1965, *per capita* consumption of these services has increased at about the same rate as money incomes. As industrial workers are among the better paid of Soviet state employees, it is to be expected that the social wage will form a smaller part of their total income than it does of less well-paid groups in the urban population.

In 1940, the value of educational and other services available to the average collective farmer and his family added less than 5 per cent to his personal income. As with industrial workers, this was approximately twice the proportion provided by cash transfers. But the rural population derived far smaller benefits from the state's welfare services than did those living in urban areas. In the post-Stalin period, *kolkhozniki* too have benefited from new priorities; indeed, the change in the structure of total income is more striking for collective farmers than it is for industrial workers. Although a major part of the integration of the collectivised peasantry into normal Soviet social institutions had been completed by the date of Khrushchev's dismissal, the share of the social wage in total *kolkhoznik* income (and, hence, the access of peasants and their dependants to educational and medical facilities) has continued to increase under Brezhnev. Table 8.3 suggests that the process of assimilating the rural population to a Soviet style of life is now far advanced.

The figures in Table 8.3, for all their interest, can only cast light on one aspect of the contribution that social consumption expenditures make to popular living standards. By their nature, they are restricted to the average impact of cash transfers and welfare services. But it is also important to ascertain who benefits, to analyse the distribution of expenditures. This is taken up in the next two sections.

3. INCOME SUPPORT: ENTITLEMENT AND VALUE

In the 1970s, more than half of recorded social consumption expenditure in the USSR was disbursed in the form of cash transfers. As has been shown above, these transfers made a significant contribution to the income of the average family, and their importance has increased in the post-Stalin period. Almost exclusively, Soviet transfers are intended to provide an alternative source of income for those suffering from temporary or permanent incapacity; little of this expenditure is designed to supplement the earned incomes of individuals or families with exceptional needs. This feature of the Soviet system, together with the fact that benefits are more or less closely tied to prior earnings, has meant that the value of cash transfers received by families has tended to increase with their incomes. Soviet income support has tended to reinforce rather than modify the distribution of income. Also, the search for administrative simplicity has resulted in the formulation of regulations that not infrequently give rise to horizontal inequities (the unequal treatment of individuals in similar circumstances). Both these features have been noted and criticised by Soviet economists and some attempt has been made to reduce their impact. But there is still room for substantial improvement.

Some idea of the growth and composition of income-support programmes in the USSR can be gained from Table 8.4. This shows that the nominal value of cash transfers has increased ten-fold in the last three decades. Even if allowance is made for changes in the cost of living, the increase is of the order of 960 per cent. The first three rows of the table refer to benefit programmes that are employment-related. In 1950, these accounted for 86 per cent of total expenditure; in 1977, their share had risen to 92.5 per cent. Even these figures understate the importance

TABLE 8.4   *Cash transfers in the Soviet Union: 1950–77 (milliard rubles)*

	1950	1960	1965	1970	1975	1977
Pensions	2.4	7.1	10.6	16.2	24.4	27.1
Sickness benefits	0.5	1.3	2.0	3.7	5.2	5.9
Maternity grants and benefits	0.2	0.5	0.6	0.9	1.4	1.5
Child allowances	0.4	0.5	0.5	0.4	0.4	0.4
Family income supplement	–	–	–	–	1.2	1.3
Other allowances	0.1	0.3	0.5	1.1	1.0	1.1
Total transfers[a]	**3.6**	**9.7**	**14.2**	**22.3**	**33.6**	**37.3**

a. In addition to the cash transfers listed in the table, Soviet statisticians include holiday pay and student stipends in this category.
SOURCE   McAuley, 1979, p. 280; *Vestnik Statistiki*, No. 2 (1978) 78.

of employment-related income maintenance programmes in Soviet cash transfers. As a result of the way that the table was compiled, it is probable that sick pay (and possibly maternity benefits) for *kolkhozniki* and members of the armed services is included in the 'other allowances' category rather than in the appropriate row of the table.

Paucity of statistics makes it difficult to determine the distribution of benefits, either collectively or under individual programmes. This question was explored by a number of Soviet economists during the 1960s when it was found that families with higher *per capita* incomes tended to receive more by way of cash transfers than did those in poverty. (For a review of this work, see McAuley, 1979, chapter 4.) But I know of no recent studies of this question. Consequently, I propose to outline the conditions of entitlement and regulations for determining the value of each of the major benefits. This should allow one to form some impression of the distributive impact of the Soviet social security system. The section ends with some partial evidence on the adequacy of individual programmes.

Cash transfers in the USSR fall into two main categories: old-age, disability and survivor pensions are available to those who, subject to certain additional conditions, have suffered a permanent loss of working capacity; sick pay and maternity benefits are provided for those suffering a temporary loss of working capacity. These benefits all depend upon prior employment. Child allowances and the family income supplement, on the other hand, are available irrespective of employment status. Let us examine each of these benefits in turn.

OLD-AGE PENSIONS

Civilian state employees are entitled to an old-age pension on reaching the age of sixty years (fifty-five years for women) provided that they have spent at least twenty-five years (twenty years for women) in state employment. There are lower retirement ages with correspondingly reduced employment requirements for underground miners and certain other designated categories. Those who fail to satisfy the employment requirement (because part of their adult life was spent on a *kolkhoz*, for example, or in bringing up a family) receive only a reduced pension – or none at all. When old-age pensions were introduced for collective farmers in 1965, the retirement age was set at sixty-five (sixty) years with a corresponding increase in required employment. Since 1967, however, the retirement age has been the same in both schemes.

In most cases, the value of the pension depends upon earnings in the last twelve months before the pension is granted. Those earning the minimum wage (70 rubles* a month in 1976) receive a pension of 45 rubles per month. The ratio between pension and earnings then falls by stages until the pension equals 50 per cent of earnings subject to a maximum pension of 120 rubles per month. The pensions of those entitled to early retirement are calculated according to a slightly more favourable formula – but are subject to the same minimum and maximum. Pensions for those living in rural areas are set at 85 per cent of the urban level. For those with dependants, a supplement of 10–15 per cent is paid. The 45 ruble minimum pension was introduced in 1971; between 1956 and 1971, the minimum had been 30 rubles per month. When pensions were introduced for *kolkhozniki*, a minimum of 12 rubles a month was established and a less favourable formula applied. In 1971, however, the *kolkhoznik*'s minimum was raised to 20 rubles per month and the scales used for the calculation of state pensions were adopted. These details are important since, as pointed out above, court practice has resulted in a situation in which the value of a person's pension, once awarded, is fixed for considerable periods, if not for life. The way in which the collective farm pension scheme was introduced has meant that the mass of elderly *kolkhozniki* who received pensions in the years 1965–71 were less favourably treated than those retiring after 1971 – even if their earnings while in employment were the same.

* An approximate sterling or dollar equivalent of this and subsequent ruble values is given in a note at the end of this chapter.

When the Soviet social security system was recodified in 1956, regulations were introduced to prevent individuals receiving both pension and earnings in a majority of cases. This was a practice that had developed in the later Stalin years to compensate for the totally inadequate level of the state pension. But, for a variety of reasons, the authorities have not insisted on this condition. During the 1960s, the regulations were progressively relaxed and now it is possible for all but a limited class of white-collar employees to receive a full pension while in full-time employment. Soviet specialists consider this inequitable and wasteful.

DISABILITY PENSIONS

Soviet law recognises three classes of disability: Class I involves total incapacity for work and requires permanent care or supervision; Class II involves only total incapacity for work and Class III involves partial loss of working capacity. The extent of incapacity in any particular case is determined by a medical-labour commission (consisting of a representative from the Ministry of Social Security, a representative from the relevant trade union and three medical specialists).

The regulations governing the payment of disability benefits are complex. Both entitlement and the value of the benefit depend upon the cause of incapacity and upon the individual's employment record. If disability is occasioned by an industrial accident or an occupational disease, a pension is payable irrespective of employment record. In other cases, the individual must satisfy an employment condition to qualify for a pension. Very crudely, this amounts to a requirement that he should have been employed for half the time since his twentieth birthday. The value of the pension awarded depends upon the severity of the incapacity, the individual's occupation (underground workers, for example, receive more favourable treatment), the cause of incapacity (accident victims qualify for higher pensions), prior earnings and so forth. Neglecting most of these qualifications, the range of benefits can be specified as:

Class	Minimum	Maximum
I	50	120
II	30	90
III	16	45

The minima set out above were introduced in 1965; between 1956 and

1965, they were somewhat lower. In 1973, the formulae used for calculating old-age pensions from earnings were substituted for the complex regulations set out in the 1956 Act and, at the same time, fixed ruble supplements replaced percentage additions for dependants. This latter change was of particular benefit to those with smaller pensions.

Eligibility for Class I and Class II disability pensions was extended to *kolkhozniki* at the same time as they were provided with old-age pensions. In 1967 they became entitled to Class III benefits for industrial accidents only. They are still not entitled to Class III benefits for disability due to general sickness. Both conditions of entitlement and levels of benefit for *kolkhozniki* are similar to those for state employees – but minima are somewhat lower.

Soviet legislation makes no mention of the principle of contributory negligence in industrial accident cases and, indeed, Lenin was critical of its operation in the pre-revolutionary Russian workmen's compensation scheme. But recently, spokesmen from the Ministry of Social Security have suggested that it might operate in certain circumstances. (The example given to a delegation from the UK Supplementary Benefits Commission was of a disability pension being reduced if it arose out of an accident in which the worker was drunk on the job.) It is not clear what legal authority is used to reduce benefits in this way, nor how widely the principle is appealed to.

SURVIVOR PENSIONS

Survivor pensions are payable, on the death of a state employee or collective farmer, to his dependent children, grandchildren or siblings under the age of sixteen (if these latter have no other relatives obliged by law to support them). A pension is also payable to a surviving spouse if he or she is above working age (and is not in receipt of an old-age pension). Similarly, the deceased's parents may qualify for a survivor pension if they were dependent upon him, are above working age (or otherwise incapacitated), not in receipt of an old-age pension and without other relatives obliged by law to support them. Entitlement also depends upon the deceased having a sufficient employment record – roughly half the period since his twentieth birthday. Pensions are payable irrespective of the earnings of other members of the family. For example, dependent children are entitled to a survivor pension on the occasion of their father's death irrespective of their mother's earnings. They retain this pension until they reach the age of sixteen (eighteen if in full-time education), unless they are adopted – for example, by another relative or their mother's second husband.

For a single dependant, the value of the survivor pension varied from 23 rubles to 60 rubles per month in 1973, depending upon the earnings of the deceased. For three or more dependants, the range was 70–120 rubles per month. The actual value of the pension also depends upon the deceased's occupation (underground workers and certain other categories receive more favourable treatment) and the cause of death (those whose breadwinners die as a result of an industrial accident or occupational disease receive higher pensions than others).

Survivor pensions for the dependents of *kolkhozniki* were introduced at the same time as old-age pensions. Previously, such people had been dependent on relatives or the charity of the *kolkhoz* for income support. In the early years of the collective farm scheme, benefits were lower than in the state one (for an equivalent prior earnings) but, since 1971, the two have moved closer together.

In addition to the three types of pension described above, there are also personal pensions and a limited number of occupational schemes (mainly for white-collar workers like physicians or airline personnel). These will not be described here.

SICK PAY

For state employees, benefits are paid from the first day of incapacity and continue for as long as the illness lasts, subject to medical attestation. (Alternatively, if it is decided that the incapacity is permanent, the employee may be awarded a disability pension, subject to his satisfying the eligibility criteria set out above.) Benefits are also payable in certain other circumstances: for example, to enable parents to look after children who are sick or for periods of quarantine.

Benefit levels depend upon previous earnings, the source of incapacity, length of employment and union membership. For those with a sufficient period of uninterrupted employment (eight years in 1972), benefits are paid at a rate equal to previous earnings; those with less than three years' uninterrupted employment, on the other hand, are paid only 50 per cent of earnings. Non-union members receive half the benefits paid to members. Those dismissed for infractions of labour discipline are not entitled to sick pay until they have worked in a new job for at least six months. Where incapacity is caused by an industrial accident or occupational disease, benefits are paid at 100 per cent of earnings regardless of employment record or union status. Notwithstanding the above regulations, sick pay (where paid) should not be less than 30 rubles per month (27 rubles in rural areas) or a *pro rata* amount for shorter periods of incapacity.

Sick pay was extended to collective farmers only in 1970. Benefits are paid in the same circumstances as to state employees, but only if the *kolkhoznik* would otherwise have been called upon for collective work. Benefits are further limited in duration to four months continuous incapacity or to five months' benefit in any calendar year. Other conditions of entitlement and methods of calculating benefits are similar to those used in the state system.

MATERNITY GRANTS AND ALLOWANCES

At the present time, Soviet female state employees are entitled to fifty-six days' leave before the birth of a child and a further fifty-six days after the birth. In cases of multiple births or where there have been complications, this post-natal leave is extended to seventy days. The scale of maternity leave has varied over the Soviet period, but these rates have been in force since the mid-1950s. Soviet female state employees are also entitled to take unpaid leave until their child's first birthday without losing their jobs or their continuous employment records. Before 1968, this unpaid leave period was only three months.

Since 1973, all women, irrespective of their union status or the length of time for which they have been employed, are entitled to maternity benefits equal to previous average earnings. Before that date, there were complicated scales relating the value of benefits to these two factors.

Entitlement to maternity leave was extended to female collective farmers in 1965. Paid leave was set at 112 days, but no mention was made in the relevant legislation about unpaid leave. In 1965, maternity benefits were set at two-thirds of previous earnings, subject to a minimum of 40 kopeks a day. Those with at least three years' employment were entitled to 100 per cent of previous earnings. It is not clear whether the 1973 modifications apply to collective farmers – but probably not.

In addition to the benefits set out above, maternity grants are payable to certain categories of indigent (but employed) parent. These are really a hangover from the past when average earnings were much lower than they are today, and they will not be mentioned further. Also, the authorities have stated their intention of introducing partial payment for the post-natal leave period mentioned above at some time in 1981–5, but no further details of this new income support programme are yet available.

CHILD ALLOWANCES

The rates at which these are paid have been unchanged since 1947. Mothers with two children are entitled to a payment of 20 rubles on the birth of a third child; those with three children receive 65 rubles on the birth of a fourth and a monthly allowance of 4 rubles from the child's first birthday until his fifth. Rates for both grant and monthly allowance increase until the tenth child. A separate payment of 5 (7.5 or 10) rubles per month is made to single women with one (two or three and more) children. These payments continue until the child's twelfth birthday – or until they are placed in a home or adopted.

FAMILY INCOME SUPPLEMENT

Since 1974, families with a *per capita* income of less than 50 rubles per month (the Soviet official poverty level) have been entitled to a payment of 12 rubles per month per child until the child's eighth birthday. (Children start school in the USSR in the autumn after their seventh birthday.) It is estimated that one-third of all children in the relevant age group were entitled to this benefit in 1974.

Descriptions of the various benefits payable under the Soviet social security system confirm that the primary purpose of cash transfers in the USSR is to provide an alternative source of income for individuals experiencing one of a number of recognised forms of incapacity to work. Only to a limited extent are they intended to provide additional income for families with exceptional needs or for those whose primary incomes are insufficient to guarantee a minimum standard of living. (In fact, only parenthood qualifies for additional financial support, and such support has only been provided recently and is still available in only limited amounts. In this sense, the Soviet social security system can be said to conform to the socialist principles set out in Section 1.) This characteristic of supplementing the distribution of earnings, rather than acting as a universal safety-net, is reinforced by the principle that benefits should be related to earnings.

The Soviet social security system acts as a supplement to the wage and salary system in providing incentives for certain kinds of labour-market behaviour in another sense too. As I have shown, for many programmes,

either the value of the benefits paid or entitlement itself is made
dependent upon certain characteristics that are irrelevant to the purpose
of the benefit itself. For example, the purpose of sick pay is to provide
means of subsistence for persons temporarily unable to work for their
living. The 'needs' of the sick are unaffected by whether they are union
members or not, whether they have been employed in the same job for
more than eight years or not, whether they have recently been dismissed
for an infraction of labour discipline or not. The intention in making
sickness benefits depend on all these factors can only be to provide an
additional incentive for behaviour that the authorities regard as
desirable. Similarly, since benefits are paid out of the state's social
insurance fund, the fact that victims of industrial accidents are paid 100
per cent of previous earnings cannot serve as a 'punishment' for
enterprises who allow such accidents to happen. Whether a man breaks
his leg on the factory floor or on the way to the grocery store, his
needs are the same – in a rational system, his benefits should be the same
too.

The same strictures could be levelled at most of the other benefits
described above. At best, the use of social security programmes to
encourage desirable behaviour in non-recipients (after all, once one falls
sick it is too late to join the union) undermines the purposiveness of the
system, reduces its ability to satisfy the tasks it was intended to. At
worst, such an approach can be the source of considerable horizontal
inequity.

In addition to the general shortcomings of the Soviet social security
system alluded to in the last couple of paragraphs, the way in which the
regulations governing individual programmes have been interpreted has
been the source of additional problems. There is some doubt about the
adequacy of the old-age pension scheme in the early Soviet period, about
the equity of arrangements for disability pensions and about the
sufficiency of income support for pregnant women and those with small
children.

Table 8.5 contains figures on the total number of pensioners (old-age,
disability and survivor) for a number of years, together with estimates of
the population of pensionable age. In 1930, there were only 19,000 old-
age pensioners in the USSR as a whole, and even in 1939, some twenty-
two years after the first Soviet decree on pensions, there were only
200,000 of them. This suggests that pension regulations were interpreted
rigidly, that to qualify for a pension, twenty-five years employment by
the *Soviet* state was required; no allowance appears to have been made
for employment in Tsarist times. As a result, little more than 1 per cent

TABLE 8.5 *Number of pensioners: USSR, 1930–78 (millions)*

| | Number of persons in receipt of a pension | | | | |
| | | | Under *kolkhoz* law | | Persons of pensionable age[a] |
	All	Old-age	All	Old-age	
1930	1.9	–	–	–	–
1939	3.4	0.2	–	–	16.9[b]
1950	19.8	0.8	–	–	–
1959	19.9	4.0	–	–	14.9
1965	26.5	8.2	–	–	–
1966	32.0	16.1	7.9	7.0	–
1970	40.1	23.7	12.1	10.5	36.3
1978	46.7	30.8	11.5	10.0	44.0[b]

a. Men aged 60 and over, women aged 55 and over.
b. For 1939, the number of women aged 55–9 years was estimated; for 1978, the number of persons of pensionable age was estimated from data giving those aged 60 and over in 1975, in I. Kalinyuk, 1977, p. 16.

SOURCES Cols 1–4: *Vestnik statistiki* No. 2 (1979) 79; Col. 5: from various population censuses.

of those of pensionable age in 1939 were in fact in receipt of an old-age pension.

Even as late as 1959, only a fifth of all pensioners were old-age pensioners and little more than a quarter of the population of pensionable age was in receipt of an old-age pension. But, with the introduction of pensions for collective farmers and with the continued maturation of the state's scheme, both the share of old-age pensions in the total number of pensions and the proportion of the relevant age cohort in receipt of a pension has risen to more normal levels. In the late 1970s, there were more than thirty million old-age pensioners in the USSR, more than three-fifths of the total. Still, even at this date, only about 70 per cent of those of pensionable age were in fact receiving an old-age pension. Some of the remainder may well have been in receipt of a disability or survivor pension, but these cannot have been numerous. Perhaps as many as a quarter of those over the age of sixty (fifty-five for women) must be dependent on their own earnings or the earnings of a relative for their support. For this group, certainly, the absence of any developed system of public assistance in the Soviet Union may often be the cause of considerable hardship.

Although the situation is changing, the figures in Table 8.5 show that for much of its existence the Soviet social security system has been primarily concerned with the provision of disability (and survivor) pensions. In 1939, more than 90 per cent of all pensions were of this variety, and twenty years later, in 1959, almost 80 per cent still were. (Much of the expansion in the number of pensioners between 1939 and 1959 can be ascribed to the awarding of disability pensions to those wounded in the Second World War.) I have come across no discussion of how adequately the Soviet system fulfils this function in the sense of providing income-support for those suffering a permanent loss of working capacity. But Soviet specialists have singled out the regulations governing the payment of disability pensions as a source of horizontal inequity. It is claimed that the same prior earnings and the same degree of incapacity can give rise to as many as thirty or fifty different rates of benefit, depending upon other circumstances (Lantsev, 1976, p. 91). If the object of the scheme is to provide income-support for the incapacitated, such variety is undesirable. Soviet specialists have also been critical of the way that regulations have resulted in substantial numbers of pensioners receiving no more than the minimum. The plight of those with dependent children has received special mention. Both the introduction of the family income supplement and the switch to fixed ruble supplements for dependents will have done something for this latter group, however.

Thus one may conclude that, although there has been a substantial expansion of expenditure on programmes designed to provide long-term income support, existing regulations leave substantial numbers of individuals (and their families) without cover or with only inadequate assistance. The system is often misguided and sometimes unfair. There have been improvements in recent years, but much remains to be done.

The maternity benefits programme, too, does not appear to have coped satisfactorily with the demands placed upon it – although the modifications already introduced and those announced for the next five-year plan period should mitigate some of its worst shortcomings. Table 8.6 reports the results of one small survey into the impact of parenthood on family living standards. It is based on a sample of 525 women giving birth to their first child in the town of Tambov. Thus, both geographically and demographically, it is unrepresentative of the recipients of maternity benefits; it may also be unrepresentative sociologically as well. But, the official initiatives alluded to above suggest that the unfortunate situation it reveals may not have been untypical of the period to which it refers. The table shows that, for the Tambov sample at least, parenthood was associated with a significant reduction in family living standards because it involved the wife's withdrawal from the labour force.

TABLE 8.6   *Distribution of families by* per capita *income before and after the arrival of a first child: Tambov*

| | Income *per capita* (rubles a month) | | | |
	−50	50−70	70−100	100−
Women with general secondary education or less:				
Income on marriage	13.4	16.5	55.1	15.0
Income after wife's withdrawal from the labour force	64.8	28.9	4.7	1.6
Women with more than general secondary education:				
Income on marriage	6.9	16.2	50.6	26.3
Income after wife's withdrawal from the labour force	62.5	29.4	6.2	1.9

NOTE   the table is based on a sample of 525 women giving birth to their first child in the town of Tambov. The sample was probably taken in the late 1960s or early 1970s. In the distributions relating to family income after the wife's withdrawal from the labour force, allowance is made for maternity pay, but it is assumed that the wife remains at home with her child until its first birthday.

SOURCE   I. Katkova, 1978, p. 42.

Availing themselves of the opportunity to take unpaid leave during their child's first year would have meant poverty for more than three-fifths of the sample, in spite of the maternity benefits available under the state's social security system. The source does not make clear, unfortunately, which particular features of the pre-1973 system were responsible for this result. But the fact that benefits are to be extended into the unpaid leave period suggests that it was more than just the normal Soviet practice of trying to use social security to encourage desirable behaviour among non-recipients.

As pointed out above, the Soviet social security system does not include provision for the payment of income support to those without work. Soviet spokesmen claim that this is justified because there is no unemployment in the USSR. This is not altogether true, although it is certainly the case that unemployment, especially long-term unemployment, is much less prevalent than in a majority of market economies. But every year substantial numbers of Soviet citizens leave their jobs and it takes them time to find alternative employment. In the interim, I would suggest, they are unemployed. In the late 1960s and early 1970s, labour turnover was running at the rate of 20 per cent or so per annum in Soviet industry, and total separations were perhaps some 10 per cent higher. Turnover in other branches of material production was of the same order of magnitude, but it was probably less in sectors like education or medical services. Those who left their jobs spent an average of one month looking for new ones. As a rough order of magnitude, then, these two figures imply that some 1.5–2.5 per cent of the Soviet labour force is without work at any one time. There is also evidence that some people experience longer-term difficulties in finding work. This so-called structural unemployment is more prevalent in small towns than in the larger urban centres, is more common in Central Asia than in European parts of the country. It is difficult to put a figure on it (partly because it may overlap with the frictional unemployment mentioned above), but I doubt whether it would exceed 0.5 per cent of the labour force. Not all of these people, the frictional and the structurally unemployed, would qualify for unemployment pay under the British (or any other) scheme, but a proportion of them would. The Soviet authorities can be justly proud of their ability to maintain high and stable levels of employment, but the absence of income-maintenance during the period without work imposes hardship on the individuals involved and their families. It is a shortcoming of the Soviet social security system.

In recent years, there have been reports in the Western press of individuals who have been denied pensions or who have had the value of their pensions reduced on political grounds. Since the newspaper reports have not been particularly explicit, it has not always been clear what has been involved; but I think that this could have occurred as a result of one of two procedures. First, the general social security regulations appear to imply that an individual convicted of a crime and sentenced to loss of freedom may forfeit his accumulated employment record (upon which the value of almost all cash transfers depend). If this is the case, and the wording of the relevant clauses is obscure, then insofar as political dissidence is treated as a criminal offence, this principle might be applied to those sentenced to imprisonment for their ideas or activities. In such circumstances, loss of pension rights is the result of 'due process', however inequitable one might think the law is on this point. On the other hand, as is suggested by the issue of drunkenness and contributory negligence mentioned above, Soviet practice may diverge from the letter of the law. Loss of pension rights may be the result of what is called, somewhat euphemistically, administrative measures. In such cases, the courts may be powerless to help. There is little reason to believe, however, that instances of loss of pension rights, either as a result of legal or of administrative procedures, are widespread. It is much more likely that the bulk of those without pensions are women whose family responsibilities have prevented them from accumulating a sufficient employment record, or ex-*kolkhozniki* with insufficient service to qualify for a pension under either scheme. However distressing the Soviet approach may be in individual cases, it is rigidity and not malice that results in its major failures.

The analysis of this section has shown, then, that on the eve of the Second World War, some twenty or twenty-five years after the October Revolution, social security programmes made at best a modest contribution to the incomes of Soviet families. The help that was provided was concentrated on the urban population. The state did little or nothing to ameliorate the conditions of the elderly and incapacitated in rural areas. In the post-Stalin period, the relative importance of the state's income-maintenance programmes has increased in both rural and urban areas. There has been a growing similarity in the treatment afforded to *kolkhozniki* and industrial workers (and, probably, state employees generally).

Levels of support have risen, but there are still shortcomings in individual programmes. There are still substantial numbers of persons of pensionable age who are not in receipt of an old-age pension. The average level of disability pensions appears to be low and regulations give rise to considerable horizontal inequity. The existing maternity benefit scheme does not make it possible for parents to have children without frequently suffering financial hardship. No financial support is available for the limited numbers of the unemployed. Soviet specialists have commented on all of these shortcomings; the authorities are therefore aware of them. But diminished growth rates in the recent past and the prospect of further decline in the future means that there is little scope for radical improvements in the short run even if these were thought desirable. But, as was pointed out above, such is not the case. The Soviet concept of socialism precludes making entitlement closely dependent on need and there is little open advocacy of such a policy. The absence of a well-developed system of public assistance, which might provide support for those who fail to benefit from existing programmes, the misfits, incompetents and awkward cases, is deliberate. Neither compassion nor egalitarianism will come to guide the Soviet social security system in the near future.

4. WELFARE SERVICES: SCOPE AND LIMITATIONS

The second major component of Soviet social consumption is the provision of goods and services, either free of charge or at subsidised prices. These welfare services, as one may call them, accounted for a little less than 50 per cent of total expenditure in the 1970s, and their relative share has fallen in the post-Stalin period. But, of course, the absolute value of expenditure for these purposes has risen significantly since 1950.

In Table 8.1, expenditure on welfare services was grouped under three main headings (expenditure on social security, representing the provision of residential accommodation for the elderly and certain other groups, being the fourth, minor, category), but these reflect the identity of the 'spending ministry' as much as the nature of the service provided. A more meaningful, functional classification would identify, separately, education, both general and vocational, medical services, pre-school child-care and housing. State provision in all these areas constitutes a significant addition to the incomes of Soviet families.

In addition, one ought, perhaps, to mention the provision of canteens and retail outlets by enterprises and the provision of rest-homes and sanatoria by the trade unions. These also add to the living standards of the families that have access to them. Little is known about the subsidy element in canteen pricing but, in view of the total contribution to social consumption from enterprise funds and given the other charges on this contribution (for example, holiday pay, part of the cost of pre-school child-care and housing subsidies), it cannot be large. The same applies to the bulk of restricted-access retail outlets, although it is not clear how much allowance one ought to make for the apparently greater reliability of supplies that characterises some of these stores. Similarly, given the explicit trade union contribution to social consumption, the provision of rest-homes and sanatoria can add little to average living standards – however much it may add to the welfare of the families that use them. As a result, these 'fringe benefits' will be ignored here.

In a chapter of this length it is clearly impossible to give a satisfactory account of all the major welfare services listed above. Rather, one must be content with an impressionistic assessment of Soviet achievements, of the extent to which Soviet policy conforms to the role set out for it in Section 1. In doing this, I propose to examine each of the major services in turn.

EDUCATION

At the time of the October Revolution, the Tsarist empire had, at best, a rudimentary educational system. In the past sixty years or so, the Soviet authorities have been successful in establishing a complete network of

TABLE 8.7   *Educational attainment: Soviet occupied population, 1939–77*

	Occupied population with educational level (%)			
	Higher		Secondary (comp. or incomp.)	
	Urban	Rural	Urban	Rural
1939	3.2	0.3	21.0	6.0
1959	5.9	1.1	50.5	30.5
1970	9.0	2.5	65.8	47.4
1977	11.6	3.9	71.9	63.4

SOURCE   *NK SSSR za 60 let*, Moscow, 1977, p. 56.

general educational establishments and of developing a system of vocational education. Some idea of the development of general education in the USSR can be gained from the figures in Table 8.7. In 1939, perhaps 10 per cent of the population had had some secondary education, and a further 1 per cent could claim further education. As might be expected, those with post-primary education were disproportionately concentrated in the towns. Twenty years later, some 40 per cent of the population could claim secondary education and a further 3 per cent or so had received further training. Now, almost 70 per cent of the occupied population has received secondary education and perhaps as many as 9 per cent have spent time at a post-secondary educational establishment. The present goal of the Soviet authorities is universal secondary education and it seems possible that this will be achieved in the not too distant future. At the same time, although there are still differences in educational attainment between the rural and urban populations, distinctions have been greatly attenuated. It is also the case that the Soviet authorities have virtually eliminated differences in educational attainment between the sexes. In 1977, some 77.9 per cent of the occupied male population had some post-primary education, while for occupied women the figure was 78.1 per cent. In this respect, then, the Soviet system appears to provide for equality of opportunity. (On the other hand, recent studies of the social composition of the student bodies at institutions of higher education, suggest that children of the intelligentsia and white-collar workers are disproportionately represented. The educational system, at least in its upper reaches, appears to reinforce existing social stratification. See Chapter 6 for discussion of this question.)

General education clearly affects an individual's capacity to undertake particular types of occupation. But this is also influenced by vocational training, and the Soviet authorities have made a determined effort to develop the latter. Although substantial numbers of Soviet citizens now receive some form of industrial training, doubts have been expressed both about the adequacy of the instruction given and about the equity of recruitment procedures.

On leaving one's secondary school in the USSR, there are five channels by which a person can effect the transition to full-time employment. First, he or she can proceed to a further educational institution; alternatively, he or she can proceed to an institution providing secondary specialist education (at the age of fifteen or eighteen); or, again, he or she can enter a so-called *PTU* (roughly, a trade school) at the age of fifteen; finally, he or she can enter the labour market directly. It is difficult to provide accurate figures on the relative importance of these different channels of access to the labour market, but one plausible set of estimates for the 1970s suggests the following distribution (the assumptions on which they are based will be spelled out at length in McAuley, forthcoming, chapter 8):

Transfer to	*Boys*	*Girls*
Further education	8	8
Secondary specialist education	11	14
PTU	57	19
Work	24	58
Total	**100**	**100**

Thus, at the present time, about a quarter of all boys and three-fifths of all girls go directly from school to work. Somewhat less than a fifth of boys and slightly more than a fifth of girls go on to secondary specialist or higher educational establishments. Almost three-fifths of boys and only a fifth of girls go on to the *PTU*.

Some of the boys and girls who move directly from school to work may well be enrolled in some form of (Soviet-type) apprenticeship scheme. But it is argued that these do little more than equip their graduates with good working habits and basic industrial skills. For all the limitations that have been levied at them on the grounds of restricted and outmoded curricula, it is agreed that qualified, highly-skilled workers require *PTU* training. It is the skilled workers who have the highest wages and who, in time, are promoted to supervisory positions. The present Soviet institutional framework does not provide equality of opportunity for vocational training for the two sexes in this field.

MEDICAL SERVICES

The Soviet authorities have made a considerable investment in the provision of medical services. There has been substantial growth in all the main physical indicators of the level of services provided and, in many instances, Soviet figures now exceed those of other industrial states. For example, in 1940, there were 7.9 physicians per 10,000 population in the USSR; by 1976, this had risen to 33.5. In Britain in 1971, on the other hand, there were only 15.7 physicians per 10,000 population and in the USA (in 1973) only 21.

The widespread availability of medical care, however, has not resulted in a commensurate reduction in morbidity. In Soviet industry in the early 1970s, the average worker lost some 10–12 days per year through sickness and, although the figures are not strictly comparable, this is significantly higher than the British figure of 7.7 days per worker per year. Further, there is some evidence to suggest that morbidity in the Soviet Union is significantly higher among women than among men (although, again, an adequate basis for this general conclusion scarcely exists in the published statistics. It is based on figures for the Baltic republics which may not be typical of the USSR as a whole. For more detail, see McAuley, forthcoming, chapter 10.)

If the available evidence points towards higher morbidity among employed women than men in the Soviet Union, published statistics also reveal that men suffer from higher mortality. Age-specific death-rates for men are as much as three times those for women in the prime working-age groups, and death-rates for men in early middle age have increased by 10 or 20 per cent in the last decade or so. There has been a worrying increase in mortality from cardio-vascular disorders and also from accidents. These observations, taken together, suggest that the medical services in the Soviet Union have not been able to satisfy fully the demands put upon them, although it is unclear how far unsatisfied demand contributes to the lack of equality of opportunity.

PRE-SCHOOL CHILD-CARE

Soviet government policy has, for a long period, stressed the desirability of pre-school child-care facilities. They are good for children in that they help to inculcate collectivist attitudes; they are good for parents in that they contribute to sexual equality in the labour market. Soviet spokesmen often also stress the considerable resources that the state devotes to the provision of these facilities. In fact, pre-school child-care has been less freely available in the USSR than official pronouncements and the comments of casual observers may have led one to believe. The figures in Table 8.8 show that in 1940, some two million children were enrolled in day-nurseries and kindergartens. Over the next thirty-five years, enrolment increased six-fold – but much of this increase took place in the 1960s and 1970s. Substantial provision is a relatively recent phenomenon.

The rates of growth in the provision of pre-school child-care implied by Table 8.8 are impressive, but the table also reveals two weaknesses in Soviet policy. In 1940 and even in the 1970s, pre-school child-care is largely an urban service. For much of the period covered by the table, only a fifth of the children in such establishments lived in rural areas. Second, although the figures are approximate, only a minority of children in the relevant age-groups can attend day-nurseries or kindergartens.

TABLE 8.8   *The provision of pre-school child-care facilities: USSR, 1940–75*

	Children enrolled in ('000)			Age-Cohort Enrolled (%)		
	All	Urban	Rural	All	Urban	Rural
1940	1 953	1 422	531	6.42	–	–
1950	1 788	1 380	408	–	–	–
1959	3 886	3 122	764	11.72	22.34	3.98
1970	9 281	7 380	1 901	30.63	50.74	12.07
1975	11 523	8 980	2 543	–	–	–

NOTES AND SOURCES   *Narodnoe obrazovanie* . . . , Moscow, 1977, pp. 119–21; *Itogi 1959*, p. 49; *Itogi 1970*, vol. II, Table 3. For 1939, the relevant age-cohort was calculated as 70 per cent of those aged 0–9 years; for 1959–70, it was calculated as the sum of the cohort aged 0–4 years and 40 per cent of that aged 5–9 years.

It is possible to argue that the scale of effort implied by the Soviet figures for 1970 is of the same order of magnitude as government expenditure on the education of this age-group in a country like Britain – although, no doubt, resources are allocated differently. In the

UK, primary education starts at the age of five; thus two-sevenths (28.6
per cent) of those aged 0–7 years will be enrolled in the infant
departments of primary schools. Although nursery education is not
widespread in the UK, 5.4 per cent of the under-fives attend day-
nurseries, kindergartens or play-groups. So almost one third of the
relevant age-group are involved in some form of child-care facility. If
these calculations are accepted, the figures in Table 8.8 imply that for
much of the Soviet period, the assistance given to mothers in caring for
their children by the Soviet state has been less than that afforded by the
British government. Before the 1960s, this was even true for the urban
population and, of course, the greater availability of child-care facilities
in urban areas since that date has been achieved partly through the
neglect of the interests of rural women and children. For all the
achievement in this area, the Soviet authorities are still some way short
of being able to guarantee equality of access to pre-school facilities and
this surely adversely affects equality of opportunity.

HOUSING

The inadequacy of Soviet housing, both in terms of quality and
quantity, is so well-known that it will not be elaborated upon here.
However, the figures in Table 8.9 suggest that gross shortages are a
feature of the past. By the 1970s, the total stock of housing was sufficient
to guarantee the minimum sanitary norm to all. Further, the Soviet
policy of charging only nominal rents for state accommodation means
that the cost of housing forms only a small part of the budget of the
average urban household.

But this very policy of nominal rents, when combined with the
mechanisms used to allocate housing space, has meant that the better-
off members of society have benefited disproportionately from the
housing subsidy programme. A substantial proportion of the new
housing built in the USSR is financed by enterprises and other
organisations. It is then transferred to local authorities to manage. But
the enterprises who finance its construction frequently insist on the right
to decide upon the initial tenants (and, sometimes, their successors).
They use this new housing as an incentive to attract skilled labour or
managerial personnel. This policy can lead to substantial differences in
the amount of space available to different occupational groups. Skilled
workers may well be better housed than the unskilled and, in certain
circumstances, may improve their conditions even further. Since all
groups pay the same nominal rents, the better housed receive the larger

subsidy. It is not possible to give precise figures on the amount of distortion there is in the allocation of the Soviet housing stock, but there are indications that it is considerable. A national survey found that, in 1967, when, according to Table 8.9, the stock was sufficient to guarantee the urban population 10 m² per person, only 27 per cent of worker households had access to more than 9 m² *per capita*. This implies that this privileged group, together with the intelligentsia and some white-collar employees, must have been substantially better housed than the urban proletariat (Sarkisyan, 1972, p. 140).

TABLE 8.9   *Adequacy of Soviet housing supply: 1940–75*

	Actual housing stock as % of need			
	Total		Urban	
	Minimum	Rational	Minimum	Rational
1940	55	33	66	39
1950	60	35	75	44
1960	72	45	94	56
1970	95	56	111	65
1975	–	–	120	71

NOTES AND SOURCES   Cols 1–2 from Revaikin, 1974, p. 112; Cols 3–5 were derived by applying the space-norms implicit in Revaikin's figures to the urban population and comparing with actual urban housing stock. Housing stock figures from *NK SSSR*, 1963, p. 515, *NK SSSR*, 1975, p. 576. The minimum need is based on a norm of 10.1 m² per person; the rational need is based on a norm of 17.2 m² of total (useful) space per person.

This brief and impressionistic survey of the major welfare services in the Soviet Union demonstrates that in each area there has been a substantial increase in provision in the past twenty or thirty years. There have been increases in pre-school child-care and educational facilities, in the housing stock, in the availability of medical services. Further, attempts have been made to reduce urban–rural disparities in provision. But there still remains inequality of access; the goal of guaranteeing equality of opportunity has not yet been achieved. Existing institutions tend to reinforce as often as counteract social and sexual inequality.

5. SOCIAL SECURITY AND SOCIAL WELFARE IN THE USSR: AN ASSESSMENT

A long conclusion would be out of place in a chapter of this nature. But the analysis of the preceding pages does permit one to draw certain conclusions. In broad terms, both the Soviet social security system and the wider provision of welfare services are consistent with the perception of socialism first articulated in the 1930s, but developed and made more consistent since Stalin's death. According to this, both the structure and level of income-support payments should reinforce the structure of incentives built into the wage and salary system. Both cash transfers and the provision of welfare services should take as their goal the establishment of equality of opportunity and not the reduction of existing inequality.

Both areas have been characterised by significant increases in the absolute volume of resources committed to them, and this increase has resulted in a reduction, if not elimination, of the grosser forms of social discrimination that characterised Stalin's Russia. There are few remaining differences in the treatment of *kolkhozniki* and state employees, the urban and rural populations.

But the construction or reconstruction of what one may call a meritocratic socialist welfare system has not been without its difficulties. The use of pensions, sick pay and maternity benefits to provide incentives for desirable labour-market behaviour has reduced their ability to satisfy their primary functions. The same is true, *mutatis mutandis*, of the housing subsidy scheme. Unwillingness to develop the public assistance side of social security has reduced the state's ability to mount an effective anti-poverty programme.

In his play *Pygmalion*, Geroge Bernard Shaw has the dustman Doolittle make a distinction between the deserving and the undeserving poor. The former are those who adopt the attitudes of the dominant class in society and attempt to live by their precepts; the undeserving poor are the rest. Adapting these concepts, it is possible to conclude that the Soviet welfare state has been designed to cope with the needs of deserving families. It offers little help, or even understanding, to the undeserving. There is little overt sympathy expressed for the inadequate or the incompetent, for those whom one might call social deviants, few attempts made to explain their behaviour in terms of the social and economic pressures to which they are subject.

A NOTE ON THE VALUE OF THE RUBLE

The discussion of individual cash transfer programmes in Section 3 of this chapter gives the value of various benefits in terms of rubles. Since it is difficult for those unfamiliar with the USSR to appreciate what the ruble is worth, this note attempts to provide a comparison of the value of the ruble with that of the pound sterling and the US dollar.

Since the ruble is formally inconvertible, the official exchange rate provides less insight into comparative values than is normally the case. In consequence, this note relies on a purchasing-power parity comparison of the ruble and the pound for 1964–5. The exchange rate that this yields is adjusted for differing inflation rates in the two countries to give relative values of their currencies for other years. Dollar values have been derived by converting pounds into dollars at the official rate of exchange. There are many shortcomings with these procedures, but they do provide some idea of the value of the ruble (and hence of Soviet social security benefits) in the years 1950–79.

To compute a purchasing-power parity rate of exchange, one must first obtain a bundle of goods and services bought by a typical household

TABLE 8.10 *The value of the ruble, the pound and the dollar: 1950–79*

	Value of 1 ruble (in £s)		Value of 1 R in $
	Soviet weights	UK weights	
1950	0.17	0.15	0.45
1960	0.29	0.25	0.76
1965	0.32	0.28	0.84
1970	0.37	0.33	0.71
1975	0.64	0.56	1.15
1979	1.06	0.92	2.23

NOTES AND SOURCES The sterling value of the ruble in 1965 is taken from P. Hanson, *The Consumer in Soviet Society* (Evanston Ill., 1968) p. 56. This has been adjusted for other years by the ratio of the retail price indexes for the two countries. The UK index was taken from *Economic Trends*, various years; the Soviet index was taken from G. Schroeder and B. Severin, 'Soviet Consumption and Income Policies in a New Perspective' in *JEC Soviet Economy in a New Perspective* (Washington DC, 1976) p. 636. (The figure for 1979 was extrapolated on the basis of the inflation rate in 1970–5.) The dollar value of the ruble given above is the average of the two sterling values converted at the official rate of exchange for the last day of the relevant year.

in the two countries. These bundles are then priced in each country and the ratio of their values yields the ppp rate of exchange. Thus, if it were the case that the typical bundle purchased by a British household in 1964 cost £20.00 in London and would have cost R78.00 in Moscow, the ppp value of the ruble would be £0.26. Since patterns of expenditure differ between countries, ppp comparisons usually yield two exchange rates – one based on the consumption of British households, for example, and one on that of Soviet families. These two rates are given in cols 1 and 2 of Table 8.10.

REFERENCES

V. A. Acharkan, 'Sotsialisticheskii printsip raspredeleniya po trudu i sotsial-noye obespecheniye', *Sotsialisticheskii trud*, No. 11 (1974) 119–29.
Itogi vsesoyuznoi perepisi naselenia 1959 goda (Moscow, 1962).
Itogi vsesoyuznoi perepisi naselenia 1970 goda (Moscow, 1972).
I. Kalinyuk, 'Starenie naselenia SSSR', *Narodonaselenia*, No. 19 (1977) 14–24.
I. Katkova, 'Materinskii ukhod za novorozhdennym', *Narodonaselenia*, No. 21 (1978) 38–46.
V. S. Kulikov, *Rol finansov v povyshenii blagosostoyania sovetskogo naroda* (Moscow, 1972).
M. S. Lantsev, *Sotsialnoe obespechenie v SSSR* (Moscow, 1976).
A. McAuley, *Economic Welfare in the Soviet Union* (London and Madison, Wis., 1979).
———*Women's Work and Wages in the USSR,* forthcoming.
V. F. Maier, *Dokhody naseleniya i rost blagosostoyaniya naroda* (Moscow, 1968).
V. F. Maier and B. V. Rakitskii, 'Obshchestvennye fondy potreblenia i rost blagosostoyania naroda', in *Oplata truda pri sotsialisme: voprosy teorii i praktiki* (Moscow and Warsaw, 1976) pp. 190–206.
Narodnoe khozyaistvo SSR, Statisticheskii ezhegodnik (Moscow, various years).
Narodnoe obrazovanie, nauka i kultura v SSSR (Moscow, 1977).
N. E. Rabkina and N. M. Rimashevskaya, *Osnovy differentsiatsii zarabotnoi platy i dokhodov naselenia* (Moscow, 1972).
B. V. Rakitskii, *Obshchestvennye fondy potreblenia kak ekonomicheskaya kategoria* (Moscow, 1967).
A. S. Revaikin, *Neobkhodimyi produkt, ego velichina i struktura pri sotsializme* (Petrozavodsk, 1974).
G. S. Sarkisyan, *Uroven, tempy i proportsii rosta realnykh dokhodov pri sotsializme* (Moscow, 1972).

9 Workers' Social Perceptions

Max Ralis

'These days, you can't even find beans in our stores', says a 40-year-old mechanic from Omsk in Western Siberia. 'It's getting to be a problem to get hold of soap and *kasha* [buckwheat: a basic and much appreciated food in Russia]', adds a 38-year-old worker from Voronezh in the once-famous Black Earth region. And things are summed up by a 30-year-old skilled worker from Simferopol in the Crimean peninsula: 'Our material life is more difficult than you can imagine.'

Moving north to Leningrad, a 31-year-old bus driver complains: 'Basic consumer goods are unavailable.' 'What we lack most of all are basic consumer goods,' echo a 41-year-old skilled worker from Irkutsk in Eastern Siberia and a 29-year-old mechanic from Cheboksary, east of Gorki. A 30-year-old worker from Berdyansk on the Sea of Azov is more specific: 'We lack staple items such as cotton, rice, and basic foodstuffs.' 'We lack everything,' says an electrician from Engels on the Volga river. A 43-year-old driver from Kirov puts things somewhat differently: 'All our problems are material ones.'

From the Far East, in Vladivostok, a 30-year-old worker recounts: 'Last year, our stores were empty right up to the month of August, and we feared the worst. Then, at last, meat and tinned goods appeared.' And, in the eastern suburbs of Moscow, a 42-year-old woman worker from Elektrostal predicts: 'If things don't improve rapidly, we will be without noodles, rice and bread.' In Ivanovo, a town dominated by the textile industry, things are no better: 'Food and vegetables are very rare and very expensive,' observes a woman worker. While a 41-year-old woman foreman from Kiev remarks: 'We lack vegetables, meat, and many other things.' 'Difficulties in obtaining dairy products and meat are unlikely to diminish,' forecasts a 30-year-old woman from Kursk, a town midway between Moscow and Kiev. 'Items like coffee and chocolate are so expensive that they are bought only for special occasions like marriages or christenings,' says a 30-year-old Orenburg woman.

These comments, like those in the following pages, were all made spontaneously by Soviet workers in conversation with Westerners. In my opinion, they reflect accurately the views of the Soviet working class on the different facets of life in the Soviet Union. In reporting them here, I have obviously had to exercise my own judgement in the matter of selection and arrangement. Some ambiguous comments have had to be discarded and there are, of course, innumerable ways of arranging these remarks in sequence. However, I have deliberately done nothing to avoid what may seem an excessively repetitive effect, in order to convey how typical the observations made really are, and how frequently they recur in the mouths of workers from opposite ends of the country, with varying professional skills, and of different nationalities. (Unless otherwise stated, it can be assumed that the speaker is a Russian.) At this stage, one fact of paramount importance is already apparent: the perceptions expressed by these Soviet workers of the society in which they live seem to be at variance with the official rosetinted view of reality.

A member of the Communist Party, a 50-year-old Ukrainian skilled worker from Balakova on the Volga, does not complain directly about material conditions, but notes instead what their consequences may be: 'Lack of foodstuffs, including meat and dairy products outrages our women.' And another CP member, a 43-year-old Ukrainian lathe operator from Kharkov, states bluntly: 'Our stores are empty. We are missing not only run-of-the-mill consumer goods, but even basic commodities such as milk, sugar and matches.' A Russian CP member (45) residing in Minsk, the Belorussian capital, finds that ideological comfort is not enough: 'For heaven's sake, life isn't easy!'

From Lvov, a 47-year-old Ukrainian foreman and party member complains: 'Finding socks, or wool for socks, is a real problem.' This complaint is reiterated by workers in various parts of the country, reaching its highest point in the lament of a 31-year-old mechanic from Odessa: 'If we had more socks and more foreign clothing, our country would be the best in the world.' A telling comment, coming as it does from a resident of the Black Sea port that has the reputation of supplying everything from arms to advanced electronic equipment – and is also the hub of the Soviet black-market industry.

But in rural areas, things are no better. An agricultural worker (41) from the Dnepropetrovsk area remarks on the lack of fruit and milk products, and a farmworker (35) from Dudinka in the Crimean peninsula reports that: 'Even in summer we lack fruit and vegetables.' Another farmworker (49) from Aleysk on the foothills of the Altai mountains in Siberia, says: 'We have neither fruit, vegetables, nor even dairy products.' An explanation for this paradoxical situation is provided by a woman farmworker (aged 45) from the Kirovsk region: 'Even we farmworkers have trouble finding eggs, chicken, butter and other products, since farmers who have such things prefer to sell them in town for higher prices than they can decently ask from the neighbours.' 'Dairy products are sold for too high a price', confirms a Krasnodar farmworker and CP member in his late thirties, and 'It's no easier for agricultural workers to get butter, eggs and so on than it is for anyone else', adds an agricultural worker (49), also a CP member, from the Yalta region. Finally, according to a 35-year-old farmworker from an area near Tambov: 'The problem of a salaried worker is that he has to go into town to buy food.'

Discontent in rural areas is not confined only to subjects such as the poor supply of food products. Dissatisfaction with conditions in *sovkhoz* (state-owned farms) and *kolkhoz* (collective farms) is widespread. A 31-year-old Estonian *Kolkhoznik* points to the poor quality of technical equipment available, and a Karelian from Teryoki complains of the lack of tools and technical equipment in his *sovkhoz*: 'Our agriculture is far from being fully mechanized,' says a farmworker and CP member (47) from Yaransk (between Kirov and Gorki). 'We are still using old-fashioned machinery,' adds a 42-year-old Novgorod farmworker. Another grievance, voiced by a 46-year-old farmworker from Balezino in the Udmurt ASSR and a Ukrainian from Dnepropetrovsk, is lack of fertilizer; while workers from Tula and Krasnodar refer to the difficulty of finding seeds.

A few rural inhabitants voice the view that they are underprivileged compared to urban residents in general. 'Owing to the lack of consumer goods, the rural population has a lower living standard,' claims a 42-year-old mechanic from Ivanovo. 'Distribution circuits for consumer goods favour big cities,' adds a Karelian farmworker from Petrozavodsk, who calls for a 'just and democratic solution to the problem'. A Latvian farmworker from Liepaya sees the problem in more radical terms: 'The rural population is underprivileged since all the decisions are made in the cities.'

Some agricultural workers, not content simply to enumerate sources of discontent, attempt to elucidate the causes of the situation and to attribute responsibility where they feel it belongs. 'Our agricultural problems stem from poor management,' states a 40-year-old farmworker from the Yalta area. 'Agriculture is mismanaged,' agrees a 42-year-old *sovkhoz* mechanic from the Sverdlovsk region. 'We still have some problems with the organization of our agriculture,' admits a metalworker and party member (51) from Berezniki.

'If the land belonged to individual farmers, they would make better use of it,' claims a woman farmworker (39) from deep in rural Crimea, 'and the middlemen, and by that I mean the administration, would not interfere. As things stand, the government officials who are supposed to be running things in fact do nothing at all. But they are living off the peasants. And that is the heart of the problem.' Finally, a 40-year-old CP member from the Krasnodar region, compares Soviet agricultural development to that of France: 'It will take at least 50 years for our country to reach [French] agricultural production levels.'

At this point, it seems opportune to explain in what way these comments were obtained. In the context of a larger social survey involving over 5000 Soviet citizens travelling in Western Europe, respondents were asked what they liked most and least about their own country. About 10 per cent of the total sample were members of the working class, and it is upon their responses alone that this chapter is based.

As may be realized, in the Soviet Union it is very difficult to engage people in the kind of conversation that will shed light on their perceptions of and reactions to the society in which they live. Soviet citizens are aware of being constantly under surveillance, especially in their intercourse with foreigners, and are hence unlikely to voice their opinions freely. But if such questions are put to them, without undue insistence, during a trip abroad, in the course of a casual conversation with a foreign acquaintance, very often they will consent, in such a relaxed setting, to voice freely their feelings, attitudes and opinions. (As this implies, none of the respondents with whom we talked in the course of the survey were made aware that they were being directly questioned; no questionnaire was shown them, and questions were introduced as unobtrusively as possible into the general drift of conversation.)

In the case of this particular question ('What do you like most and least about your own country?'), the subject was broached by means of a projective question that, as will be seen, could not, for obvious reasons, have been used within the Soviet Union. Rather than tackle the subject head-on, care was taken to approach it obliquely, in order to create a favourable psychological climate. Once the social researcher, a Westerner with a knowledge of Russian, had established contact with the Soviet visitor and managed to place relations on a suitably friendly footing, he asked the Soviet visitor what he liked most about the Western country in which he was presently travelling, following this with the query of what he liked least about it. This provided an appropriate lead into the question, 'what do you like most and least about the Soviet Union?'

In practically all cases, the Soviet visitor replied openly and spontaneously to the question. (Obviously there is a difference between what someone really feels and what he says he feels but, in practice, there is no satisfactory way of distinguishing between the two, and no attempt has therefore been made to do so.)[1] A few people refused outright to reply, or else evaded giving a direct answer. Both parts of the question (praise and criticism) were equally subject to evasion in these cases. One example of non-response came from a Ukrainian textile worker (33) from Lvov: 'I prefer to avoid answering this question, since I am on vacation, and I don't feel like reopening the wound.'

The idea embodied in this remark was expressed more precisely by a 38-year-old worker from Petropavlovsk in the Far East: 'I regret my trip to France, since it has opened my eyes to the extent of our misery.' And a 35-year-old Bryansk worker adds: 'Admittedly our people live in misery, but their happiness derives from the fact that they are not aware of it.'

Travel abroad, in other words, can be a mixed blessing. If this Bryansk worker is to be believed, it is perhaps fortunate for the Soviet people that relatively few of them do in fact get the chance to go abroad.[2] Foreign travel is both a distinction and a privilege. Authorization to go abroad as a tourist is dependent on the approval of one's place of work, of the Communist Youth Organization (Komsomol) or the party organization (as appropriate), and various other official bodies. As far as workers are concerned, it should also be borne in mind that the costs involved are frequently higher than they are easily able to bear. Nevertheless, most of the workers we talked to were tourists, although there were also a number of delegates, members of friendship societies, and participants in technical-exchanges programmes involving automobile and textile plants in Italy, and factories in France and elsewhere.

A further advantage of contacting Soviet citizens travelling abroad is that certain towns and cities in the Soviet Union are out of bounds to foreigners, including journalists and diplomats. However, residents of these 'closed' cities sometimes get the chance to travel abroad, and it was while they were travelling in various parts of Western Europe that we were able to talk to them. This meant that we were able to obtain the reactions of working people from all over the Soviet Union, and not just certain parts of it.

I would like here to forestall possible objections on the part of Westerners reading the remarks made by these Soviet workers. Some people in the West tend to believe that independently-thinking Soviet citizens will be prevented from travelling abroad, or else assume that rigorous surveillance of Soviet tourists abroad will preclude their expressing their ideas openly. Other Westerners tend to sympathize with social institutions in the USSR and hence reject the possibility of Soviet citizens abroad voicing their own criticisms of conditions at home. People in both these groups may find it hard to accept that Soviet workers really see things the way they do. Hence the frequent use of verbatim quotations in this chapter in an attempt to convince these sceptics that Soviet workers perceive different options and alternatives, that nothing is either all black or all white, and that in a country of over 200 million people it is as impossible to enforce uniformity as it is to eliminate all traces of heresy.

It should perhaps also be mentioned here that, although the 1970 Soviet census indicates that over 83 million people are engaged in manual labour,[3] the Soviet classifications do not correspond to accepted Western norms. Hence, we have omitted from the present study members of the service industries, such as barbers, photographers, municipal employees, despatchers, hospital personnel and so on, and restricted ourselves to those classified habitually as 'manual workers' in the West. A further point worth noting is that none of the respondents quoted here had higher education. Although a few of the skilled workers had technical qualifications, the great majority of workers had had less than ten years' schooling.

'Theoretically,' says a 31-year-old worker from Kurgan (Western Siberia), 'a worker makes as much as an engineer. But, in practice, an engineer makes two or three times as much a worker.' In reality, the Soviet working class does not therefore seem to be the privileged class it is claimed to be in official propaganda. 'I believe that we will be deprived of production bonuses this year because we lack the raw material we need to fulfil the Plan,' says a 39-year-old foreman from Ivanovo, and concern with diminishing bonuses is also reflected in comments by workers from Kirov and Togliatti. But although there is widespread dissatisfaction with salary levels and bonus payments, as well as a feeling that salaries are being overtaken by the rising cost of living, this is not always the heart of the problem.

'It is difficult to obtain shoes and clothing,' says a 39-year-old farmworker and CP member from Yalta; 'to have money is not enough, you've still got to find the goods.' And a 55-year-old skilled worker from

Kemerovo in Western Siberia takes up the refrain: 'To buy shoes and children's clothing, you need good contacts, or else you have to stand endlessly and repeatedly in a queue.' Other items are also difficult to find. 'We have great difficulties in procuring all household goods,' says a 47-year-old skilled worker and CP member from Barnaul, also in Western Siberia. 'To find washing machines or refrigerators is a real problem,' adds another worker (46) from Orenburg, in the same region. While a Minsk electrician (36) complains: 'We lack practically all domestic equipment and hardware supplies.' And in Groznyy, Bryansk, Moscow, Odessa, Tallin, Kalinin, Ivanovo, Tambov and many other cities, the situation is exactly the same.

All these problems stem, of course, from insufficient production and inefficient distribution circuits. With inadequate supplies of consumer goods available, what happens is that when some coveted item is put on sale in a store, long queues of would-be purchasers immediately form. In the Soviet Union, standing in a queue is an accepted part of the daily routine. 'I hate standing in queues,' complains a 31-year-old farmworker from Krasnodar. 'The queues in front of stores are getting longer and longer,' comments a 50-year-old worker from Segezha in the Karelian ASSR. 'The queues [in front of stores] haven't gone, and they aren't likely to either,' observes a skilled woman worker (50) from Vladivostok, one of the 'closed' cities referred to earlier on.

And even by standing in a queue, one has no guarantee of eventually being able to make one's purchases. 'Even though there are long queues in front of our stores, you don't always find what you are looking for,' says a 24-year-old skilled worker from Voronezh. 'The situation is catastrophic,' continues a 33-year-old Togliatti worker dramatically; 'even now that we have started to trade with foreign countries, we still aren't succeeding in getting goods into our stores.' An alternative solution is to resort to the black market. 'Since the stores are practically empty, the black market is flourishing,' explains a Murmansk foreman in his fifties. And the whole frustrating situation is aptly summed up by a 30-year-old worker from Togliatti, remarking wistfully on a visit to France: 'If we had only half of what you have, we would never, never complain.'

Although it is evident from these comments that the situation with regard to distribution and production of consumer goods in the USSR is far from satisfactory, it should not be deduced that all foodstuffs and household goods are permanently missing from all the stores in the country. These observations were gathered over a three-and-a-half-year period, between February 1975 and August 1978. Thus, if on a certain date, matches were not available in a certain district of Kiev, and the would-be purchaser was sufficiently annoyed to complain about it to a foreigner on a trip to the West a few days or a few weeks later, this does not necessarily mean that matches were missing from every store in Kiev, which is, after all, a city of over 2 million people.

Not surprisingly, it is the women who suffer most from a situation like this. 'Life is difficult for women,' comments a woman skilled worker (30) from Moscow. 'They have a job to hold down, the housework to do, not to mention queueing in stores.' 'I loathe standing in queues, and yet we have to queue a lot,' says a woman worker from Orekhovo-Zuyevo, 50 miles east of Moscow. 'Women have a hard life, what with their jobs, the housework, the queues in stores to buy food and clothing; and then, to top it all, the men get drunk and beat them,' adds a 44-year-old Chita woman. And a 40-year-old woman worker from Ulyanovsk puts it even more bluntly: 'In the Soviet Union, women are still slaves, because life is difficult, and the men don't help. For men, it's easy. They have their job, their newspaper, radio and television, their vodka, and all the housework is left for the women to do.' 'Men may dress better now,' affirms a 26-year-old woman from Orenburg, 'but underneath they're still beasts. A lot of them still beat their wives.'

Some men, however, show awareness of the difficulties faced by Soviet women, at least to the extent that it affects them personally. 'We lack everything,' says, for example, a 44-year-old Kharkov mechanic; 'consequently, our women complain, and this leads to problems in the home.' 'Women don't have enough time for their families, since almost all of them have jobs outside the home,' adds a 29-year-old Muscovite. 'Women especially have a hard time of it in our country,' admits an unskilled worker (44) from Zhdanov in the Ukraine. 'The difficulty of shopping makes life very tedious for our women,' agrees a skilled worker (34) from Saransk. Finally, in the words of a Ukrainian mechanic from Dneprodzherzinsk: 'Our women age fast because they work too hard.'

Material difficulties are compounded by poor housing conditions and overcrowding, a problem evoked by workers from many different areas. A Karelian worker from Vyborg complains of too small apartments, and an Estonian from Tallin of lack of apartments. Another Estonian, also from Tallin, refers in more general terms to 'poor housing conditions', and a 21-year-old woman from Ivanovo says briefly: 'We've got some housing problems.' 'We suffer from inadequate housing space,' explains a 40-year-old CP member from Pechora in the Komi ASSR, and a 33-year-old worker from Yaroslavl puts it more graphically: 'Lack of housing is a great problem. In my own case, a four-room apartment is shared between four families, ten persons in all.' A 36-year-old mechanic from Krivoy Rog is in an even worse position: 'Our salaries are miserable. We lack everything. There are eight of us living in two rooms.' 'We still have to build a good many apartments to catch up with people's needs,' admits a building worker and CP member (51) from Rostov.

The problem is not only one of quantity, but also of quality. 'Apartments are not solidly built,' complains a woman factory worker (39) from Leningrad. Possibly the answer lies in the shortage of building materials evoked by a 36-year-old mason from Minsk: 'Construction materials are hard to obtain, which is why even a mason can't have his own house'; and also by a farmworker from Novikovo on Sakhalin Island in the Far East: 'We have to pick up stones from ruins, because we have nothing else to build with. It's nothing to be proud of.'

And what do Soviet workers find to be proud of, to appreciate or to admire, in their country? Often replies tend to be somewhat stereotyped (especially comments made by members of the Communist Party), and run on the lines of 'the great communist system', free education, free medical care, lack of unemployment and so on. Many respondents referred simply to 'my friends', 'my family', 'the Russian people'. Certain characteristics of the Russian people, such as hospitality or generosity, are also singled out for mention.

As will be seen further on, many workers reject the notion of all-pervading state control regulating every aspect of the citizens' lives ('We can't live our own lives,' says a 34-year-old Gorki foreman). Others, however, seem to derive a certain reassurance from the certitude that everything is managed for them by the state. 'There is order, and citizens feel secure,' says a 51-year-old building worker from Rostov. Economic security is also important. 'Our economic system is stable. We don't live luxuriously, but neither do we risk starvation,' remarks a 44-year-old Moscow tailor. 'We have far fewer material goods,' continues a 30-year-old Engels transport worker, 'but people are better off in the sense that they have fewer problems.' (It is perhaps no coincidence that these three respondents are all members of the Communist Party.)

If positive reactions to the Soviet Union seem to be unfairly neglected in favour of negative attitudes in this study, one reason for this is that people in general tend to be more inventive in detailing their burdens than their blessings! Additionally, it is often the case that people without higher education encounter greater difficulty in manipulating abstract concepts. It comes as no surprise therefore that, with a few exceptions (notably political comments on lack of freedom and so on), the critical comments expressed here are almost uniformly concrete and factual in nature. Based on first-hand experience, they point up what is missing from Soviet society and in what way things could be improved. On the other hand, remarks praising conditions in Soviet society are more likely to refer to abstract notions, as we have seen above. They tend to be expressed in impersonal terms, impregnated with the language and slogans of communist propaganda. Lacking in personal conviction, they seem to us imperfect instruments with which to measure the individual's true perceptions of his social environment.

Although a number of workers praise the fact that medical care is entirely free, a 42-year-old agricultural worker and CP member from Kalach near the town of Voronezh puts his finger on a factor that goes a good way towards obviating this advantage: 'We lack most basic medicaments, and that is serious.' 'Our problem is to find the medicaments once they have been prescribed,' agrees a 51-year-old worker from Tula. 'Certain medicaments and B12 vitamins are unobtainable,' says a Vitebsk skilled worker (48), and the absence of medicaments is confirmed by women workers from Lvov and Orekhovo-Zuyevo: 'You can't always find the medicine you're looking for,' says the latter.

A specific complaint concerning the unavailability of certain optic lenses is voiced by a 38-year-old agricultural worker from the Altai mountains and a 50-year-old woman CP member from Yaroslavl, who said: 'Certain optic lenses are difficult to find. My younger brother almost went blind.' Another instance of deficiencies leading to disease was mentioned by a Leningrad printing worker and CP member aged 40: 'In my profession, what we lack most is milk. Many people get lung diseases for lack of milk and a good diet.' A vaguer fear is expressed by a 42-year-old Donetsk foreman: 'Cancer is spreading more and more in the Soviet Union.'

In a country which holds certain records of longevity, where certain inhabitants of the Caucasus region attain great ages, it is perhaps surprising to encounter concern about ageing. But it should not be forgotten that the difficult material life also takes its toll. Thus, a 52-year-old skilled worker from Rostov reflects: 'We age rapidly in the USSR.' 'At 50, a man is finished,' adds a 30-year-old Leningrad foreman. A Khabarovsk woman worker (37) concludes: 'People are ageing faster, and longevity on the whole is diminishing.' While a woman unskilled worker from Yaroslavl sees it in terms of a social problem: 'Retirement age should be reduced, because the way things are right now, you're dead before you can benefit from retirement.'

It is not unlikely that a week or two in France or Italy has brought the attention of many Soviet workers to social conditions in the West, as compared to those in their own country. 'Family allowances don't exist at home,' remarks a skilled worker (46) from Kursk; 'even with five kids you get nothing at all.' The same complaint is made by a 33-year-old Togliatti worker. 'We don't have a thirteenth month and our bonuses are decreasing,' objects an unskilled worker (39) from Minsk. An Orenburg worker (32) considers that holiday time is insufficient, and a 57-year-old Ivanovo skilled worker, thinking ahead no doubt to his impending retirement, comments: 'Our pensions aren't high. Most people have to go on working after they retire to make ends meet.'

More serious social problems, such as alcoholism, also preoccupy a large number of workers, although their viewpoints are not necessarily the same. 'Our famous vodka is a bit too expensive,' complains a 31-year-old Belgorod worker. 'According to rumour, the price of vodka is about to go up. This will be a catastrophe,' adds a worker from Ivanovo, also in his thirties. But a 40-year-old foreman and CP member from Kirov takes the opposite view: 'There is too much drunkenness and laziness at my place of work, and the management is too lax about it.' 'Young people drink even more than the older generation,' claims a 30-year-old skilled worker from Ivanovo.

An explanation is provided by a 34-year-old engine driver and CP member from Odessa: 'It is true to say that people drink too much, but it happens because they have too much money.' And this comment is indirectly borne out by a 48-year-old skilled worker from Arkhangelsk in the far north: 'Admittedly vodka is rather expensive, but that is no reason to do without.'

The problem of alcoholism in the Soviet Union is notoriously related to the rigorous climatic conditions and the virtual absence of other forms of entertainment for the long winter evenings. The lack of leisure-time facilities is a subject of discontent among younger workers especially. 'In general, there are not enough entertainment facilities,' observes a 32-year-old Novgorod worker. 'There is a shortage of amusement facilities for young people,' complains a 39-year-old Smolensk worker. 'At night, entertainment is limited,' says another Novgorod resident. 'It is difficult to find leisure-time activities,' agrees a Ukrainian mechanic from Rostov in his late twenties.

Some of the workers voiced more specific hankerings. A 35-year-old skilled worker from Orenburg complains that: 'Sporting equipment is hard to find, unattractive and expensive', while a skilled worker, also in his thirties, from Chiatura in Georgia remarks: 'Soviet television is monotonous, and so is everything else.' 'We have no Westerns or suspense films,' laments a 25-year-old skilled worker from Gorki. And from Saransk, another skilled worker (32) regrets the absence of Westerns and James Bond films: 'Our films are not as good [as Western ones],' opines a woman farmworker (29) from the Ivanovo region; 'they are monotonous; there's no action.'

Another grievance is the lack of Western music. A 29-year-old Tula skilled worker, admitting that there are a good many cultural clubs where people can listen to music, points out that the music in question is folk music only. 'On the black market, pop records sell for exorbitant prices such as 10–15 rubles a record,' complains a 27-year-old Ulyanovsk worker. 'Occasionally, one finds jazz and rock records on the black market, but at a high cost,' confirms a skilled worker (36) from Omsk. 'The only way to get jazz records is on the black market, but the prices there are exaggerated and constantly changing,' says another skilled worker (32) from Voroshilovgrad.

Leisure activities are further restricted by the lack of transport facilities. 'We lack bicycles, motorcycles, not to mention cars; and so our leisure time is monotonous,' says a young Kharkov foreman. Many manual workers display a fascination with automobiles, which are seen as immensely desirable, especially by skilled workers, mechanics and younger workers. But for most of them, a car is something out of their reach. 'A car is a great luxury,' remarks a Ukrainian skilled worker (29) from Voroshilovgrad.

Part of the problem is the waiting time, and part is the price. 'A car is something to dream about,' reflects a 32-year-old Ukrainian woman from Kherson; 'even if I saved half my salary, I would still have to work all my life long to be able to afford one.' 'Cars are expensive and practically unobtainable; even people with money have to wait three or four years,' adds a Kishinev mechanic (26). 'There is still a long waiting period to buy a car,' agrees a 27-year-old skilled worker from Krasnovodsk in the Turkmen SSR. Another skilled worker of the same age, from Tashkent in the Uzbek SSR, goes straight to the root of the matter: 'We are a long way behind in automobile construction.' While a 34-year-old worker from the automobile plant in Togliatti complains that: 'Not only do automobile workers have to pay the same price for a car as other people, they even have to wait as long.'

But those who eventually win this coveted prize find themselves faced with other problems. Inadequate transport facilities and poor roads complicate the lives of millions of Soviet citizens, and complaints from professional drivers and others highlight the absence of facilities for motorists in the USSR. 'I have to go some 30 kilometres to work and back, and it takes me between three and four hours,' says a 50-year-old agricultural worker, living to the north of Kalinin. 'We have no highways, but there aren't many cars either,' says a Tula skilled worker (30). Lorry drivers from Moscow and Leningrad complain of bad roads. A 38-year-old cab driver and CP member from Kiev points to the lack of garages and service stations, and an Uzbek driver of the same age from Tashkent feels that the standard of garage maintenance is too low. While those wishing to motor for pleasure should bear in mind the remark made by a Ukrainian skilled worker from Taganrog, who says that: 'Tourism inside the Soviet Union is very expensive.'

But on the mind of more people is tourism outside the Soviet Union. 'The greatest achievement in the history of our country is to be able to take tourist trips abroad,' declares a Chiatura skilled worker (39). Many people saw it as an extremely positive development that simple workers from distant parts of the country should now be given the opportunity to travel abroad. However, a 32-year-old Ukrainian worker from Kiev put his finger on the limitations of this arrangement: 'It remains a privilege to travel abroad.' This feeling of dissatisfaction was shared by a great many of his fellow travellers. Remarks about the limited possibilities for foreign travel were made by an Estonian woman building worker from Tartu, a 27-year-old Moscow printing worker, a 24-year-old Leningrad building worker, and a 34-year-old Ukrainian farmworker from the Kharkov area, to mention only a few. 'I dislike this system that prevents me from visiting a country as much as I want,' states a 30-year-old Leningrad cab driver. 'We cannot travel as much as we would like,' adds an Estonian driver from Tallin. 'I would have liked to visit other European countries,' explains a 29-year-old worker from Ivanovo.

Permission to travel abroad is difficult to obtain in principle, and opportunities to travel abroad are rare. Travellers often cannot select the country they want to visit. There is no choice of destination; they are generally obliged to settle for the country advertised in the trade union or party cells. In addition to this, passports are hard to come by and also expensive, and foreign-currency allowances are extremely tight.

General complaints concerning travel restrictions were voiced by a factory worker from Kharkov, a mechanic from Leningrad, a roadworker from Repino (near Moscow), an Estonian woman factory worker from Vilyandi, and many others. 'It is still rare to travel abroad,' observes a 28-year-old skilled worker from Vyborg. 'In all probability, when you get a chance to travel abroad, it'll be your first and last trip,' comments a Ukrainian fitter (47) from Belopolye. But even this, to the mind of a 35-year-old woman worker from Khabarovsk, is already something to be thankful for: 'If you behave correctly and work efficiently, you get the chance to travel abroad at least once in your lifetime.' While a more optimistic point of view is taken by a 42-year-old skilled worker from Murmansk: 'you are only authorized to travel abroad once every three to four years.'

'When you get the chance to travel abroad – which is rare, sometimes no more than once in a lifetime – you are so restricted in foreign currency that you're prevented from really enjoying your trip to the full.' This comment, by a 37-year-old Ukrainian mechanic from Rostov, sums up the disappointment felt by many travellers at having the occasion thus summarily spoilt for them. 'They don't give us enough foreign currency,' confirms a skilled worker (38) from Odessa. 'They allot you a ridiculously small amount of foreign currency to travel abroad,' adds a 53-year-old Tula skilled worker. 'Unfortunately we get very little foreign currency, and we can only dream of buying souvenirs,' complains a woman worker from Orekhovo-Zuyevo.

Some travellers are concerned with the image projected by Soviet tourists abroad, and others feel themselves hard done by in comparison to people of other nationalities. 'They allow us so little currency that we look really poor when we travel abroad,' says a 25-year-old Sverdlovsk mechanic. While an Estonian sailor (30) from Tartu observes: 'We have nowhere near as much foreign currency as merchant sailors from other countries.'

Other visitors have been more outspoken against what they feel is a gross injustice. 'Our bosses are bastards!' says a 39-year-old skilled worker from Novocherkassk; 'they paid out our spending money – a ludicrous 200 French francs per person – on the last day of our trip.' 'These bastard officials only give you a minimum of foreign currency,' grumbles a 31-year-old driver from Nikolayev in the Ukraine. 'The devils allowed us only 110 French francs each for a ten-day trip to France. It's ridiculous', says a 39-year-old woman farmworker from a village in the Altai region, while a 33-year-old agricultural worker from Yefremov in the Tula region complains of only 75 French francs spending money.

Travelling abroad is an eye-opener in more ways than one. A 25-year-old woman from Orekhovo-Zuyevo was prompted by her experiences in Italy to make the following comment: 'It is curious that people seem to lose their faith in a religious country like Italy, whereas in our communist country people tend to look for it.' Other comparisons were drawn between the Soviet Union and the West by other respondents, depending on their own preoccupations. Thus, a Ukrainian sailor in his thirties from Odessa remarks: 'Compared to Western countries, the turnover of workers in Russia is amazing.' A female agricultural worker and CP member (39) from the Sovetsk area, north of Kaliningrad, deploring the lack of orthodoxy of foreign communist parties, declares: 'Our government should not label other parties as communist. They don't deserve it.'

Other observers are struck by the discrepancy between the way in which life in the West has been described to them and what they see for themselves to be the reality of the situation. 'We were made to believe that communism is better than capitalism but, seeing what I have seen, I have doubts,' says a 30-year-old agricultural worker from near Temir-tau in Kazakhstan. 'Our dreams of a better life are unfounded, because Soviet reality has nothing to do with your reality,' says a 33-year-old Tashkent electrician sadly. 'We are always told that foreigners live miserably, and now I see that it is the opposite. It is silly to lie to us,' comments a 31-year-old Cherkassy woman. And, echoing comments made earlier, a woman agricultural worker, an Ossetian from the Caucasus, concludes: 'It would be better if they didn't let us travel abroad. After a trip like this, you feel even more miserable than you did before.'

The social perceptions of Soviet workers related so far have focused primarily upon their own living conditions and touched only incidentally upon political matters. In the following pages, we will deal with political preoccupations.

Comments relating to various aspects of the Soviet political and economic system were abundant. Dislike of the system, nationality tensions, restrictions on free speech and freedom of information were frequently evoked. But the very fact that citizens of the Soviet Union travelling abroad should venture to hold forth on such topics at first sight runs counter to the experiences and observations of Western tourists to the Soviet Union. Talking to Soviet people on their own home ground, Westerners tend to bring back with them the impression that people think things are better now than they have ever been and are likely to improve still further. Is it possible that the observations of Western travellers are, for one reason or another, superficial or misguided?

As a rule, Western travellers generally meet privileged Soviet citizens and are entertained in specially selected places. It is unlikely that their Soviet hosts would give vent to any critical thoughts. Any workers whom they may encounter would probably speak in a spirit of patriotism, if not in the name of the ruling party. How can we reconcile these two conflicting perspectives? The answer is perhaps best resumed in the words of Hadley Cantril, an eminent social psychologist: 'A person's reality world can only be altered through experience, not through indoctrination and dictum alone.'[4]

'Brezhnev fell into the trap he set at Helsinki and, as a result, he has to let us travel abroad,' as a 40-year-old Ukrainian skilled worker from Chernigov gleefully remarks. (Asked what he liked least about his country, the same source replied: 'Let me turn the question the other way round. Is there anything that *does* work in our country?') But for other respondents, the Helsinki Agreements have had no impact at all in the Soviet Union. 'It is obvious that there is no chance at all of the Helsinki Agreements being applied in our country,' declares a 40-year-old Gorki foreman, while another foreman, a Ukrainian from Dnepropetrovsk, reacts in the following way: 'Brezhnev got the better of the capitalist countries in getting them to sign the Helsinki Agreements, which he himself is not going to put into practice.' The 'system' is a focus of criticism for a good many of the Soviet workers we talked to. 'That shit system', said a Moscow factory worker, asked what he disliked most about his country. An Estonian minor from Pyarnu (28) describes the system as 'treacherous', a foreman from Petrozavodsk (27) says quite openly that he dislikes the system, while a Moscow lorry driver condemns the 'one-party system', and a 24-year-old worker from Izhevsk denounces the 'hegemony' of the party. 'I don't like today's system, with its norms and political education,' declares a 50-year-old agricultural worker, an Estonian from the Tallin area. 'People are conditioned to think all the same way. This is contrary to human nature and progress,' says a 29-year-old Ukrainian electrician from Odessa.

Credit can probably be given to the relaxed atmosphere in the West which encouraged the Soviet visitors to touch on political questions, in spite of the warning not to do so that some of them, at least, seem to have received. 'It is pointless to give us instructions not to discuss politics with foreigners,' comments a Ukrainian unskilled worker from Chernovtsy. 'Most people do not take much interest in politics anyway, and those who do are reluctant to discuss the subject.' The implication seems to be that a Soviet citizen does not discuss politics unless he knows exactly who he is talking to and is sure that the person is a friend or family member that he can trust entirely – or unless he is in a situation that guarantees his anonymity.

'There is no real freedom in the Soviet Union', said a 31-year-old factory worker from Yaroslavl, and his statement was echoed by a good many other respondents, including a female house-painter from Novgorod, a Leningrad sailor, a Ukrainian cab-driver from Kishinev, a Karelian forestry worker, an Estonian fisherman from Tallin, and a mechanic, a stoker and a tailor, all from Moscow. One aspect of this lack of freedom is the restriction placed on travel both within the Soviet Union and abroad. 'I am prevented from doing what I want to do and going where I want to go,' protests a 48-year-old Latvian skilled worker from Riga. 'We lack the freedom to travel as much as we want and as much as is necessary,' contributes a 30-year-old Estonian farmworker living near Tartu. An Estonian skilled worker complains of both travel restrictions and lack of free speech for, of course, another constraint is the impossibility of speaking openly. 'Everyone is watching you,' explains a 30-year-old Moscow unskilled worker. 'Everyone is watching each other,' elaborates an Estonian sailor from Pyarnu. 'Although Stalin has been dead for well over twenty years, people have still not lost the habit of denunciation,' claims a 31-year-old worker from Odessa.

An all-encompassing feeling of oppression emerges from the comments made by some of the workers. 'I don't really feel free,' says a 37-year-old mechanic from Rybinsk, a town north of Moscow. 'Contrary to what they tell us, we are simply not free,' states a Leningrad foreman flatly. 'We are subject to all kinds of restrictions,' says a Leningrad cab driver (44). 'What I dislike most is all the restrictions that simply don't exist in Western countries,' adds a woman bakery worker (31) from Moscow. But the most graphic comment comes from a 30-year-old Estonian farmworker from the Tallin region: 'Living in the Soviet Union, you feel as if you were in prison.'

For many members of Soviet minority nationalities, this atmosphere of oppression is embodied in concrete form in the shape of Russian rule, Russian influence and Russian privileges, which are seen as a direct threat to their potential for national self-determination. 'Throughout the entire Soviet Union, the Russians have a privileged status. This is not democratic,' points out a 39-year-old Latvian seaman from Riga. 'In Lithuania, at least, the Russians are privileged. In another two or three generations, Pan-slavism will have taken over our country completely,' adds another Balt, a Lithuanian, a 30-year-old skilled worker from Kaunas. 'The trend is pro-Russian and anti-Georgian, which doesn't give us much hope for the future,' says a 27-year-old Georgian worker from Tbilisi gloomily. 'Russian influence is too great,' says a Latvian sailor (30) from Ventspils. 'There are too many Russians around,' complains a 52-year-old Estonian farmer from the Tallin area. Finally, a Ukrainian sailor from Odessa uses the same words to describe what he most dislikes about his country as an unskilled Ukrainian worker from Rostov: 'The Russians in general.'

Privileges and discrimination take many forms. Thus, a Georgian cab driver from Leningrad affirms that the Russians are given special treatment in assignment of apartments, and a Lithuanian worker from Kaunas complains of discrimination against Lithuanian literary clubs. A 30-year-old worker from the Komi ASSR feels that the cultural position of the national minorities is severely compromised, and a Ukrainian worker from Poltava is worried by 'censorship and the absence of a free Ukrainian press'. Resentment of the control exercised by the central government is apparent in the remark of a Tatar mechanic (27) living on a *kolkhoz* near Samarkand: 'The Moscow government knows more about the circumstances and possibilities in Uzbekistan than the people who live there!' 'We are autonomous, but it's not the same as having a state of one's own,' remarks a 39-year-old Karelian worker from Petrozavodsk bitterly. (Karelia is an 'autonomous' republic, which means that its legal status is inferior to that of a fully-fledged union republic, such as Estonia, Georgia or Uzbekistan.)

Another characteristic of the totalitarian system is, of course, the state monopoly of information. 'We don't have enough freedom,' says a 37-year-old mechanic from Moscow; 'people need truthful information.' A Ukrainian glass-blower (52) from Rovno and a Leningrad skilled worker (40) complain of 'limited information'. 'We don't have access to good Western information', laments an Estonian foreman of the same age from Tallin, and a 29-year-old Leningrad electrician puts it more precisely: 'You can't listen freely to Western [radio] stations.'

Lack of free information implies lack of contact with the outside world in general. 'We have too few contacts with foreign countries', is the opinion of a 33-year-old mechanic from Molodechno in the Belorussian SSR; and a woman worker from Ivanovo puts the idea in more concrete terms: 'It would be desirable to have more tourist travel in both directions, east – west.'

'We have very good laws in the Soviet Union. The problem is that nobody abides by them,' remarks a 40-year-old skilled worker from Segezha in Karelia. The problem of discrimination towards members of national minorities has already been evoked in some detail, and a Karelian printing worker living in Kiev adds succinctly: 'There are injustices at all levels.' Complaints about the bureaucracy in general are formulated by an Estonian sailor from Pyarnu, a Karelian baker from Petrozavodsk, and a skilled worker from Leningrad, who say: 'The bureaucracy in general doesn't work properly.' More touches are added to the overall picture of corruption and inefficiency by a 28-year-old driver from Yaroslavl, who comments: 'To make a career in our country depends not on whatever individual gifts one may possess, but on selling oneself, prostituting oneself.' And a 45-year-old Belorussian woman CP member mentions 'Party careerists and opportunists', as the facet of Soviet life she dislikes the most. Finally, a Tula ironsmith remarks: 'Highly-placed officials and military officers have unlimited power – and they know how to use it.'

Nor are the country's leaders themselves exempt from criticism. 'The attitude of the present leaders lacks clarity,' notes a Belorussian steelworker (30) from Gomel. 'They are neither leftist, rightist nor centrist. It's impossible to place them.' And he adds: 'The true communists in our country, those of the Lenin school, are pro-Chinese, and they are quite right.' Conversely, support for the present leadership was voiced by a 42-year-old Voroshilovgrad mechanic: 'Brezhnev wants to co-operate with the West, but unfortunately those around him are not always in agreement with this policy. When Brezhnev goes, the situation may well deteriorate. The struggle for power will start up immediately.'

Criticism of government policy covers a wide variety of issues. 'Our leaders talk about making peace in the world, while at the same time they are busy turning our country into the world's leading arms manufacturer,' observes a Ukrainian worker (20) from Nikolayev. 'Military expenses are excessive', feels a 33-year-old farmworker from a state farm in the Tajik SSR, while a 32-year-old Kuybyshev worker adds: 'I think the salaries of professional soldiers are too high.' 'There are so many soldiers in our town that at times one thinks we must be at war,' says a skilled worker in his forties from Blagoveshchensk, on the Chinese frontier in the Far East.

'We spend too much money on space conquest,' objects a 27-year-old Berdyansk mechanic. A 37-year-old Belorussian foreman from Brest deplores the government's negative attitude to emigration, and a woman worker from Orenburg in the Urals comments: 'To show that we are doing well, many of our products are exported, with the result that the Soviet people are deprived.' Although this last comment is based on a misconception, the speaker's sense of injustice is no less real for that.

Finally, a good deal of resentment seems to be aroused by the Soviet government's policy of aid to developing countries. 'Without our assistance to . . . developing countries, we would already have caught up with the US in agricultural production,' claims a 40-year-old foreman and CP member from Leninabad in the Tajik SSR. (However, another party member of the same age, a *sovkhoz* foreman from

Nyuvchim in the Komi ASSR, reflects: 'Our attempts to catch up with the US are utopian.') 'We are giving too much aid to Third World countries at the expense of our own people,' says a Togliatti worker. 'We give too much assistance to developing countries,' agrees a 23-year-old Ukrainian mechanic from Kharkov. A foreman from Alma-Ata, aged 29, sees a more concrete link between cause and effect: 'We give too much to India and Vietnam. That's why we lack vegetables.'

It is hoped that these perceptions of Soviet society speak for themselves, and no attempt has been made to draw any conclusions from them. In any case, it would be misleading to generalize from such a small-scale survey as this. But although we do not claim that these respondents were representative of the Soviet population (or even the Soviet working class) as a whole, their comments indicate that workers of different ages and nationalities, living in different parts of the Soviet Union, share much the same preoccupations. Overall, their reactions seem to point to the acceptance of certain values (much importance is placed on material well-being, for instance, and also on 'freedom' in the widest sense of the word), and also attest to a widespread recognition of the inadequacies and defects of their country.

NOTES

1. Renato Tagiuri, *Person Perception and Interpersonal Behavior* (Stanford University Press, 1958) p. 317.
2. For example, the *New York Times* of 25 October 1979 reports that 70,000 Americans visit the Soviet Union every year, while fewer than 5000 Soviet citizens visit the United States. It can be assumed that most of the Americans visiting the USSR were tourists, but it is unlikely that this was the case with Soviet visitors to the USA.
3. *Raspredileniye naseleniya SSSR po zanatiyam* (Distribution of the Population of the USSR by Occupation) Ed. Statistika (Moscow, 1973).
4. Hadley Cantril, *Soviet Leaders and Mastery Over Man* (Rutgers University Press, 1960) p. 110.

Supplement: Retail Prices in Moscow and Four Western Cities in March 1979

Keith Bush*

INTRODUCTION

The purpose of this survey is to facilitate the comparison of Soviet and Western living standards by recording the retail prices of selected consumer goods and services in Moscow and four Western cities at a given time and computing the work-time equivalents of these prices.

The first section outlines the nature of the sample taken and explains the methods used. It then lists some of the major qualifications that apply to this, or indeed to any, international survey of consumer goods and services. The section ends with a tally for a weekly family basket of food, beverages and cigarettes at estimated Soviet levels of consumption, priced in terms of work-time units, together with a monthly rent and two prominent consumer durables. Four appendices follow.

Appendix 1 gives the retail prices in local currencies of 176 consumer goods and services in Washington, Moscow, Munich, Paris and London, as observed in early March 1979. In Appendix 2, these prices are converted into US dollars at the official interbank foreign exchange rates prevailing on 1 March, 1979. In Appendix 3, the retail prices are expressed in work-time equivalents based on estimates of average take-home pay in January 1979 of industrial workers, male and female, in the respective countries. Appendix 4 supplies the data and the sources from which the figures for take-home pay were derived.

* Mr Bush is director of research of Radio Liberty in Munich. This study is the latest of his periodic comprehensive surveys of retail prices and wages in five countries.

THE SAMPLE

The survey has in the main been confined to goods and services that can be purchased in all five cities. This has restricted the range of goods that might have been included: for instance, frozen and convenience foods, the mainstay of many Western households, have been largely excluded because they are not widely available in Moscow. In the Western cities, prices have been surveyed whereever possible in at least five suburban supermarkets of the kind with more moderately-priced products, and an average price has been computed. (Hypermarkets appear to account for a growing share of retail trade in foodstuffs, soft goods and durables in the US, France and Germany, but they are unknown in the USSR and seldom to be found in the UK.) In Moscow, the prices for foodstuffs were those recorded at state retail stores: here prices are stable except for those on 'new' and 'improved' products and, because of slight seasonal variations, those on certain vegetables and fruit. The abbreviation 'na' means that the good or service was not found at the store or establishment surveyed; it does not necessarily signify that the item could not be purchased somewhere in that particular city. Parentheses have been used to designate the prices of items that have in the past been seen on sale in Moscow but that could not be found by any surveyor in any state retail store in Moscow at the time of this survey.

Prices have been recorded for the standard quantity or package sold. In many instances, this is larger in the US than in Western Europe or Moscow, which may introduce a slight bias in favour of the US owing to quantity discounts. Against this could be set the cost of individual transportation.

Obvious loss leaders have been excluded from this survey, and container charges have been deducted. State, local and value-added taxes, if levied, have been included. For the US and Western Europe, a common brand name has been chosen for the survey, where possible. If multiple tickets or carnets are commonly used, the price of a specific journey with these, rather than with an individual ticket, has been noted.

Although every effort has been made to ensure correspondence between the goods and services selected for examination in the five cities, the greatest shortcoming in any survey of this nature is the lack of comparability of many items. This incomparability is in large part attributable simply to differing national tastes. For example, the vegetables, fruit and meat on sale in Paris looked infinitely more appetizing to this writer than the goods on display in the other cities. The processing and packaging of foodstuffs in Western Europe and in the USSR continue to lag behind American standards. The 'drive-away' price has been noted for a basic Ford 'Fairlane' in the US, a Ford 'Granada' in Western Europe and a 'Volga' GAZ-24 in the USSR: all of these models are of roughly the same size and engine capacity, but it is difficult to compare their finish, their performance, their serviceability and their resale value. Should a Chevrolet 'Chevette' be equated with a VAZ-2101 'Zhiguli'? And so on.

The retail prices of goods and services have been recorded in capital cities (with the exception of Munich) and then converted into units of work-time using *national* average earnings. At first glance, this may seem questionable, to say the least. Yet while the charges for consumer services in these large cities were found to be appreciably higher than in outlying towns, the reverse was the case for many staple foodstuffs, soft goods and durables. Thus a housewife in Sens may find it worth her while to stock up in Paris, and her counterpart in Landsberg will often fill the car with supplies on a shopping expedition to Munich.

Another important consideration is the non-availability in Moscow at any given time of many of the items listed, except on special occasions such as the October Revolution anniversary holidays and, perhaps, during the 1980 Olympics. Since the state retail prices for such deficient items are known from periodic surveys, it has been deemed preferable to record those prices (distinguished by parentheses) rather than leave too many gaps in the lists. Similarly, the nominal charge for a double room in a Moscow hotel is astonishingly low, but then it is almost impossible for a Soviet citizen to get a room there without special authorization.

The monthly rents refer to modest, unfurnished three-room apartments in one of the least expensive suburbs (such as the 20th arrondisement in Paris). A floor space of 50 square metres was specified. This comes close to the current Soviet urban *per capita* average housing space of nearly nine square metres of 'living space' and thirteen square metres of 'total space'. It is smaller than most housing occupied by a family of four in the West. The first figure given relates to uncontrolled and unsubsidized housing: this category has no real equivalent in Moscow, where housing is virtually a rationed good. The second rent is for accommodation that is subsidized, or under rent control, by the local authorities. (Curiously, we were assured by the Housing Resources Division of the Washington, DC government that rents of housing under rent control in March were somewhat higher than those on the free market.)

TAKE-HOME PAY

The critical measure take-home pay has been derived from the average gross earnings of industrial (manufacturing) workers, male and female. This approach is far from ideal: there are, for instance, precious few, if any, industrial workers living in Washington, DC. The choice was made, however, because industrial workers form the largest single category of wage-earners in most industrialized nations and it is the only category for which roughly comparable data exist. For the purpose of the survey, it might have been more desirable to set the average number of wage-earners in each family against the average number of family members: for all Soviet workers and employees – that is, including those working on *sovkhozes* – the respective averages are believed to be 1.6 and 3.5. Yet no comparable figures could be found for industrial workers and their families in any of the countries surveyed. Moreover, where mothers work outside the home, the attendant costs of child care would have to be considered.

The calculations for take-home pay relate to January 1979. At the time of writing, this was the latest month for which preliminary estimates of gross earnings had been published in some of the countries and also the first month in which certain new rates of deductions were applicable. The figure for average earnings for the UK refers to adult male workers: no comparable weighted average data were available for male and female workers. Since earnings of female manual workers in British industry in April 1978 were only 60.2 per cent of corresponding male earnings, the UK figures employed are high and not comparable.

From the average gross earnings, the direct income tax payable by a worker with three non-earning dependants (namely, a housewife and two children aged nine and six years) has been deducted. No itemized deductions have been made. State taxes for Washington, DC, and church taxes for West German workers, have been deducted. A transportation allowance for Paris has been added. For the four Western countries, the obligatory social security contribution by the employee has been subtracted from after-tax earnings. Medical insurance premiums guaranteeing basic health care coverage for workers and their families are obligatory in Western Europe; no specific contribution is levied in the USSR. Here, for the sake of comparability, we have deducted from the American worker's pay a group high-option family coverage insurance premium. This provides basic hospital and out-patient coverage but excludes dental care. A further specific deduction is made from the gross earnings of the German, French and British workers for unemployment insurance. No such charge is made in the USSR, where unemployment officially ceased in 1930. In the US, the employer bears the total cost of unemployment insurance.

Family allowances are payable in the three West European nations cited, but not in the US. A family income supplement has been payable since September 1974 in the USSR, where the *per capita* family income is less than fifty rubles a month. This takes the form of a flat rate of twelve rubles a month for each child until the child's eighth birthday. Of course, in most workers' families, as in the West, the wife also holds a job outside the home; this would in most cases raise the *per capita* incomes above the fifty-ruble level.

For the purpose of juxtaposition with retail prices, the calculation of take-home pay employing the methodology described above is probably the fairest measure that can be derived from the available data. The use of 'total income' – that is to say, money wages plus transfer payments – would probably not change the relative positions to any significant degree. For the share of state transfer income in total post-tax personal income in each of the five countries under review has shown a remarkable degree of convergence in recent years.

WEEKLY FAMILY BASKET

To give an indication of purchasing power in the five countries surveyed, the following table assembles a weekly 'basket' for a family of four (and for the statistically average family of 3.5 persons), plus one month's rent and the two most expensive consumer durables – all in the work-time equivalents given in Appendix 3. The basket of food, beverages and cigarettes is at estimated Soviet levels of consumption (it thus excludes, *inter alia*, coffee) and is limited to those items priced in the survey. It tends to confirm the pattern of expenditure of Soviet families that have an average of 1.6 wage-earners and that spend over one-half of their disposable income on food, drink and cigarettes.

Weekly basket (for four persons) of consumer goods at Soviet level of consumption in March 1979, expressed as work-time units

Item	Kilograms	Washington	Moscow (Minutes of work-time)	Munich	Paris	London
Flour	1.0	5	28	4	8	8
Bread	6.0	48	72	30	84	72
Noodles	2.0	26	58	16	28	40
Beef	1.0	63	132	60	108	123
Pork	1.5	60	188	95	131	125
Minced beef	1.0	43	128	48	73	57
Sausages	1.0	31	145	40	53	43
Cod	1.0	50	50	42	75	86
Sugar	4.0	20	236	32	40	44
Butter	0.5	24	119	23	27	29
Margarine	1.0	31	118	17	25	24
Milk (litres)	10.0	70	180	50	60	90
Cheese	1.0	71	197	60	65	58
Eggs, cheapest (units)	17.0	14	100	10	31	26
Potatoes	9.0	18	63	18	36	36
Cabbage	2.0	10	18	6	20	18
Carrots	0.5	4	5	3	5	6
Tomatoes	0.5	9	33	9	9	19
Apples	1.0	11	40	8	8	15
Tea	0.1	11	50	16	23	6
Beer (litres)	3.0	24	60	21	30	66
Gin/vodka (litres)	1.0	52	380	54	105	161
Cigarettes (units)	120	54	138	96	42	132

(Hours of work-time)

Weekly basket, as above	12.5	42.3	12.6	18.1	21.4
Weekly basket for 'statistically average' family of 3.5 persons	10.9	37.0	11.0	15.8	18.7
Rent monthly	52.5	12.5	25.2	44.4	22.6
Colour TV	86.3	712.6	135.3	221.7	177.4

(Months of work-time)

Small car	4.1	35.0	7.0	8.1	8.5

Dynamic Comparison

Unfortunately, the prices given are not strictly comparable in some respects with earlier series. First of all, for logistic reasons, the survey has been carried out at a different time of the year. Moreover, many different brands of foodstuffs and models of durables have come on to the market in the meantime and it has not been possible to quantify their qualitative differences from previous models.

Appendix 1:   Retail Prices of Goods and Services in Local Currencies

Unit of measurement: one kilogram, except where otherwise noted
na denotes a product not generally available.
Parentheses denote a known price for a product not on sale in early March.

Item	Remarks	Washington (dollars)	Moscow (rubles)	Munich (marks)	Paris (francs)	London (pounds)
Grain products						
Wheat flour		0.37	0.42	0.69	2.85	0.21
White bread		0.58	0.28	0.78	4.80	0.33
Rye bread		1.52	0.18	1.18	11.40	0.32
Noodles	Macaroni type	1.01	0.44	1.38	4.90	0.54
Rice	Polished	0.92	0.88	1.99	4.85	0.48
Cornflakes		1.94	na	3.96	20.09	0.64
Oatmeal	Flocken, krupa	0.95	0.37	1.60	10.10	0.32
Meat and poultry						
Beef	Best for roasting	4.82	(2.00)	9.99	36.50	3.30
Steak	Sirloin	6.38	(2.96)	22.00	32.40	3.92
Veal	No bone	7.68	(2.30)	11.98	33.80	2.42
Pork	Best for roasting	3.06	1.90	10.50	29.20	2.23
Pork chops	With bone	4.16	(2.64)	7.90	22.00	1.83
Mutton		na	1.60	12.00	35.60	1.77
Lamb		4.82	na	16.00	45.00	2.85
Chicken	Frozen	1.08	3.40	3.14	11.70	0.92
Turkey	Frozen	1.74	(2.60)	5.50	14.60	1.08
Bacon	Lean, sliced	3.06	2.00	8.90	16.40	2.26
Ham	Cooked, sliced	5.28	3.70	14.90	38.60	3.02
Minced beef	Hamburger	3.28	1.95	7.96	24.60	1.52

Corned beef	Canned	2.89	2.60	5.37	6.05	1.86
Luncheon meat	Canned	3.47	2.91	6.63	22.50	0.93
Sausages, pork	Most common	2.40	2.20	6.60	17.90	1.14
Sausages	Frankfurters	2.40	2.50	9.80	17.50	1.76
Fish, fresh or frozen						
Cod	Frozen, fillet	3.76	0.77	6.96	25.20	2.30
Herring		1.96	1.45	3.96	44.40	1.35
Fish fingers	Frozen	2.62	na	6.30	29.25	2.18
Fish, canned						
Salmon	Pink	4.40	4.08	37.50	30.27	2.50
Herring	In tomato sauce	na	2.60	4.15	13.22	0.82
Tuna		3.58	(3.49)	10.70	24.25	2.71
Sardines	Cheapest, 115g	0.35	0.40	0.61	3.12	0.18
Sugar and confectionery						
Sugar	Granulated, white	0.40	0.90	1.39	3.30	0.30
Cocoa	Or cocoa drink	9.46	5.10	5.59	13.60	4.36
Chocolate	100 g, plain	0.56	1.17	0.99	1.80	0.34
Chocolate	100 g, milk	0.56	1.17	0.99	2.30	0.34
Ice cream	Plain vanilla	1.36	1.92	4.56	12.60	0.43
Fats						
Butter	Best	3.63	3.60	7.56	18.00	1.52
Margarine		2.40	1.80	2.76	8.40	0.64
Vegetable oil	Litre	1.22	1.98	1.79	4.70	0.70
Olive oil	Litre	3.80	1.80	9.27	15.20	1.86
Lard		1.43	1.72	na	na	0.54

Appendix 1 *(Continued)*

Item	Remarks	Washington (dollars)	Moscow (rubles)	Munich (marks)	Paris (francs)	London (pounds)
Milk and milk products						
Milk, fresh	Litre, packaged	0.52	0.28	0.89	2.10	0.24
Milk	Litre, canned	1.33	0.52	2.56	10.00	0.54
Cream, fresh	½ litre	1.16	0.37	1.11	4.20	0.53
Yoghurt	150 g, plain	0.21	0.15	0.44	1.05	0.11
Cheese, fresh	Gouda type	5.45	3.00	9.90	21.90	1.56
Cheese, fresh	Camembert type	12.32	(2.77)	8.45	19.20	2.48
Cheese, cottage		1.74	1.40	4.90	8.30	1.24
Cheese, processed		3.47	3.00	7.95	24.30	1.40
Eggs						
Eggs, largest (65–70 g)	10	0.80	1.50	1.89	7.85	0.54
Eggs, cheapest (45–50 g)	10	0.63	0.90	0.98	6.30	0.39
Vegetables, fresh or canned						
Potatoes, old		0.17	0.10	0.40	1.28	0.11
Carrots		0.55	0.15	0.99	3.15	0.29
Cabbage		0.42	0.14	0.44	3.50	0.25
Onions		0.28	0.12	1.80	2.40	0.26
Beetroot		na	0.03	1.20	6.40	0.48
Tomatoes		1.30	(1.00)	2.98	5.90	1.01
Cauliflower		1.25	(0.40)	2.60	7.70	0.58
Jar of carrot	Baby food, 200 g	0.25	0.17	1.19	3.00	0.19

Baked beans	In tomato sauce	0.55	0.66	2.06	7.88	0.29
Tomato soup	Canned	1.23	na	3.16	8.33	0.57
Tomato juice	Litre	0.69	0.63	1.98	12.50	0.39
Vegetables, frozen						
Peas		1.74	1.05[1]	6.60	11.33	0.64
Beans		1.96	0.94[1]	5.00	12.00	0.88
Spinach		1.15	(0.42[1])	2.20	13.11	0.75
Fruit, fresh						
Apples, eating		0.86	0.60	1.30	2.65	0.41
Apples, cooking		0.86	0.60	1.19	2.15	0.35
Oranges		0.44	(1.40)	1.29	2.75	0.44
Bananas		0.44	(1.10)	0.98	4.50	0.50
Lemon	One large	0.07	(0.35)	0.18	0.90	0.09
Grapefruit	One large	0.18	(1.40)	0.39	1.85	0.10
Fruit, dried						
Prunes	Unpitted	1.95	2.00	6.72	13.50	1.21
Raisins		4.69	1.24	3.98	12.80	1.03
Fruit, preserved						
Peaches	Canned or bottled	1.10	1.22	1.16	8.47	0.45
Plums	Canned or bottled	1.03	1.72	1.70	9.29	0.46
Jam	Strawberry	2.31	0.96	4.42	7.22	0.70
Honey		1.82	(6.00)	3.18	14.20	1.32

[1] In cans or jars.

Appendix 1 *(Continued)*

Item	Remarks	Washington (dollars)	Moscow (rubles)	Munich (marks)	Paris (francs)	London (pounds)
Seasoning						
Salt	Cheapest, granulated	0.22	0.10	0.98	1.65	0.09
Pepper, ground	Cheapest, 100 g	0.88	0.72	2.20	6.95	0.49
Mustard	Ready-mixed	1.71	1.60	11.80	11.67	1.77
Vinegar	Litre	0.50	0.72	2.60	2.20	0.26
Mayonnaise	Litre	2.18	1.80	1.98	16.20	1.17
Tea and coffee						
Tea	100 g	0.81	0.76	2.62	7.85	0.17
Tea bags	100	1.99	(3.00)	3.98	14.95	0.77
Coffee, ground		5.83	20.00	13.98	29.20	4.36
Coffee, instant	100 g	1.23	6.00	3.99	10.90	0.85
Cup of coffee in café, one		0.25	0.20	1.50	1.60	0.20
Beverages						
Wine, red	Litre	1.53	2.03	2.49	3.60	1.65
Wine, white	Litre	1.53	2.03	2.49	4.15	1.65
Beer, domestic	Litre, bottled	0.59	0.30	1.18	3.35	0.60
Cognac	0.7 litre	8.00	11.36	19.99	38.50	6.37
Scotch whisky	0.7 litre	7.49	na	17.99	39.90	4.48
Champagne	0.8 litre	5.00	4.67	6.65	39.50	4.45
Gin	0.7 litre	3.99	4.50	9.99	36.00	4.30
Vodka	0.5 litre	3.99	5.77	8.99	35.50	4.30
Mineral water	Litre	1.99	0.40	0.99	0.93	0.15

Apple juice	Litre	0.50	0.83	0.89	2.60	0.38
Orange juice	Litre, cheapest	0.63	1.79	0.99	3.95	0.38
Cola		0.58	(0.31[1])	0.79	2.75	0.46
Tobacco etc.						
Cigarettes	20, most popular	0.71	0.35	2.70	2.30	0.60
Tobacco, pipe	100 g	1.66	0.62	7.50	5.75	2.75
Matches	Safety, box of 50	0.01[2]	0.01	0.10	0.45	0.03
Cosmetics, drugs etc.						
Toilet soap	150 g, small bar	0.35	0.35	0.99	1.75	0.17
Detergent	1 kg, for clothes	0.71	1.41	1.93	2.20	0.57
Detergent	Litre, for dishes	1.38	na	1.71	5.50	0.56
Scouring powder		1.49	(1.60)	3.70	3.31	0.42
Toothpaste	270 g	1.24	1.03	5.40	12.25	1.06
Razor blades	10	1.26	0.50	5.68	3.10	0.72
Cotton wool	200 g	1.05	0.30	1.98	2.80	0.36
Toilet paper	2-roll pack	0.45	(0.28)	0.69	3.10	0.25
Toilet tissues	100	0.42	(0.64)	1.50	3.00	0.33
Sanitary pads	10	1.00	(0.25)	2.48	2.55	0.23
Contraceptives for one month, oral		3.79	(1.74)	9.00	5.15	0.69
Aspirin	100, cheapest	0.45	0.60	11.50	7.30	0.20
Tranquillizers	50, Valium-5	6.10	(3.40)	13.00	13.75	0.20[3]
Lipstick		2.00	(1.10)	12.00	11.00	1.35

[1] Small bottle, presumably 0.2 litre.
[2] Book matches with advertisement.
[3] National Health Service flat rate; on prescription only.

Appendix 1 *(Continued)*

Item	Remarks	Washington (dollars)	Moscow (rubles)	Munich (marks)	Paris (francs)	London (pounds)
Nail varnish	¼ fluid oz	1.00	0.24	12.00	13.00	1.10
Fluid make-up	Small bottle	1.75	0.60	13.00	14.00	1.25
Eye shadow	Small bottle	1.95	0.60	12.50	14.60	0.95
Deodorant	Roll-on	1.37	(3.23)	10.00	10.00	1.25
Q-tips	100	0.60	na	0.99	6.20	0.43
Perfume	½ fluid oz	18.00	30.00	69.00	45.00	13.90
Transportation						
Medium car		3 810	na	16 415	51 388	5 108
Small car		3 299	5 635	12 590	28 990	2 578
Annual insurance	Small Car	300	na	560	1 500	62.00
Annual road tax	Small car	20.00	11.35	188	400	50.00
Bicycle	Men's, cheapest	69.99	55.50	199	620	39.40
Petrol	Super, 10 litres	2.14	2.00	9.20	26.80	1.85
Petrol	Regular, 10 litres	1.85	1.50	8.79	24.50	1.67
Car wash	Outside only	2.75	1.00	4.50	6.00	0.40
Puncture repair	No wheel change	5.00	4.12	5.00	10.00	1.25
Garaging	One hour, covered	1.50	na	1.80	4.00	0.10
Parking meter	One hour, city centre	0.50	na	0.20	3.00	0.40
Garaging	One month, covered	40.00	17.50	50.00	150.00	5.00
Taxi fare	2 m/3 km	1.85	0.60	4.60	12.00	1.80
Bus fare	2 m/3 km	0.40	0.05	0.88	1.25	0.25
Subway fare	2 m/3 km	0.40	0.05	0.88	1.25	0.30
Train fare	60 m/100 km, economy	6.12	4.20	13.00	23.00	3.40
Air fare	300 km, economy	44.20	8.40	144.00	245	19.00

Clothing

Stockings	1 pair	1.30	1.70	1.98	4.50	0.30
Panty hose	1 pair, cheapest	1.67	(6.50)	0.89	4.30	0.28
Men's shirt	Long sleeve	12.00	9.60	32.00	39.00	5.00
Men's socks	1 pair, nylon	1.25	1.70	0.98	3.75	0.95
Men's shoes	1 pair, leather	35.00	30.00	92.00	179.00	18.00
Men's raincoat	Dacron/cotton	70.00	70.00	98.00	245.00	25.00
Men's office suit	2-piece, dacron rayon	90.00	61.80	259.00	379.00	39.95

Consumer durables

Refrigerator	Large, 360 litre	379.95	345	898	na	184.50
Refrigerator	Med., 240 litre	250	295	450	1 435	99.95
Refrigerator	Small, 120 litre	199	190	198	535	56.95
Washing machine	Cheapest	319.95	360	199	1 795	105.95
Electric razor		32.00	38.00	80.00	210	17.95
Television	Black and white 59 cm/23 inch	120	230	298	1 550	108
Television	Colour 59 cm/23 inch	398	650	1 350	4 490	284.95
Camera film	Colour, 20 exp.	1.65	0.35	5.20	11.40	2.60

Miscellaneous

Red roses	12, short-stem	12.00	(8.40)	12.00	21.60	2.60
Light bulb	100-watt, clear	0.40	0.30	0.99	1.90	0.18
Morning paper		0.20	0.03	0.60	1.80	0.10
Suburban movies	Best seat	3.50	0.50	8.00	17.00	1.50

Housing and services

Rent, monthly	50 sq. m unfurn.	215	na	600	1 300	60.00
Rent, monthly	Subsidized, unfurn.	242	11.39	252	900	36.36

Appendix 1 *(Continued)*

Item	Remarks	Washington (dollars)	Moscow (rubles)	Munich (marks)	Paris (francs)	London (pounds)
Hotel room	Double, w/bath	39.66	(2.50)	120	264	30.00
Electricity	1/12 annual bill	15.00	2.10	31.00	56.00	10.50
Fuel oil	1/12 annual bill	—¹	1.49	80.00	170	16.60
Water	1/12 annual bill	—¹	1.20	5.00	15.00	3.00
Telephone rent	Per month	13.00	0.83	27.00	70.00	3.30
Local call	Pay telephone	0.20	0.02	0.20	0.40	0.02
Telegram	30 words domestic	6.00	1.35	18.00	15.60	2.81
TV and radio licence	Annual black & white	nil	nil	168	178	11.00
Postage stamp	letter, first-class, domestic	0.15	0.04	0.60	1.20	0.09
Shirt laundered	White, cotton	0.70	0.12	2.50	4.20	0.35
Use of launderette	3.5 kg	0.50	0.35	1.30	8.00	0.40
Dry cleaning	Man's overcoat	4.95	1.30	4.50	25.80	1.45
Baby-sitter	Per hour, excl. fare	1.50	1.00	8.00	12.00	1.00
Cleaning woman	Per hour, excl. fare	4.40	3.00	10.00	16.00	1.50
Haircut	Men, no extras	4.00	0.50	8.00	22.00	0.80
Shampoo & set	Women, no extras	10.00	5.00	20.00	43.70	1.90
Manicure	Women	6.00	0.50	8.00	25.30	1.00

¹ Included in rent.

Appendix 2: Retail Prices of Goods and Services Converted to US Dollars

Unit of measurement: one kilogram, except where otherwise noted

Item	Remarks	Washington	Moscow	Munich	Paris	London
Grain products						
Wheat flour		0.37	0.64	0.37	0.68	0.42
White bread		0.58	0.42	0.42	1.14	0.67
Rye bread		1.52	0.27	0.64	2.71	0.65
Noodles	Macaroni type	1.01	0.67	0.75	1.16	1.09
Rice	Polished	0.92	1.33	1.07	1.15	0.97
Cornflakes		1.94	na	2.14	4.77	1.29
Oatmeal	Flocken, krupa	0.95	0.56	0.86	2.40	0.65
Meat and poultry						
Beef	Best for roasting	4.82	3.03	5.40	8.67	6.68
Steak	Sirloin	6.38	4.48	11.88	7.70	7.93
Veal	No bone	7.68	3.48	6.47	8.03	4.90
Pork	Best for roasting	3.06	2.87	5.67	6.94	4.51
Pork chops	With bone	4.16	3.99	4.27	5.23	3.70
Mutton		na	2.42	6.48	8.46	3.58
Lamb		4.82	na	8.64	10.69	5.77
Chicken	Frozen	1.08	5.14	1.70	2.78	1.86
Turkey	Frozen	1.74	3.93	2.97	3.47	2.18
Bacon	Lean, sliced	3.06	3.03	4.81	3.90	4.57
Ham	Cooked, sliced	5.28	5.60	8.05	9.17	6.11
Minced beef	Hamburger	3.28	2.95	4.30	5.84	3.07
Corned beef	Canned	2.89	3.93	0.97	1.44	3.76
Luncheon meat	Canned	3.47	4.40	3.58	5.34	1.88

Appendix 2 (Continued)

Item	Remarks	Washington	Moscow	Munich	Paris	London
Sausages, pork	Most common	2.40	3.33	3.56	4.25	2.31
Sausages	Frankfurters	2.40	3.78	5.29	4.16	3.56
Fish, fresh or frozen						
Cod	Frozen, fillet	3.76	1.16	3.76	5.99	4.65
Herring		1.96	2.19	2.14	10.55	2.73
Fish fingers	Frozen	2.62	na	3.40	6.95	4.41
Fish, canned						
Salmon	Pink	4.40	6.17	20.25	7.19	5.06
Herring	In tomato sauce	na	3.93	2.24	3.14	1.66
Tuna		3.58	5.28	5.73	5.76	5.48
Sardines	Cheapest, 115 g	0.35	0.61	0.33	0.74	0.36
Sugar and confectionery						
Sugar	Granulated, white	0.40	1.36	0.75	0.78	0.61
Cocoa	Or cocoa drink	9.46	7.72	3.02	3.23	8.82
Chocolate	100 g, plain	0.56	1.77	0.53	0.43	0.69
Chocolate	100g, milk	0.56	1.77	0.53	0.55	0.69
Ice cream	Plain vanilla	1.36	2.90	2.46	2.99	0.87
Fats						
Butter		3.63	5.45	4.08	4.28	3.07
Margarine	Best	2.40	2.72	1.49	2.00	1.30
Vegetable oil	Litre	1.22	3.00	0.97	1.12	1.42
Olive oil	Litre	3.80	2.72	5.01	3.61	3.76
Lard		1.43	2.60	na	na	1.09

Milk and milk products

Milk, fresh	Litre, packaged	0.52	0.42	0.48	0.50	0.49
Milk	Litre, canned	1.33	0.79	1.38	2.38	1.09
Cream, fresh	¼ litre	1.16	0.56	0.60	1.00	1.07
Yoghurt	150 g, plain	0.21	0.23	0.24	0.25	0.22
Cheese, fresh	Gouda type	5.45	4.54	5.35	5.20	3.16
Cheese, fresh	Camembert type	12.32	4.19	4.56	4.56	5.02
Cheese, cottage		1.74	2.12	2.65	1.97	2.51
Cheese, processed		3.47	4.54	4.29	5.77	2.83

Eggs

Eggs, largest (65–70 g)	10	0.80	2.27	1.02	1.86	1.09
Eggs, cheapest (45–50 g)	10	0.63	1.36	0.53	1.50	0.79

Vegetables, fresh or canned

Potatoes, old		0.17	0.15	0.22	0.30	0.22
Carrots		0.55	0.23	0.53	0.75	0.59
Cabbage		0.42	0.21	0.24	0.83	0.51
Onions		0.28	0.18	0.97	0.57	0.53
Beetroot		na	0.05	0.65	1.52	0.97
Tomatoes		1.30	1.51	1.61	1.40	2.04
Cauliflower		1.25	na	1.40	1.83	1.17
Jar of carrot	Baby food, 200 g	0.25	na	0.64	0.71	0.38
Baked beans	In tomato sauce	0.55	1.00	1.11	1.87	0.59
Tomato soup	Canned	1.23	na	1.71	1.98	1.15
Tomato juice	Litre	0.69	0.95	1.07	2.97	0.79

Appendix 2 *(Continued)*

Item	Remarks	Washington	Moscow	Munich	Paris	London
Vegetables, frozen						
Peas		1.74	1.59[1]	3.56	2.69	1.29
Beans		1.96	1.42[1]	2.70	2.85	1.78
Spinach		1.15	0.64[1]	1.19	3.11	1.52
Fruit, fresh						
Apples, eating		0.86	0.91	0.70	0.63	0.83
Apples, cooking		0.86	0.91	0.64	0.51	0.71
Oranges		0.44	2.12	0.70	0.65	0.89
Bananas		0.44	1.66	0.53	1.07	1.01
Lemon	One large	0.07	0.53	0.10	0.21	0.18
Grapefruit	One large	0.18	2.12	0.21	0.44	0.20
Fruit, dried						
Prunes	Unpitted	1.95	3.03	3.63	3.21	2.45
Raisins		4.69	1.88	2.15	3.04	2.08
Fruit, preserved						
Peaches	Canned, bottled	1.10	1.85	0.63	2.01	0.91
Plums	Canned, bottled	1.03	2.60	0.92	2.21	0.93
Jam	Strawberry	2.31	1.45	2.39	1.71	1.42
Honey		1.82	9.08	1.72	3.37	2.67
Seasoning						
Salt	Cheapest	0.22	0.15	0.53	0.39	0.18
Pepper, ground	Cheapest, 100 g	0.88	1.09	1.19	1.65	0.99
Mustard	Ready-mixed	1.71	2.42	6.37	2.77	3.58

Vinegar	Litre	0.50	1.09	1.40	0.52	0.53
Mayonnaise		2.18	2.72	1.07	3.85	2.37
Tea and coffee						
Tea	100 g	0.81	1.15	1.41	1.86	0.34
Tea bags	100	1.99	4.54	2.15	3.55	1.56
Coffee, ground		5.83	30.26	7.55	6.94	8.82
Coffee, instant	100 g	1.23	9.08	2.15	2.59	1.72
Cup of coffee in cafe, one		0.25	0.15	0.81	0.38	0.40
Beverages						
Wine, red	Litre	1.53	3.07	1.34	0.86	3.34
Wine, white	Litre	1.53	3.07	1.34	0.99	3.34
Beer, domestic	Litre, bottled	0.59	0.45	0.64	0.80	1.21
Cognac	0.7 litre	8.00	17.19	10.79	9.14	12.89
Scotch whisky	0.7 litre	7.49	na	9.71	9.48	9.06
Champagne	0.8 litre	5.00	7.07	3.59	9.38	9.00
Gin	0.7 litre	3.99	6.81	5.39	8.55	8.70
Vodka	0.5 litre	3.99	8.73	4.85	8.43	8.70
Mineral water	Litre	1.99	0.61	0.53	0.22	0.30
Apple juice	Litre	0.50	1.26	0.48	0.62	0.77
Orange juice	Litre	0.63	2.71	0.53	0.94	0.77
Cola	Litre, cheapest	0.58	0.47[1]	0.43	0.65	0.93
Tobacco etc.						
Cigarettes	20, most popular	0.71	0.53	1.46	0.55	1.21
Tobacco, pipe	100 g	1.66	0.94	4.05	1.37	5.56
Matches	Safety, box of 50	0.01[2]	0.02	0.05	0.04	0.06

[1] Small bottle, presumably 0.2 litre.
[2] Book matches with advertisement.

Appendix 2 *(Continued)*

Item	Remarks	Washington	Moscow	Munich	Paris	London
Cosmetics, drugs etc.						
Toilet soap	150 g, small bar	0.35	0.53	0.53	0.42	0.34
Detergent	1 kg, for clothes	0.71	2.13	1.04	0.52	1.15
Detergent	Litre, for dishes	1.38	na	0.92	1.31	1.13
Scouring powder		1.49	2.42	2.00	0.79	0.85
Toothpaste	270 g	1.24	1.56	2.92	2.91	2.14
Razor blades	10	1.26	0.76	3.07	0.74	1.46
Cotton wool	200 g	1.05	0.45	1.07	0.67	0.73
Toilet paper	2-roll pack	0.45	0.42	0.37	0.74	0.51
Toilet tissues	100	0.42	0.97	0.81	0.71	0.67
Sanitary pads	10	1.00	0.38	1.34	0.61	0.47
Contraceptives for one month, oral		3.79	1.15	4.86	1.22	1.40
Aspirin	100, cheapest	0.45	0.91	6.21	1.73	0.40
Tranquillizers	50, Valium-5	6.10	5.14	7.02	3.27	0.40[1]
Lipstick		2.00	1.66	6.48	2.61	2.73
Nail varnish	¼ fluid oz	1.00	0.36	6.48	3.09	2.23
Fluid make-up	Small bottle	1.75	0.91	7.02	3.33	2.53
Eye shadow	Small bottle	1.95	0.91	6.75	3.47	1.92
Deodorant	Roll-on	1.37	4.89	5.40	2.38	2.53
Q-tips	100	0.60	na	0.53	1.47	0.87
Perfume	½ fluid oz	18.00	4.54	37.26	10.69	28.10
Transport						
Medium Car		3810	14293	8868	12205	10333
Small Car		3299	8525	6798	6888	5215

[1] National Health Service flat rate; on prescription only.

Annual insurance	Small car	300	na	302.40	356.30	125.43
Annual road tax	Small car	20.00	17.17	101.52	95.01	101.15
Bicycle	Men's, cheapest	69.99	83.97	107.46	147.27	79.71
Petrol	Super, 10 litres	2.14	3.03	4.97	6.37	3.74
Petrol	Regular, 10 litres	1.85	2.27	4.75	5.82	3.38
Car wash	Outside only	2.75	1.51	2.43	1.43	0.81
Puncture repair	No wheel change	5.00	6.23	2.70	2.38	2.53
Garaging	One hour, covered	1.50	na	0.97	0.95	0.20
Parking meter	One hour, city centre	0.50	na	0.11	0.72	0.81
Garaging	One month, covered	40.00	26.48	27.00	35.63	10.12
Taxi fare	2 m/3 km	1.85	0.91	2.48	2.85	3.64
Bus fare	2 m/3 km	0.40	0.08	0.48	0.30	0.51
Subway fare	2 m/3 km	0.40	0.08	0.48	0.30	0.61
Train fare	60 m/100 km, economy	6.12	6.35	7.02	5.46	6.88
Air fare	300 km, economy	44.20	12.71	77.76	58.19	38.44
Clothing						
Stockings	1 pair	1.30	2.57	1.06	1.07	0.61
Panty hose	1 pair, cheapest	1.67	9.83	0.48	1.02	0.57
Men's shirt	Long sleeve	12.00	14.52	17.28	9.26	10.12
Men's socks	1 pair, nylon	1.25	2.57	0.53	0.89	1.92
Men's shoes	1 pair, leather	35.00	45.39	49.68	42.52	36.41
Men's raincoat	Dacron/cotton	70.00	105.90	52.92	58.19	50.58
Men's office suit	2-piece, dacron rayon	90.00	93.49	139.86	90.02	80.82
Consumer durables						
Refrigerator	Large, 360 litres	379.95	521.94	485.06	na	373.24
Refrigerator	Med., 240 litres	250.00	446.29	243.00	340.86	202.20

Appendix 2 (Continued)

Item	Remarks	Washington	Moscow	Munich	Paris	London
Refrigerator	Small, 120 litres	199.00	287.44	106.92	127.08	115.21
Washing machine	Cheapest	319.95	544.63	528.12	426.37	214.34
Electric razor		32.00	57.49	43.20	49.88	36.31
Television	Black & white, 59 cm/23 inch	120.00	347.96	160.92	368.17	218.48
Television	Colour, 59 cm/23 inch	398.00	983.36	729.00	1066	576.45
Camera film	Colour, 20 exp.	1.65	0.53	2.81	2.71	5.26
Miscellaneous						
Red roses	12, short-stem	12.00	12.71	6.48	5.13	5.26
Light bulb	100-watt, clear	0.40	0.45	0.53	0.45	0.36
Morning paper		0.20	0.05	0.32	0.43	0.20
Suburban movies	Best seat	3.50	0.76	4.32	4.04	3.03
Housing and services						
Rent, monthly	50 sq. m unfurn.	215	na	324.00	308.79	121.38
Rent, monthly	Subsidized, unfurn.	242	17.23	136.08	213.78	73.56
Hotel room	Double, w/bath	39.66	3.78	64.30	62.71	60.69
Electricity	1/12 annual bill	15.00	3.18	16.74	13.30	21.24
Fuel oil	1/12 annual bill	—[1]	1.49	43.20	40.38	33.58
Water	1/12 annual bill	—[1]	0.18	2.70	3.56	6.07
Telephone rent	Per month	13.00	1.26	14.58	16.63	6.68
Local call	Pay telephone	0.20	0.03	0.11	0.10	0.04
Telegram	30 words, domestic	6.00	2.04	9.72	3.71	5.68

TV and radio licence	Annual, black & white	nil	nil	90.72	42.28	22.25
Postage stamp	Letter, first-class, domestic	0.15	0.06	0.32	0.29	0.18
Shirt laundered	White, cotton	0.70	0.18	1.35	1.00	0.71
Use of launderette	3.5 kg	0.50	0.53	0.70	1.90	0.81
Dry cleaning	Man's overcoat	4.95	1.97	2.43	6.13	2.93
Baby-sitter	Per hour, excl. fare	1.50	1.51	4.32	2.85	2.02
Cleaning woman	Per hour, excl. fare	4.40	4.54	5.40	3.80	3.03
Haircut	Men, no extras	4.00	0.76	4.32	5.23	1.62
Shampoo & set	Women, no extras	10.00	7.56	10.80	10.38	3.84
Manicure	Women	6.50	0.76	4.32	6.01	2.02

[1] Included in rent.

Appendix 3: Retail Prices of Goods and Services in Units of Work-Time
Minutes unless otherwise specified

Item	Remarks	Washington	Moscow	Munich	Paris	London
Grain products						
Wheat flour		5	28	4	8	8
White bread		8	18	5	14	12
Rue bread		20	12	7	34	12
Noodles	Macaroni type	13	29	8	14	20
Rice	Polished	12	58	12	14	18
Cornflakes		25	na	24	59	24
Oatmeal	Flocken, krupa	12	24	10	30	12
Meat and poultry						
Beef	Best for roasting	63	132	60	108	123
Steak	Sirloin	83	195	132	96	146
Veal	No bone	100	151	72	100	90
Pork	Best for roasting	40	125	63	87	83
Pork chops	With bone	54	173	48	65	68
Mutton		na	105	72	105	66
Lamb		63	na	96	133	106
Chicken	Frozen	14	223	19	35	34
Turkey	Frozen	23	171	33	43	40
Bacon	Lean, sliced	40	132	54	49	84
Ham	Cooked, sliced	69	243	90	114	113
Minced beef	Hamburger	43	128	48	73	57
Corned beef	Canned	38	171	11	18	69
Luncheon meat	Canned	45	191	40	67	35
Sausages, pork	Most common	31	145	40	53	43
Sausages	Frankfurters	31	164	59	52	66

Fish, fresh or frozen						
Cod	Frozen, fillet	50	50	42	75	86
Herring	Frozen	26	95	24	132	50
Fish figures		34	na	38	87	81
Fish, canned						
Salmon	Pink	57	268	226	90	93
Herring	In tomato sauce	na	171	25	39	31
Tuna		47	230	64	72	101
Sardines	Cheapest, 115 g	5	27	4	9	7
Sugar and confectionery						
Sugar	Granulated, white	5	58	10	11	
Cocoa	Or cocoa drink	123	336	34	40	163
Chocolate	100 g, plain	7	77	6	5	13
Chocolate	100 g, milk	7	77	6	7	13
Ice cream	Plain vanilla	18	126	27	37	16
Fats						
Butter	Best	47	237	45	53	57
Margarine		31	118	17	25	24
Vegetable oil	Litre	16	130	11	14	26
Olive oil	Litre	49	118	56	45	69
Lard		19	113	na	na	20
Milk and milk products						
Milk, fresh	Litre, packaged	7	18	5	6	9
Milk	Litre, canned	17	34	15	30	20
Cream, fresh	¼ litre	15	24	7	12	20
Yoghurt	150 g, plain	3	10	3	3	4
Cheese, fresh	Gouda type	71	197	60	65	58
Cheese, fresh	Camembert type	160	182	51	57	93
Cheese, cottage		23	92	30	25	46
Cheese, processed		45	197	48	72	52

Appendix 3 *(Continued)*

Item	Remarks	Washington	Moscow	Munich	Paris	London
Eggs						
Eggs, largest (65–70 g)	10	10	99	11	23	20
Eggs, cheapest (45–50 g)	10	8	59	6	18	15
Vegetables, fresh or canned						
Potatoes, old		2	7	2	4	4
Carrots		7	10	6	9	11
Cabbage		5	9	3	10	9
Onions		4	8	11	7	10
Beetroot		na	2	7	19	18
Tomatoes		17	66	18	17	38
Cauliflower		16	na	16	23	22
Jar of carrot	Baby food, 200 g	3	na	7	9	7
Baked beans	In tomato sauce	7	43	12	23	11
Tomato soup	Canned	16	na	19	25	21
Tomato juice	Litre	9	41	12	37	15
Vegetables, frozen						
Peas		23	69	40	34	24
Beans		26	62	30	36	33
Spinach		15	28	13	39	28
Fruit, Fresh						
Apples, eating		11	40	8	8	15
Apples, cooking		11	40	7	6	13
Oranges		6	92	8	8	16
Bananas		6	72	6	13	19

Lemon	One large	1	23	1	3	3
Grapefruit	One large	2	92	2	5	4
Fruit, dried						
Prunes	Unpitted	25	132	40	40	45
Raisins		61	82	24	38	38
Fruit, preserved						
Peaches	Canned or bottled	14	80	7	25	17
Plums	Canned or bottled	13	113	10	28	17
Jam	Strawberry	30	63	27	21	26
Honey		24	395	19	42	49
Seasoning						
Salt	Cheapest, granulated	3	7	6	5	3
Pepper, ground	Cheapest, 100 g	11	47	13	21	18
Mustard	Ready-mixed	22	105	71	35	66
Vinegar	Litre	7	47	16	6	10
Mayonnaise	Litre	28	118	12	48	44
Tea and coffee						
Tea	100 g	11	50	16	23	6
Tea bags	100	26	197	24	44	29
Coffee, ground		76	1 316	84	87	163
Coffee, instant	100 g	16	395	24	32	32
Cup of coffee in cafe, one		3	7	9	5	7
Beverages						
Wine, red	Litre	20	133	15	11	62
Wine, white	Litre	20	133	15	12	62
Beer, domestic	Litre, bottled	8	20	7	10	22
Cognac	0.7 litre	104	747	120	114	238

Appendix 3 *(Continued)*

Item	Remarks	Washington	Moscow	Munich	Paris	London
Scotch whisky	0.7 litre	98	na	108	118	167
Champagne	0.8 litre	65	307	40	117	166
Gin	0.7 litre	52	296	60	107	161
Vodka	0.5 litre	52	380	54	105	161
Mineral water	Litre	26	27	6	3	6
Apple juice	Litre	7	55	5	8	14
Orange juice	Litre, cheapest	8	118	6	12	14
Cola	Litre, cheapest	8	20[1]	5	8	17
Tobacco etc.						
Cigarettes	20, most popular	9	23	16	7	22
Tobacco, pipe	100 g	22	41	45	17	103
Matches	Safety, box of 50	—[2]	1	1	1	1
Cosmetics, drugs etc.						
Toilet soap	150 g, small bar	5	23	6	5	6
Detergent	1 kg, for clothes	9	93	12	6	21
Detergent	Litre, for dishes	18	na	10	16	21
Scouring powder		19	105	22	10	16
Toothpaste	270 g	16	68	33	36	39
Razor blades	10	16	33	34	9	27
Cotton wool	200 g	14	20	12	8	13
Toilet paper	2-roll pack	6	18	4	8	9
Toilet tissues	100	5	42	9	9	12
Sanitary pads	10	13	17	15	8	9
Contraceptives for one month, oral		49	50	54	15	26

[1] Small bottle, presumably 0.2 litre.
[2] Book matches with advertisement.

Aspirin	100 cheapest	6	40	69	22	7
Tranquillizers	50, Valium-5	79	223	78	41	7[3]
Lipstick	½ fluid oz	26	72	72	33	50
Nail varnish	Small bottle	13	16	72	39	41
Fluid make-up	Small bottle	23	40	78	42	47
Eye shadow	Small bottle	25	40	75	43	35
Deodorant	Roll-on	18	213	60	30	47
Q-tips	100	8	na	6	18	16
Perfume	½ fluid oz	234	197	415	133	518

Transportation (Months of work-time)

Medium car		5	59	9	14	17
Small car		4	35	7	8	9
Annual insurance	Small car (*hours*)	65	na	56	74	39
Annual road tax	Small car	4	12	19	20	31
Bicycle	Men's, cheapest (*hours*)	15	61	20	31	24
Petrol	Super, 10 litres	28	132	55	79	69
Petrol	Regular, 10 litres	24	99	53	73	62
Car wash	Outside only	36	66	27	18	15
Puncture repair	No wheel change	65	271	30	30	47
Garaging	One hour, covered	20	na	11	12	4
Parking meter	One hour, city centre	7	na	1	9	15
Garaging	1 month, covered (*hours*)	9	19	5	7	3
Taxi fare	2 m/3 km	24	40	28	36	67
Bus fare	2 m/3 km	5	3	5	4	9
Subway fare	2 m/3 km	5	3	5	4	11
Train fare	60 m/100 km	80	276	78	68	127
Air fare	300 km, econ. (*hours*)	10	9	17	12	12

Clothing

Stockings	1 pair	17	112	12	13	11
Panty hose	1 pair, cheapest	22	427	5	13	11

[3] National Health Service flat rate: on prescription only.

Appendix 3 (*Continued*)

Item	Remarks	Washington	Moscow	Munich	Paris	London
Men's shirt	Long sleeve	156	631	192	115	187
Men's socks	1 pair, nylon	16	117	6	11	35
Men's shoes	1 pair, leather (*hours*)	8	33	9	9	11
Men's raincoat	Dacron/cotton (*hours*)	15	77	10	12	16
Men's office suit	2-piece, dacron rayon (*hours*)	20	68	26	19	25
Consumer Durables (Hours of work-time)						
Refrigerator	Large, 360 litres	83	378	90	na	115
Refrigerator	Med., 240 litres	54	323	45	71	62
Refrigerator	Small, 120 litres	43	208	20	26	35
Washing machine	Cheapest	69	395	98	89	66
Electric razor		7	42	8	10	11
Television	Black & white, 59 cm/23 inch	26	252	30	77	67
Television	Colour, 59 cm/23 inch	86	713	135	222	177
Camera film	Colour, 20 exp. (*minutes*)	21	23	31	34	97
Miscellaneous (Minutes of work-time)						
Red roses	12, short-stem	156	553	72	64	97
Light bulb	100-watt, clear	5	20	6	6	7
Morning paper		3	2	4	5	4
Suburban movies	Best seat	46	33	48	50	56
Housing and services						
Rent, monthly	50 sq. m unfurn. (*hours*)	47	na	60	64	37

Rent, monthly	Subsidized, unfurn. (*hours*)	53	12	25	44	23
Hotel room	Double, w/bath (*hours*)	9	3	12	13	19
Electricity	1/12 annual bill	195	138	186	166	392
Fuel oil	1/12 annual bill	—¹	65	48	50	62
Water	1/12 annual bill	—¹	8	30	44	112
Telephone rent	Per month	169	55	162	207	123
Local call	Pay telephone	3	1	1	1	1
Telegram	30 words, domestic	78	89	108	46	105
TV and radio licence	Annual, black & white	nil	nil	1011	527	411
Postage stamp	Letter, firstclass, domestic	2	3	4	4	3
Shirt laundered	White, cotton	9	8	15	12	13
Use of launderette	3.5 kg	7	23	8	24	15
Dry cleaning	Man's overcoat	64	86	27	76	54
Baby-sitter	Per hour, excl. fare	20	66	48	36	37
Cleaning woman	Per hour, excl. fare	57	197	60	47	56
Haircut	Men, no extras	52	33	48	65	30
Shampoo & set	Women, no extras	130	329	120	129	71
Manicure	Women	78	33	48	75	37

¹ Included in rent.

Appendix 4:   Average Gross And Take-Home Pay – January 1979

	(a) US (dollars)	(b) USSR (rubles)	(c) FRG (marks)	(d) France (francs)	(e) UK (pounds)
1. Average gross monthly earnings	1121.38	165.64	2288.00	3494.66	380.90
2. *minus* Income, state and church tax	145.70	16.73	233.86	43.83	79.25
3. *minus* Social security contributions	68.74	nil	205.92 ⎫		
4. *minus* Medical insurance premium	108.00	nil	128.13 ⎬ 401.32		24.75
5. *minus* Unemployment insurance payment	nil	nil	34.42 ⎭		
6. *plus* Family allowance	nil	12.00	130.00	549.50	26.00
7. Average monthly take-home pay	**798.94**	**160.91**	**1810.77**	**3599.01**	**302.90**
8. Monthly take-home pay converted to US $	798.94	243.43	978.11	854.87	612.79
9. Take-home pay ($) per work-hour	4.61	1.38	5.39	4.81	3.25
10. Take-home pay (c) per work-minute	7.68	2.30	8.98	8.02	5.42

SOURCES AND NOTES
(1a) The average gross weekly earnings in January 1979 were $258.80 (*US Department of Labor News*, 2 February 1979).
(1b) The average gross monthly earnings for industrial workers, male and female, at the end of 1977 were 171.80 rubles (*Narkhoz 77*, p. 385). To this is applied the 3.2 per cent increase recorded for all workers and employees in 1978 (*Pravda*, 20 January 1978) and 0.2 per cent for January 1979. The gross monthly average includes about 12 rubles for paid vacation (see *Zhurnalist*, No. 8 (1974) 79).
(1c) Statistisches Bundesamt, Wiesbaden and the Ifo-Institut, Munich.
(1d) SVP. Includes transport allowance of Frs 23.
(1e) For adult males. *Department of Employment Gazette*, February 1979, pp. 126–7, and estimates provided by *The Economist*.
(2a) *Employers' Tax Guide*, Circular E, revised November 1978.
(2b) Derived from B. Pashkevich and F. Gilitsky, *Spravochnik rashchetchika po zarabotnoi plate* (Nauki i tekhnika, Minsk, 1968) pp. 220–59, as amended by *Prilozhenie k postanovleniyu Soveta Ministrov SSSR ot 25 dekabrya 1972 g.*, No. 882, p. 6.
(2c) Gesamtabzugstabelle.
(2d) SVP.
(2e) *The Economist Diary 1979*, pp. 21, 22.
(3a) *Employers' Tax Guide*.
(3c) Gesamtabzugstabelle.
(4a) Insurance company brochure. Basic family medical and hospital coverage, other than dental care.
(4c) Gesamtabzugstabelle.
(4d) SVP.
(4e) Leaflet NI 40, *National Insurance Contributions for Employees*, March 1978.

(5a) Paid by the employer.
(5c) Gesamtabzugstabelle.
(6b) A family income supplement is paid when the *per capita* family income is below 50 rubles a month. This takes the form of a flat rate of 12 rubles a month paid for each child in a low-income family until the child reaches the age of eight (*Pravda*, 27 September 1974).
(6c) Arbeitsamt, Munich.
(6d) SVP.
(6e) Department of Health and Social Security.
 (8) The official interbank foreign exchange rates at close of business on 28 February 1979 and, hence, valid for 1 March 1979, were: US $ = 0.661 rubles; DM, 1.8513; frs, 4.21; and 0.4943 pounds (drawn or derived from *IHT*, 1 March 1979; *Ekonomicheskaya gazeta*, No. 11, (1979) 22, and a Paris bank).
 (9) The most recent actual average weekly hours of work in industry reported were: US, 40.6 hours in November 1978; USSR, 40.6 hours in 1977; FRG, 41.9 hours in October 1977; France, 41.0 hours in March 1978; and UK, 44.2 hours in October 1978 (*USDL News*, 8 December 1978; *Narkhoz 77*, p. 388; *UN Monthly Bulletin of Statistics*, August 1978, p. 16; and *Department of Employment Gazette*, February 1979, p. 126).

Index

A